T0074670

GPU Pro 360

Guide to Mobile Devices

GPU Pro 360

Guide to Mobile Devices

Edited by Wolfgang Engel

CRC Press
Taylor & Francis Group
Boca Raton London New York

CRC Press is an imprint of the
Taylor & Francis Group, an **informa** business
AN A K PETERS BOOK

CRC Press
Taylor & Francis Group
6000 Broken Sound Parkway NW, Suite 300
Boca Raton, FL 33487-2742

Printed and bound in India by Replika Press Pvt. Ltd.

Printed on acid-free paper

International Standard Book Number-13: 978-0-8153-5281-5 (Paperback)
International Standard Book Number-13: 978-0-8153-5283-9 (Hardback)

Library of Congress Cataloging-in-Publication Data

Names: Engel, Wolfgang F., editor.
Title: GPU pro 360 guide to mobile devices / edited by Wolfgang Engel.
Description: Boca Raton : Taylor & Francis, CRC Press, [2018]
Identifiers: LCCN 2017060054| ISBN 9780815352815 (pbk. : alk. paper)
   | ISBN 9780815352839 (hardback : alk. paper)
Subjects: LCSH: Computer graphics. | Graphics processing units--Programming.
   | Pocket computers--Programming. | Mobile computing. | Rendering (Computer graphics)
Classification: LCC T385 .G68885 2018 | DDC 621.39/96--dc23
LC record available at https://lccn.loc.gov/2017060054

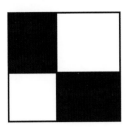

Contents

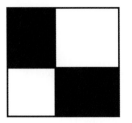

Introduction

With all devices now touch-driven and offering few physical keys, the effective usage of touch screens is critical. The chapter, "Touchscreen-Based User Interaction," by Andrea Bizzotto, provides basic insight into the complexities and solutions required to achieve the best possible user-interaction and experience through a touch-based interface.

"Optimizing a 3D UI Engine for Mobile Devices," by Hyunwoo Ki, offers early insights into optimizing a user interface for mobile devices, looking at the importance of font rendering engines and "dirty region"-based optimizations to avoid rendering more than is actually required.

The chapter, "A Shader-Based eBook Renderer," by Andrea Bizzotto illustrates a vertex-shader-based implementation of the page-peeling effect of a basic eBook renderer. It covers high-quality procedural antialiasing of the page edges, as well as some tricks that achieve a polished look. Two pages can be combined side-by-side to simulate a real book, and additional techniques are introduced to illustrate how to satisfy additional constraints and meet power-consumption requirements.

The next chapter, "Post-Processing Effects on Mobile Devices," by Marco Weber and Peter Quayle describes a general approach to implement post-processing on handheld devices by showing how to implement a bloom effect with efficient convolution.

Joe Davis and Ken Catterall show in "Shader-Based Water Effects" how to render high-quality water effects at a low computational cost. Although there are many examples of water effects using shaders that are readily available, they are designed mainly for high-performance graphics chips on desktop platforms. This chapter shows how to tailor a technique discussed by Kurt Pelzer (in ShaderX^2, "Advanced Water Effects," 2004) to mobile platforms.

In "Realistic Real-Time Skin Rendering on Mobile," Renaldas Zioma and Ole Ciliox share how they implemented skin rendering using physically based shading models for the Unity "The Chase" demo. Their method makes use of approximations and lookup textures in order to balance the arithmetic and texture load.

In "Deferred Rendering Techniques on Mobile Devices," Ashley Vaughan Smith explores various techniques for doing deferred rendering on mobile devices. This chapter steps through deferred shading, light pre-pass rendering, and light indexed rendering, and also details extensions that allow efficient read-access to individual render targets to further improve performance.

In "Bandwidth Efficient Graphics with the ARM Mali GPUs," Marius Bjørge presents new ARM Mali GPU extensions that allow applications to efficiently read and write data to the on-chip tile buffer. Applications can read the current color, depth, and stencil values as well as treat the tile buffer as a local storage with full read and write access. The chapter also contains example use-cases such as soft particles and deferred shading.

In "Efficient Morph Target Animation Using OpenGL ES 3.0," James L. Jones shows how OpenGL ES 3.0 can be used to do morph target animation efficiently on mobile devices. Transform feedback is used to blend a set of poses, and the chapter also describes how to batch blend multiple poses to reduce the number of passes.

In "Tiled Deferred Blending," Ramses Ladlani describes a method for doing deferred blending. Blended primitives are first tiled to screen-space tiles, and then each tile is rendered while blending the primitives in a single fragment shader pass. The method has proven efficient on immediate mode renderers where blending involves an expensive read-modify-write operation with the framebuffer.

In "Adaptive Scalable Texture Compression," Stacy Smith presents ASTC, a new texture compression format that has been accepted as a Khronos standard. ASTC is set to pretty much replace all existing compressed texture formats. It supports bit rates ranging from 0.89 bpp up to 8 bpp for both LDR and HDR textures. This chapter explains how it works, how to use it, and how to get the most out of it.

In "Optimizing OpenCL Kernels for the ARM Mali-T600 GPUs," Johan Gronqvist and Anton Lokhmotov go into the details of writing efficient OpenCL kernels for the ARM Mali-T600 GPUs. This chapter introduces the ARM Mali-T600 GPU series and goes into a deep discussion of the performance characteristics of various OpenCL kernels.

"Hybrid Ray Tracing on a PowerVR GPU" by Gareth Morgan describes how an existing raster-based graphics engine can use ray tracing to add high-quality effects like hard and soft shadows, reflection, and refraction while continuing to use rasterization as the primary rendering method. The chapter also gives an introduction to the OpenRL API.

"Implementing a GPU-Only Particle-Collision System with ASTC 3D Textures and OpenGL ES 3.0" by Daniele Di Donato shares how the author used OpenGL ES 3.0 and ASTC 3D textures to do bandwidth-friendly collision detection of particles on the GPU. The 3D texture stores a voxel representation of the scene, which is used to do direct collision tests as well as to look up the nearest surface.

"Animated Characters with Shell Fur for Mobile Devices" by Andrew Girdler and James L. Jones presents how the authors were able to optimize a high-quality animation system to run efficiently on mobile devices. With OpenGL ES 3.0, they made use of transform feedback and instancing in order to reach the performance target.

"High Dynamic Range Computational Photography on Mobile GPUs" by Simon McIntosh-Smith, Amir Chohan, Dan Curran, and Anton Lokhmotov explores HDR computational photography on mobile GPUs using OpenCL and shares some very interesting results.

In "Efficient Soft Shadows Based on Static Local Cubemap," Sylwester Bala and Roberto Lopez Mendes introduce a novel soft shadow technique that makes use of local cubemaps. The technique allows for very nice looking smooth shadows at minimal performance cost.

In "Physically Based Deferred Shading on Mobile," Ashley Vaughan Smith and Mathieu Einig describe how to implement physically based deferred shading on a power-constrained mobile device using extensions such as pixel local storage and framebuffer fetch. The chapter also explains how these extensions can be used to implement deferred decal rendering very easily on mobile GPUs.

Lastly, I would like to thank all the contributors in this book for their great work and excellent chapters.

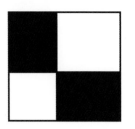

Web Materials

Example programs and source code to accompany some of the chapters are available on the CRC Press website: go to https://www.crcpress.com/9780815352815 and click on the "Downloads" tab.

The directory structure follows the book structure by using the chapter numbers as the name of the subdirectory.

General System Requirements

The material presented in this book was originally published between 2010 and 2016, and the most recent developments have the following system requirements:

- The DirectX June 2010 SDK (the latest SDK is installed with Visual Studio 2012).

- DirectX 11 or DirectX 12 capable GPUs are required to run the examples. The chapter will mention the exact requirement.

- The OS should be Microsoft Windows 10, following the requirement of DirectX 11 or 12 capable GPUs.

- Visual Studio C++ 2012 (some examples might require older versions).

- 2GB RAM or more.

- The latest GPU driver.

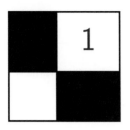

Touchscreen-Based User Interaction
Andrea Bizzotto

1.1 Introduction

The touchscreen plays a major role in user interaction on mobile devices. Although some of these systems come with high-level APIs that could be used by the programmer to detect gestures, others provide just raw access to the samples read from the hardware. This chapter illustrates a mathematical framework that can be used to estimate the motion and position of the input pointer on screen (see Figure 1.1). An application for controlling the position of a camera in a three-dimensional spherical coordinate system is presented as an usage example.

1.2 Motion Estimation

Let us approach the problem of estimating the motion on screen, given a set of samples described by three values:

- The time when the sample was read.

- The position of the sample along the x axis.

- The position of the sample along the y axis.

The context of this problem is a main-loop based graphics application. With this respect, the platform-specific touchscreen implementation might provide one sample per-frame, or multiple samples (as it is the case if the touchscreen subsystem is independent from the main loop).

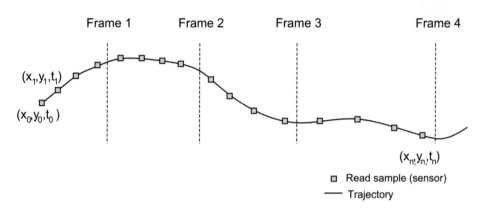

Figure 1.1. Touchscreen input: while the user drags the pointer on screen, the new samples become available and at the beginning of each frame they can be used to estimate the motion and position.

A very simple approach would be to calculate the motion as the velocity between two consecutive samples as in Equation (1.1), where t_i is the time of the sample i, $s(t_i)$ the corresponding position and $v(t_i)$ the velocity:

$$v(t_n) = \frac{s(t_n) - s(t_{n-1})}{t_n - t_{n-1}}. \tag{1.1}$$

Given the small screen size of mobile devices and their relatively high resolution, reading consecutive samples can result in different x- and y-coordinates, even if the pointer is not moving on screen. This effect was observed on OMAP Zoom platforms, where a set of samples with slightly different positions was returned even when the input position was fixed.

We can take in account this behavior in our model by assuming that the samples are affected by Gaussian noise, whose variance is platform-dependent. If on a particular device this side effect does not exist, our model is still valid as it means that the variance of the noise is zero. Since we want our motion estimation algorithm to be virtually unaffected by the presence of noise, we introduce a method for noise reduction followed by a thresholding operation.

A very common technique for noise reduction is to apply an average filter on the set of available samples, therefore reducing the error by a factor of N (where N is the size of the set).

If the user drags the pointer on screen and we want to estimate the motion of such interaction, we can use a more effective approach that reduces the noise and makes use of all the samples in a given time interval:

1. Choose a "time window" that contains all the most recent samples. To do so, we store all the samples that we want to process in an circular queue. At each frame we update our queue by adding all the samples that were read since the previous frame, and discarding the ones that are too old. If no samples are read for some time, the queue will quickly empty and we can set the motion to 0.

2. Calculate all the velocities between consecutive samples in the queue.

3. Obtain the average on those velocities.

This method is much more reliable than the previous one and introduces a trade-off between accuracy and responsiveness of the filter:

Bigger window. More samples are stored: the accuracy increases but the responsiveness of the filter decreases. Since we are using a causal filter, if ΔT is the length of the window, we are introducing a delay equal to $\Delta T/2$.

Smaller window. Fewer samples are stored: the accuracy decreases but the responsiveness increases.

```
void update(Sample *pSamples, int num, float &mx, float &my) {
  //Add the samples read in the last frame.
  queue.add(pSamples, num);
  //Deletes old samples
  queue.remove(getTime() - timeWindow);
  if (queue.size() < 2) {
    mx = my = 0.0f;
    return;
  }
  int i = 0;
  Iterator iter = queue.begin();
  Sample curr, prev = iter.data();
  while (iter.next()) {
    curr = iter.data();
    //Motion is an array that stores motions of consecutive
    samples.
    motion[i].dx = (curr.x - prev.x) / (curr.t - prev.t);
    motion[i].dy = (curr.y - prev.y) / (curr.t - prev.t);
    prev = curr;
    i++;
  }
  CalculateAverage(motion, i, mx, my);
  //Apply thresholds
  if (mx < thresholdX) mx = 0.0f;
  if (my < thresholdY) my = 0.0f;
}
```

Listing 1.1. Motion estimation routine.

The method can be made even more robust: we can define a platform-dependent threshold that is proportional to the variance of the noise, and if the estimated motion is smaller than this threshold, we set it to zero. This will guarantee that no motion is detected if the input position does not change (taking noise into account).

The complete method for updating the motion is summarized in Listing 1.1.

Such an approach has been successfully tested on several platforms. For the purpose of motion estimation, choosing a time interval of 0.2 seconds gives good results on an OMAP Zoom platform, while on the Samsung Omnia the read input coordinates are constant if the pointer doesn't move on screen, and the time interval and threshold can be smaller as no noise needs to be removed. The same applies on Windows emulation, where the mouse is used as a pointing device to simulate the touchscreen.

1.3 Position Prediction

Position estimation seems to be an easy task as the position of the last sample can be used directly. Some considerations can be made nevertheless:

- The instant when the input is processed (beginning of the new frame) is not necessarily the same as the time of the last read sample.

- The graphics pipeline takes some time to render the frame and swap the buffers, so if the input position is used to draw a target on screen (for example a cursor), it might be worth to adjust this position according to the time when the frame will be actually rendered.

These two contributions are put together in Equation (1.2), where $\triangle_{\text{read}}$ is the difference between the current time and the time of the last sample, and $\triangle_{\text{frame}}$ is the time to render the current frame, equal to the time to render the previous frame (we can assume that the framerate is locally constant):

$$\triangle_{\text{total}} = \triangle_{\text{read}} + \triangle_{\text{frame}}. \tag{1.2}$$

The predicted position is then as in Equation (1.3), where $v(t_{\text{last}})$ is the motion estimated as described and t_{last} the time of the last read sample:

$$s(t_{\text{new}}) = s(t_{\text{last}}) + v(t_{\text{last}}) \cdot (t_{\text{last}} + \triangle_{\text{total}}). \tag{1.3}$$

1.4 Application: Controlling a Camera in a Spherical Coordinate System

A possible application is to use our new motion primitives to move a camera around an object in the center of the scene. The target of the camera is therefore fixed to the origin of the world coordinate system. If required, this constraint can be relaxed by setting the target on an arbitrary point in three-dimensional space, as with a simple translation this case can be included in the former one.

The position of the camera is determined by a vector (x, y, z) of coordinates, while only the motion in the x- and y-directions of the screen is available. As it is not intuitive to map these directions to a point in a cartesian coordinate system, we can use an alternative representation for the position of the camera:

Yaw. Rotation around the y-axis.

Pitch. Rotation around the x-axis.

Radius. Distance of the camera from the origin.

This allows us to use the x- and y-motion on the touchscreen to update the yaw and pitch angles of the camera, while leaving the radius fixed or adjustable through other input controls.

Figure 1.2 shows the concept. The camera position is initially set to $(0, 0, R)^{\mathrm{T}}$. At each frame the yaw and pitch angles are updated according to the motion on the touchscreen, and the position is updated.

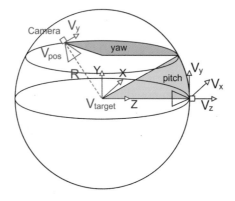

Figure 1.2. Three-dimensional spherical coordinate system: upon application of the yaw and pitch angles the camera moves from the initial position (marked in blue) to the final one (green). The camera defines a coordinate system defined by the position and the three orthonormal vectors (V_x, V_y, V_z).

To render our scene from the viewpoint of the camera we need to calculate the roto-translation matrix that transforms a point from world space coordinates to camera space coordinates. In OpenGL such a matrix is known as model-view matrix and can be computed once the position, target and up direction of the camera are known; therefore, we want to find these values first.

The spherical coordinate system is useful to update the yaw and pitch angles, but to find the model-view matrix the position needs to be expressed again in the canonical coordinate system. This is done by applying the rotation matrices that correspond to the two angles to the initial position, as in Equations (1.4), (1.5) and (1.6).

$$\mathbf{R_y}(\alpha) = \begin{pmatrix} \cos(\alpha) & 0 & -\sin(\alpha) \\ 0 & 1 & 0 \\ \sin(\alpha) & 0 & \cos(\alpha), \end{pmatrix} \mathbf{R_x}(\alpha) = \begin{pmatrix} 1 & 0 & 0 \\ 0 & \cos(\alpha) & -\sin(\alpha) \\ 0 & \sin(\alpha) & \cos(\alpha) \end{pmatrix}.$$

$$\text{(1.4)}$$

$$\mathbf{M_{rot}} = \mathbf{R_y}(\text{yaw}) \cdot \mathbf{R_x}(\text{pitch}). \tag{1.5}$$

$$\mathbf{V_{pos}} = \mathbf{M_{rot}} \cdot \begin{pmatrix} 0 \\ 0 \\ R \end{pmatrix}. \tag{1.6}$$

The target of our camera is fixed at the origin, as Equation (1.7) states, and the up direction (V_y) is determined by Equation (1.8).

$$\mathbf{V_{target}} = \mathbf{0^T}. \tag{1.7}$$

$$\mathbf{V_y} = \mathbf{M_{rot}} \cdot \begin{pmatrix} 0 \\ 1 \\ 0 \end{pmatrix}. \tag{1.8}$$

The model-view matrix is composed by a translation that shifts the coordinate system to the position of the camera and by a rotation that takes into account its relative orientation. Such rotation can be expressed as a matrix formed by three orthonormal vectors that can be immediately derived from the position, target and up direction of the camera. Equations (1.9), (1.10) and (1.11) illustrate the concept:

$$\mathbf{V_z} = -\frac{\mathbf{V_{target}} - \mathbf{V_{pos}}}{||\mathbf{V_{target}} - \mathbf{V_{pos}}||}. \tag{1.9}$$

$$\mathbf{V_x} = \mathbf{V_y} \times \mathbf{V_z}. \tag{1.10}$$

$$\mathbf{M_{view}} = \left(\begin{array}{c|c} \mathbf{V}_x^T & 0 \\ \mathbf{V}_y^T & 0 \\ \mathbf{V}_z^T & 0 \\ \mathbf{0}^T & 1 \end{array}\right) \cdot \left(\begin{array}{c|c} \mathbf{0}_{3\times3} & -\mathbf{V}_{pos} \\ \hline \mathbf{0}^T & 1 \end{array}\right). \tag{1.11}$$

It can be noticed that the vectors V_x, V_y, and V_z represent the axes of a right-handed reference frame. For this reason the direction of the camera is opposite of the vector V_z.

This mathematical framework allows the setup of an interactive system where the user can spin the camera around the observed object. The yaw and pitch angles can be updated at each frame by adding the motion on the x- and y-axes, but once the user releases the pointer, the camera movement immediately stops. It would be more realistic if the camera had a residual inertial motion, and the next section illustrates how to implement this.

1.4.1 Adding Inertia

The desired effect consists in letting the camera spin for a short amount of time, until the residual motion is zero. Such effect is best modeled by a decreasing exponential function like the one in Equation (1.12):

$$f(t) = \begin{cases} 0, & t < 0, \\ 1 - e^{-\tau t}, & t \geq 0. \end{cases} \tag{1.12}$$

If t_r is the time when the input is released and M_x the corresponding motion on the x-axis, the residual speed at any instant in time is given by $x(t) = M_x \cdot f(t - t_r)$.

This value can be integrated over time to update the yaw angle (the same procedure is valid for the y-axis / pitch angle). The integration is a discrete operation as it can be performed at each frame, and Equation (1.13) provides a method to update the angle frame by frame:

$$x(t_n) = \sum_{i=0}^{n} M_x \cdot f(t_i - t_r)(t_i - t_{i-1}) = x(t_{n-1}) + M_x \cdot f(t_n - t_r)(t_n - t_{n-1}). \tag{1.13}$$

1.5 Algorithm Overview

The general algorithm for updating the camera position within the main loop is illustrated in Listing 1.2.

The motion is estimated using the discussed technique and used to update the yaw and pitch angles. When the input is released the current time and the motion are saved and later used to add the inertial contribution to the angles

```
t = getTime ();
touchscreen.GetMotion(motionX, motionY);
if (touchscreen.Released()) {
  releaseMotionX = motionX;
  releaseMotionY = motionY;
  tr = t;
}
yaw = yaw + motionX + releaseMotionX * f(t - tr);
pitch = pitch + motionY + releaseMotionY * f(t - tr);
MView = CalculateMatrix(yaw, pitch, radius);

RenderGeometry(MView);
```

Listing 1.2. Render loop.

(appropriate scaling factors can be used when updating the angles in order to calibrate the speed of the camera position as desired). Finally, the model-view matrix can be calculated with the techique previously described and the geometry can be rendered using that matrix.

Figure 1.3 illustrates how the presented techniques have been used in an OpenGL ES 2.0 demo developed at Imagination Technologies.

Figure 1.3. Flowers demo. This demo shows procedural plant growth with detailed flowers and makes use of the described touchscreen implementation to spin the camera around the growing plant.

1.6 Conclusion

This chapter showed how to approach motion estimation by means of a robust algorithm whose parameters can be adapted on different platforms to get optimal results. The length of the time window and the threshold can be tweaked as necessary according to the requirements of the final application.

A simple OpenGL ES 2.0 demo that allows to control the camera in the spherical coordinate system previously described is available in the book's web materials on the CRC Press website, together with full source code for OMAP Zoom1, Zoom2 and Windows emulation, where the mouse is used to simulate the touchscreen interaction.

1.7 Acknowledgments

The author would like to thank Kristof Beets and the whole BizDev and DevTech teams for their work, contribution, and feedback.

2

Optimizing a 3D UI Engine
for Mobile Devices
Hyunwoo Ki

A graphical user interface (GUI) is the preferred type of user interface (UI). It provides more intuitive visual components with images or animations, as opposed to a text-based interface. Such a GUI is essential for both graphics applications (for example, games) and non-graphics applications (for example, a phonebook). It should offer us convenience as well as beauty. With advancement of embedded systems, UI design shows a trend toward presenting three-dimensional graphical looks. Because the UI is a fundamental component for all applications, a UI engine should provide high performance and low memory consumption. The major mission of our UX development group at INNOACE Co., Ltd., is developing an optimized three-dimensional UI engine and an authoring tool for various mobile devices to maximize user experience. Our core engine supports two-dimensional and three-dimensional widgets, scene management, resource management, True-

Figure 2.1. Examples using a three-dimensional UI engine base on OpenGL ES 2.0.

Type font rendering, three-dimensional transition, visibility culling, occlusion culling, widget caching, partial rendering, etc. Based on this core engine, we migrated our UI engine to various platforms, for example LINUX, Windows Mobile, Android and GPOS. We developed a hardware renderer based on OpenGL ES 2.0 for high-end smartphones and PMPs, and a software renderer for common mobile phones. This chapter presents practical optimization methods for a three-dimensional UI engine based on OpenGL ES 2.0 with our development experience (see Figure 2.1). However, we expect some features of our core engine would be useful for OpenGL ES 1.1 or software renderers.

2.1 Overview

Optimization methods presented in this chapter include rendering pipeline optimization, TrueType font rendering, widget caches with partial update, and resource management.

1. *Rendering pipeline optimization.* We describe fundamental development guidelines of OpenGL ES 2.0 for a three-dimensional UI engine. We show our usage examples of render states, shaders, textures, draw calls, and etc.

2. *TrueType font rendering.* Texts are a very important component of the UI, and rendering texts requires higher costs than rendering other widgets. Particularly, processing Asian languages (e.g., Korean and Chinese) lower engine efficiency because it must handle many font glyphs. We present our text renderer's design and implementation issues to minimize draw calls and texture changes with low memory consumption.

3. *Widget caches with partial update.* We render a composite widget to a render texture, and consider this texture as a widget cache until a sub-widget of the composite widget is changed. This widget cache accelerates rendering a composite widget. Furthermore, according to interaction and logic, we partially update this widget cache to reduce update costs.

4. *Resource management.* We developed an efficient resource management system based on DirectX, one with resource garbage collectors. For example, if a managed texture has not been used for a long time, we dispose it on memory, and this texture is automatically restored from storage when we use it. We describe design and implementation issues of our resource management system.

2.2 Optimization Methods

2.2.1 Rendering Pipeline Optimization

We describe development guidelines for OpenGL ES 2.0 for a three-dimensional UI engine with our development experience.

Render states and shaders. A lot of changes of render states, textures and shaders in a single frame cause a UI engine to drop performance. Therefore these changes should be kept to a minimum. Fortunately, UI rendering does not require many changes. Most widgets use a texture which has an alpha channel, and there is no lighting or other color blending. If we render two-dimensional styled transparent widgets in back-to-front order, we do not need a depth test. Based on these properties, general render states are as follows:

- Shader: simple texture mapping shader.

- Texture: one color texture.

- Color: 1.0, 1.0, 1.0, 1.0 (RGBA).

- Alpha blend: enabled.

- Depth Test & Depth Mask: disabled.

Our renderer manages render states and shaders in a simple way. We save the current render states, textures and shader information. When we render a widget, we compare the current render states, textures and shader with the material property of the widget. If state changes are not required, we do not call OpenGL functions.

We minimize querying current state values by calling `glGet*` functions. Instead we get the values by calling our renderer's inline functions because our renderer always clones the values. We predefine important limits of our target devices such as the maximum texture before releasing our engine package. Validation checks using the `glGetError` function are very expensive. Thus, for a release build we use the `glGetError` function only for critical (but infrequent) APIs such as the `glTexImage2D` function. For resource generation functions such as `glGenTextures` and `glGenFramebuffers`, we compare the resultant values of the functions with zero without calling the `glGetError` function. If a value is zero, it means resource generation has failed and thus we do error handling.

Because our target resolution of WVGA (480 × 800) has many pixels, fragment shaders are very costly. Therefore we keep to a minimum the number of instructions for fragment shaders. If a conditional branch such as an if statement or a discard instruction to mimic an alpha test is added, the performance will drop. Using an alpha blend with a texture that has zero alpha values instead of using an alpha test, is enough to render alpha-tested widgets in many cases. We use a small set of predefined shaders and load precompiled shader binaries. The renderer maps hash keys to OpenGL uniform IDs for each shader to quickly write shader parameters without querying uniform IDs in rendering time.

Textures. Generally, in a UI design, a texture is designed with perfect one-to-one mapping of texture texels to screen pixels. Therefore we use mipmapping and linear filtering only for scaled or rotated widgets, or three-dimensional models if an application requires it. For most widgets, to save memory we recommend not using mipmaps, and using nearest-filtering. Our target LCD's color format is 16-bit R5G6B5, and we prefer 16-bit textures (R5G6B5 or R4G4B4A4) instead of 24-bit (R8G8B8) or 32-bit (R8G8B8A8) ones in order to improve performance for texture uploading and reading. Using 24- or 32-bit textures sometimes results in a banding artifact on the screen. Bit conversion with dithering and other preprocessing using a graphic tool are required for better image quality.

Using compressed textures greatly increases engine efficiency. DXT1 compression reduces memory usage to 1/6 for R8G8B8 textures. It also reduces a texture upload time. Image decoding is also removed unlike JPG and PNG formats. For some devices (e.g., FIMG 3D from Samsung Electronics), a format conversion to replace an original image format to a hardware internal format, for example from R8G8B8A8 to B8G8R8A8, is removed. Similarly, using hardware internal formats also reduces texture loading time by ignoring format conversion. For a 480×800 resolution texture, we saved a factor of ten in loading time, including texture uploading, compared with a JPG texture on a device based on FIMG 3D. Using compressed textures also improves rendering performance because it reduces memory bandwidth and increases cache hit rates.

If your target devices support non-power-of-two (NPOT) resolution textures, we recommend to use such textures to reduce memory usage by removing empty texels for padding. Because we do not prefer mipmaps generally, we do not have to be concerned about using NPOT textures. NPOT textures (but a multiple of four texels textures) with DXT compression were very useful for thumbnail images, animated images, etc. We provide a software DXT compressor for applications, and they compress thumbnail images for list widgets when original images are stored. Although DXT compression speed is not fast, it is acceptable because image size is small and compression is done at storage time with a progress widget. Most importantly, such compression improves loading and rendering speed, and reduces memory usage.

Miscellaneous. Reducing a vertex data size is an important strategy. We always use indexed vertex arrays to reduce vertex data by sharing. We also use interleaved vertex arrays (a.k.a. packed vertex arrays) instead of separated arrays to maximize memory access efficiency. An interleaved vertex array is structured by a single large array with each vertex attribute, using a structure of the C language. Because most widgets are rendered by a simple quad or a rounded quad with texturing, level of detail of vertex data is not necessary.

Visibility culling, occlusion culling, and scissor tests increase frame rates. Basically we set a scissor box and a visibility culling area to the full screen size. Some widgets need to clip child widgets or own text. For example, several list items of a list box are located in the outside of the list box. In this case, we do not have to render these list items (visibility culling). Another list item may be located in the boundary of the list box. In this case, parts of the list items are displayed and the other parts are not displayed by clipping. We can implement such clipping using a stencil test, but it increases rendering passes and rendering costs for accessing the stencil buffer. For example, an implementation using scissor tests was more than two times faster than using stencil tests for FIMG 3D. If an application needs only rectangular clipping, we recommended using scissor tests instead of stencil tests.

We implemented a simple, user-guided occlusion culling. If a widget is assigned as an occluder, we render occluder widgets first. Then we compare other widgets' bounding boxes with occluders' ones in screen coordinates. If a widget is completely occluded by an occluder, we skip rendering this widget. Such occlusion culling is useful for a fullscreen popup or a keypad. Our keypad covers half of fullscreen in top-most order.

2.2.2 TrueType Font Rendering

Text rendering is a very important feature to deliver information for users. This section describes design and implementation issues of our TrueType font renderer.

Figure 2.2 shows our TrueType font rendering algorithm. To render a text, we render each character-sized quad (Figure 2.2(a)) and do texture mapping using corresponding font textures with alpha blending (Figure 2.2(c)). Each font texture has bitmaps of characters and is grouped by a font size and font face (font

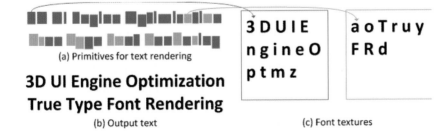

Figure 2.2. Our approach for TrueType font rendering.

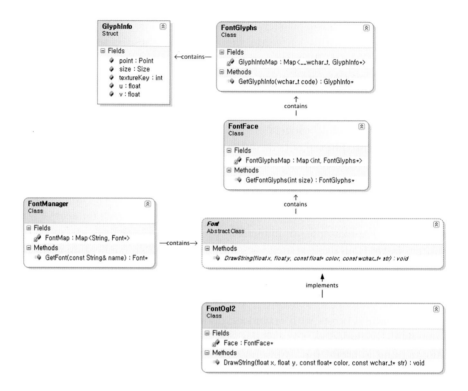

Figure 2.3. Simple class diagrams of our TrueType font renderer.

name). Each character's bitmap is written on a font texture when the character is used. If a character is already written on a font texture, we reuse it without rewriting to save memory and avoid writing.

We now describe the design of our TrueType font renderer. Figure 2.3 shows simple class diagrams. Every font and every text buffer is entirely managed by the font manager, which has containers for fonts and text buffers, and performs operations to create, destroy, and get fonts or text buffer instances. The Font class is an abstract class that has functionalities to render texts and calculate a text size. A derived class of the Font class for a certain target platform has a FontFace instance. The FontFace class has data loaded from a TTF file, and has a container for FontGlyphs instances grouped by font size. A FontGlyphs instance of a FontFace instance is added when a certain font size is first used. The FontGlyphs class has a container for GlyphInfo instances grouped by a character code. A GlyphInfo instance of a FontGlyphs instance is also added when a certain character code is first used. Therefore, we store only the information of used characters of used sizes of the specified font face. The GlyphInfo structure stores a position, a size, a texture's coordinates, and a texture key to render a character. The texture key is used to get a font texture instance quickly and safely. When we require a character for text rendering, a font texture stores the bitmap of the character. Bitmaps of characters are filled in consecutive order (see, e.g., Figure 2.2(c)).

To render a text, for each character in the text we expand work to compute world position of a quad and its texture coordinates corresponding to the bitmap of the character using information of a FontGlyphs instance. Usually there are many texts on the screen and doing such work causes a significant performance drop. We use pre-generated text buffers until a caption, an alignment, a size or other property is changed, to improve performance.

As described above, a text is rendered by drawing a quad per character and by mapping a corresponding font texture. Because a single font texture cannot store all character's bitmap data, we will often use several font textures for rendering a single text. Especially, Asian languages such as Korean and Chinese use many more unique characters than English, and as a result rendering a single text often needs many font textures. It increases the number of draw calls with texture changes and thus it significantly drops rendering efficiency, assuming each character is never overlapped by another. Rendering orders of characters are not important in text rendering. By exploiting this property, we design a text buffer by grouping vertex buffers by a same font texture. At rendering time, we set render states and shader parameters once and then we render each vertex buffer with changing font textures. Such an approach minimizes the number of draw calls and texture changes. As an example, we show the number of draw calls and texture changes for a text in Figure 2.2, before and after grouping in Figure 2.4.

Similarly, for rich text rendering, we group vertex buffers by same image texture, same line color, or same text background color (RGBA color is encoded by a 32-bit unsigned integer).

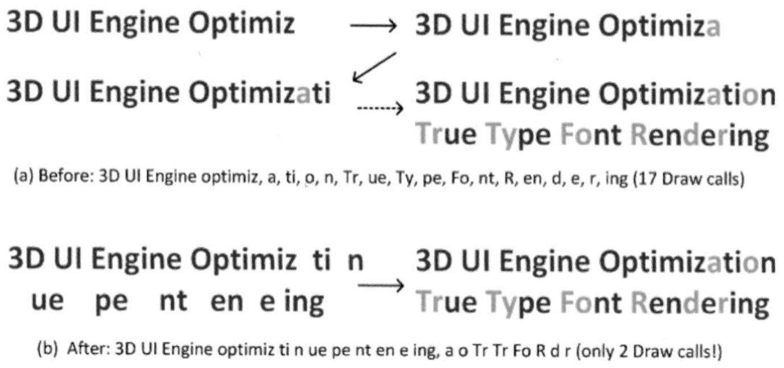
3D UI Engine Optimiz
3D UI Engine Optimiza
3D UI Engine Optimizati
3D UI Engine Optimization
True Type Font Rendering
(a) Before: 3D UI Engine optimiz, a, ti, o, n, Tr, ue, Ty, pe, Fo, nt, R, en, d, e, r, ing (17 Draw calls)
3D UI Engine Optimiz ti n
ue pe nt en e ing
3D UI Engine Optimization
True Type Font Rendering
(b) After: 3D UI Engine optimiz ti n ue pe nt en e ing, a o Tr Tr Fo R d r (only 2 Draw calls!)

Figure 2.4. Reducing draw calls using a text buffer.

2.2.3   Widget Caches with Partial Update

There are various basic widgets such as a button, a label, and an image. Some widgets are composite widgets composed of several basic or (and) other composite widgets such as a keypad and a list box. Rendering a composite widget is slower because it has a high fill area and requires many draw calls. We introduce an algorithm to replace rendering a composite widget by rendering a single image. We first create a render texture covering a composite widget entirely. Then we render a composite widget onto this render texture instead of the frame buffer. We call this render texture a *widget cache* and use it for rendering the composite widget until the appearance of the composite widget is changed. Although quality inequality exists, it is useful for us because we do not need mipmaps generally and we ignore hardware anti-aliasing, dithering, etc.

Using a widget cache significantly improves rendering performance. However, if the appearance of a composite widget frequently changes, it causes a performance drop because it requires both updating a widget cache and rendering the composite widget using this cache. In order to solve this problem, we develop partial update rendering. Pseudocode for this is shown in Listing 2.1. We describe the algorithm in detail in the next paragraph.

When a sub-widget's property (e.g., position, color, texture, and caption) is changed, we set a flag to notify that a widget cache must be updated. At rendering time (Widget::Render), we find flagged subwidgets and merge all bounding boxes of them (Widget::UpdateDirtyRectRecursive). We also merge the bounding box of the previous frame with the current merged bounding box to update the dirty area of the previous frame. This prevents footprint-like artifacts due to an animation. Now we project the merged bounding box onto screen-space to compute a dirty rectangle in screen-space. We set a visibility culling area and a scissor box for this dirty rectangle (`Renderer::SetClipRect`) and then update the widget cache by rendering the flagged subwidgets including their child widgets without clearing the widget cache (`Renderer::RenderWidgetToTexture`). For example, if we press a single button of a keypad widget, a button image is highlighted by a texture change and the dirty rectangle is the same as the bounding box of the button in screen-space (see Figure 2.5). At the cache update time, only the background widget and the button pass visibility culling tests, and an area corresponding to the bounding box of the button in screen-space passes scissor tests. These tests greatly reduce costs to update a widget cache, and thus incredibly improve rendering performance. Although such a widget cache consumes large memory space, we selectively use widget caches and destroy them when we do not use them any longer.

```
void Widget::Render()
{
    if (HasCache())
        UpdateCache();
    if (IsValidCache())
    {
        Renderer->RenderCache(widget);
        return;
    }
    for (int i = 0; i < GetChildCound(); ++i)
        GetChildAt(i)->Render();
    Renderer->Render(this);
    SetDirty(false);
}

void Widget::UpdateCache()
{
    if (! UpdateDirtyRectRecursive())
        return;
    Renderer->PushClipRect();
    Renderer->RenderWidgetToTexture(this);
    Renderer->PopClipRect();
    SetValidCache(true);
}

void Widget::UpdateDirtyRectRecursive()
{
    ClearDirtyRect();
    for (int i = 0; i < GetChildCound(); ++i)
    {
        Widget *child = GetChildAt(i);
        if (child ->IsDirty())
            MergeDirtyAABB(child->GetAABB());
        child->UpdateDirtyRectRecursive();
    }
    AABB curDirtyAABB = GetDirtyAABB();
    MergeDirtyAABB(GetPrevDirtyAABB());
    SetPrevDirtyAABB(curDirtyAABB);
    SetDirtyRect(TransformToScreen(GetDirtyAABB()));
}

void Renderer::RenderWidgetToTexture(Widget *widget)
{
    TransformWorldToFullScreen(widget);
    SetRenderTarget(widget->GetCache());
    SetClipRect(widget->GetDirtyRect());
    Widget->Render();
    SetRenderTarget(NULL);
}
```

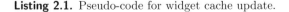

Listing 2.1. Pseudo-code for widget cache update.

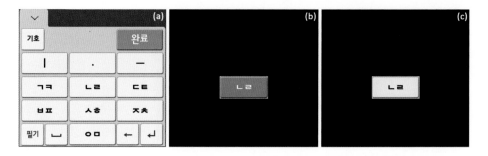

Figure 2.5. An example of partial update rendering: (a) original keypad; (b) and (c) partial update.

2.2.4   Resource Management

Imagine that during writing a multimedia mail using your cell phone, you can attach a photo from a photo-album application. Concurrently, you can hear a song and receive a message or phone call. In the described scenario, several applications need to cooperate on a small finite memory pool.

OpenGL gives most frequently used (MFU) textures high priority and assigns them as resident textures. The resident textures are placed in video memory for fast access, and the other textures are placed in system memory until these textures are used. A developer can set the priority of textures using the glPrioritizeTextures function. However, such a resource management system is not supported on OpenGL ES 2.0.

We implemented our resource management system similar to DirectX. All resources such as textures and render textures have a reference counter and a time stamp recorded when a resource is referenced. A resource has a unique key, priority, status, pool type, and memory usage. The priority is more preferential rather than the time stamp for resource sorting.

Our resource pool types are based on DirectX, but there are many differences. There are four types: *default, managed, semi-managed,* and *system*. A resource of a default type is never destroyed unless the resource manager or an application explicitly destroys it. A resource of a managed type can be disposed of at any time in order to gain available memory and can restore its memory and data. A resource of a semi-managed type can be also disposed at any time. However, it can only reallocate memory by itself and thus the renderer must restore its data before using it. A resource of a system type is similar to the default type but is always located in system memory.

For using such a resource management system, derived classes of the Resource class must implement `Dispose` and `Restore` methods. The `Dispose` method frees allocated memory and makes a resource status `LostMemory`, whereas the `Restore` method recovers a disposed resource according to its pool type. A resource of a managed type is completely restored and thus a status will be `Valid`, whereas a resource of a semi-managed type is only reallocated memory without restoring data and thus it makes a resource status `EmptyData`. The other types are never restored automatically.

Generally we use a managed type for textures loaded from image files. Our target device's memory system is a unified memory architecture (UMA) and the total memory space is insufficient to run many applications. Therefore, we restore a managed texture from an original image file instead of system memory unlike DirectX. We used nandflash storage and its access speed was sufficiently fast. Applications can use background loading using threading based on a simple user-guided prediction algorithm. UI design has a usage flow by scenarios and such flow is reflected at a structure of content. We preload the next possible components in the background. An application can customize loading methods by using texture buffer update instead of setting a texture filename. An image viewer application based on our engine used a small alternative image while an original image is loading. When we restore a texture we also restore an address mode, texture filtering, etc.

We use the semi-managed type for text buffers and widget caches. Text buffers and widget caches can be disposed and reallocated when we want. Typically we dispose of them when they disappear from the screen and reallocate them when they reappear. The data of a text buffer is restored by recomputing position and texture coordinates and rebuilding vertex buffers, and the data of a widget cache is restored by rendering widgets to a render texture when we use them. In the view of an application, the semi-managed type is the same as the managed type. However, in the view of the renderer, complex restoring—for example, processing events and business logic, traversing scenes, and rendering widgets—is needed as compared with simple file loading or memory copy for a managed type. This is the reason why we call it semi-managed rather than managed. A system type is a special type. We use it for mixing three-dimensional and two-dimensional rendering. For example, a texture of a system type is directly copied (or bit-blitting) to the frame buffer.

Our texture manager has a garbage collector and it disposes of managed textures when the textures is not used for a long time and its reference counter is less than two (see Listing 2.2). We consider total used memory, available memory space, frame time, and time stamp, and an application can control various settings for garbage collection.

All managed and semi-managed resources are managed by the resource manager. The resource manager compulsorily disposes of low prioritized resources if available memory space is insufficient to create a new resource (see Listing 2.2). It releases all resources including non-managed typed resources when an application is terminated to prevent memory leaks. An application can also control management conditions. Basically, we prepare a minimum of four times the memory rather than the required size because actual available memory space is less than a measured size due to memory fragmentation, and we also want to minimize the number of times of processing for supplying available memory.

A memory supplement process is as follows. First, the resource manager collects managed and semi-managed resources whose reference counter is less than two. Then we sort collected resources using a priority and a time stamp, and dispose of resources until available memory is sufficiently supplied (`ResourcePool::SupplyAvailableMemory`). If memory is still insufficient, we dispose of remained, managed, and semi-managed resources, ignoring their reference counter (`ResourcePool::EvictManagedResourcesAll`). We limit the maximum memory space for OpenGL.

If an application uses memory over this limit, our engine informs it of an out-of-memory error. Although memory usage does not go over the limit, if the `GL_OUT_OF_MEMORY` error happens from the `glTexImage2D` or the `glRenderBuffer Storage` function, we set available memory of our resource pool to zero and limit the maximum memory to the current memory usage (`ResourcePool::Zero AvailableMemory`). This error is due to memory fragmentation or usage by other applications.

Optionally, we also dispose of all managed and semi-managed resources when an application is hidden by other applications to supply available memory for other application and to reduce a memory fragmentation problem. At the end of the frame, we explicitly unbind all resources, such as textures, to decrease their reference counters. It helps our resource manager to release resources that are no longer in use.

```
bool Texture::Allocate()
{
    if (! ResourcePool.IsAvailable(requiredMemory))
        ResourcePool.SupplyAvailableMemory(requireMemory);
    Texture *texture = NULL;
    glTexImage2D(...);
    GLenum errorGL = glGetError();
    if (errorGL == GL_OUT_OF_MEMORY)
    {
        ResourcePool.ZeroAvailableMemory();
        ResourcePool.SupplyAvailableMemory(requireMemory);

        // retry
        glTexImage2D(...)
```

```
        errorGL = glGetError();
        if (errorGL == GL_OUT_OF_MEMORY)
        {
            ResourcePool.EvictManagedResourcesAll();

            // retry
            glTexImage2D(...)
            errorGL = glGetError();
            if (errorGL == GL_OUT_OF_MEMORY)
            {
                // TODO: error handling
                return false;
            }

            // TODO: other error handlings code
        }

        // TODO: other error handlings code
    }
    return true;
}

int ResourcePool::ZeroAvailableMemory()
{
    available = 0;
    limit = used;
    if (limit < MinLimit)
    {
        limit = MinLimit;
        EvictManagedResourcesAll();
    }
}

int ResourcePool::SupplyAvailableMemory(int required)
{
    int safe = required * 4;
    safe = MIN(safe, limit);
    if (safe < avaiable)
        return 0;
    Vector<Resource*> disposableResources;
    disposableResources.Reserve(resouces.Count());
    GatherManagedResources(disposableResources);
    disposableResources.Sort();
    int oldUsed = used;
    for (int i = 0; i < disposableResources.Count(); ++i)
    {
        Resource *resource = disposableResources[i];
        if (! resource || resource->GetRefCount() > 1)
            continue;
        resource->Dispose();
        if (safe < available)
            break;
    }
    if (safe > available)
```

```
            EvictManagedResourcesAll();
        return oldUsed - used;
    }
```

Listing 2.2. Resource pool management.

2.3 Conclusion

We presented optimization methods to implement a three-dimensional UI engine for mobile devices. They play important roles to deploy our solution on a commercial scale and make many applications more efficient. We show captured images of applications based on our three-dimensional UI engine in the book's web materials available on the CRC Press website. We spared no efforts to generalize our solution to support other platforms. However, you must improve algorithms and develop additional optimizations for your target platforms. We have been extending our business to support various platforms and have been continuing to optimize our engine for various targets. For example, we use partial update rendering for all widgets on a set-top box. For this, we assume the current page that has all widgets in the current view is one of composite widgets. Such an approach greatly increases frame rates.

We believe this chapter supplies development guidelines for not only mobile three-dimensional UI engines but also all mobile three-dimensional applications.

Bibliography

[Munshi et al. 08] Aaftab Munshi, Dan Ginsburg, and Dave Shreiner. *OpenGL(R) ES 2.0 Programming Guide*. Boston: Addison-Wesley Professional, 2008.

[Pulli et al. 07] Kari Pulli, Jani Vaarala, Ville Miettinen, Tomi Aarnio, and Kimmo Roimela. *Mobile 3D Graphics: with OpenGL ES and M3G*. San Francisco: Morgan Kaufmann, 2007.

[Beets 09] Kristof Beets, Mikael Gustavsson, and Erik Olsson. "Optimizing your first OpenGL ES Applications." *ShaderX7: Advanced Rendering Techniques*. Boston: Charles River Media, 2009.

[Catterall 09] Ken Catterall. "Optimised Shaders for Advanced Graphical User Interfaces." *ShaderX7: Advanced Rendering Techniques*. Boston: Charles River Media, 2009.

[Khronos 09] Khronos OpenGL ES. 2009. Available at http://www.khronos.org/
    opengles/.

[Imagination Technologies 09] Khronos OpenGL ES 2.0 SDKs for POWERVR
    SGX. 2009. Available at http://www.imgtec.com/powervr/insider/sdk/
    KhronosOpenGLES2xSGX.asp.

[Microsoft 09] Microsoft DirectX. 2009. Available at http://msdn.microsoft.com/
    en-us/directx/default.aspx.

A Shader-Based eBook Renderer

Andrea Bizzotto

Readers of eBooks are becoming increasingly popular. Touch screens and programmable GPUs, such as the POWERVR SGX Series from Imagination Technologies, can be combined to implement user-friendly navigation and page flipping functionality. This chapter illustrates a vertex-shader-based implementation of the page-peeling effect, and details some techniques that allow high-quality procedural antialiasing of the page edges, as well as some tricks that achieve a polished look. Two pages can be combined side-by-side to simulate a real book, and additional techniques are introduced to illustrate how to satisfy additional constraints and meet power consumption requirements.

3.1 Overview

The chapter is organized as follows: Section 3.2 introduces the mathematical model which is the basis of a page-peeling simulation, and shows how to use the vertex shader to render the effect with a tessellated grid on OpenGL ES 2.0 hardware. Section 3.3 discusses the additional constraints that need to be considered when rendering two pages side-by-side, and Section 3.4 illustrates some techniques that improve the visual look and deal with antialiasing. An approach that doesn't require a tessellated grid is illustrated in Section 3.5 to show how the technique can be adapted to work on OpenGL ES 1.1 hardware with minimal vertex overhead. Section 3.6 mentions some practical considerations regarding performance and power consumption. Finally, Sections 3.7, 3.8, and 3.9 discuss some aspects that have not been considered or that can be improved.

    Throughout the chapter, points will be represented with a capital bold letter, vectors with a small bold letter, and scalars in italic. Page, quad, and plane will be used interchangeably to describe the same entity.

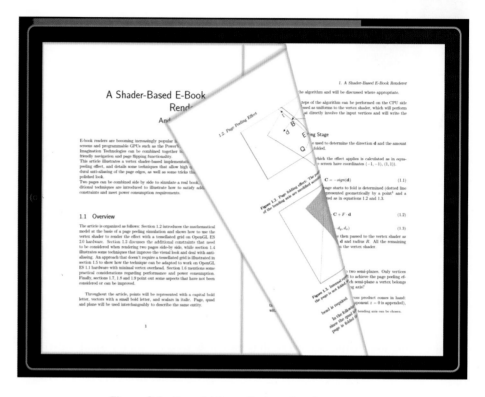

Figure 3.1. Page-folding effect rendered on screen.

3.2 Page-Peeling Effect

A page can be modeled as a quad. One corner can be selected and pulled in many directions. The mathematical model assumes that the interaction generates a bend on the page with a constant radius across the surface. When a page folds, it wraps around a semicircle by an angle that increases from $0°$ (no folding) to $180°$ (full semicircle). After that, the surface slides in parallel above the unfolded part of the page, as illustrated in Figures 3.1 and 3.2.

Since the page can be folded in any chosen direction, the original position of any arbitrary point on the quad can be modified.

In order to implement this effect on graphics hardware, the page can be represented as a highly tessellated grid whose vertices represent a discretized version of the points of the plane. The vertices' positions are modified in the vertex shader according to the folding algorithm, and the output values are then interpolated between vertices in the rasterization stage. As a smooth-looking bend is required, the tessellation factor needs to be high enough to simulate the nonlinear deformation with sufficient accuracy (as illustrated in Figure 3.3).

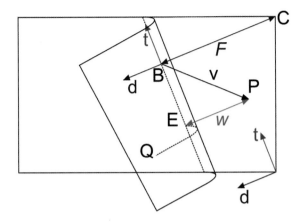

Figure 3.2. Page-folding effect: positions of the input vertices on the right of the bending axis are modified according to the model.

In the following discussion, all vectors can be considered two-dimensional since the quad initially lies on the plane with equation $z = 0$. When the page is folded, the z-coordinate does change, but this is not relevant for most stages of the algorithm and will be discussed where appropriate.

Some of the steps of the algorithm can be performed on the CPU side, and the results passed as uniforms to the vertex shader, which will perform only operations that directly involve the input vertices and will write the output position.

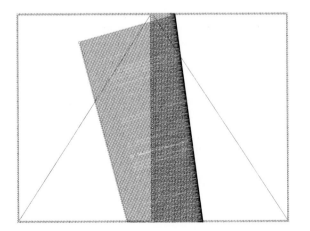

Figure 3.3. Internal representation: a tessellated grid is used as the input. When the page is not folded, two triangles can be used to render it.

3.2.1 Pre-Processing Stage

The touch screen can be used to determine the direction **d** and the amount (extent) F by which the page is folded.

First, the corner to which the effect applies is calculated as in Equation (3.1) (the corners of the screen have coordinates $(-1, -1)$, $(1, 1)$):

$$\mathbf{C} = -\text{sign}(\mathbf{d}) \tag{3.1}$$

Then, the axis where the page starts to fold is determined (dotted line in Figure 3.2). This can be represented geometrically by a point[1] and a direction, which can be calculated as in Equations (3.2) and (3.3).

$$\mathbf{B} = \mathbf{C} + F \cdot \mathbf{d} \tag{3.2}$$
$$\mathbf{t} = (-d_y, d_x) \tag{3.3}$$

The calculated values **B** and **t** are then passed to the vertex shader as uniforms, together with the direction **d** and radius R. All the remaining steps of the algorithm are performed in the vertex shader.

3.2.2 Per-Vertex Stage

The bending axis partitions the plane into two semiplanes. Only vertices in the right semiplane need to be modified to achieve the page-peeling effect. How is it possible to determine to which semiplane a vertex belongs, and what is its distance from the bending axis?

The right-handedness property of the cross product comes in handy: given two vectors **t** and **v** (to which a third component $z = 0$ is appended), the resulting vector $\mathbf{s} = \mathbf{t} \times \mathbf{v}$ will point upward if **t** follows **v**, and downward otherwise. Additionally, the length of **s** is given by Equation (3.4), where **t** is unitary:

$$|\mathbf{s}| = |\mathbf{t}||\mathbf{v}| \sin \theta_{tv} = |\mathbf{v}| \sin \theta_{tv} \tag{3.4}$$

Since **t** and **v** both lie on the same plane $z = 0$, the scalar value $w = s_z$, which satisfies $|w| = |s_z| = |\mathbf{s}|$, gives all the required information. In fact, the sign of w represents the direction of the resulting vector **s** and tells which semiplane the vertex belongs to, and its absolute value is the distance from the axis.

It can be noticed in Figure 3.2 that the relation $w = -\mathbf{d} \cdot \mathbf{v}$ also holds since the dot product calculates the projection of the vector **v** into **d**, which can be on either side of the bending axis. To summarize, both the cross and dot product can be used to get the required information as Equation (3.5) shows:

$$|w| = |\mathbf{v}| \cos \theta_{dv} = |\mathbf{d} \cdot \mathbf{v}| = |\mathbf{t} \times \mathbf{v}| = |\mathbf{v}| \sin \theta_{tv} = |s_z|. \tag{3.5}$$

---

[1]For the purposes of the algorithm, any point on the bending axis can be chosen.

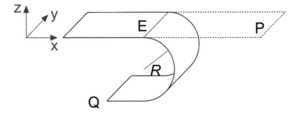

Figure 3.4. Model for bending effect: For vertices with $w > 0$ the position needs to to be recalculated by wrapping it along the curve path.

If a vertex lies on the right semiplane, it needs to be folded as illustrated in Figure 3.4.

The final vertex position $\mathbf{Q}$ needs to be updated according to the folding direction $\mathbf{d}$ and distance from the axis w. First, the projection $\mathbf{E}$ of $\mathbf{P}$ onto the bending axis is calculated as in Equation (3.6):

$$\mathbf{E} = \mathbf{B} + (\mathbf{v} \cdot \mathbf{t})\,\mathbf{t} \qquad (3.6)$$

Figure 3.4 shows that the x-, y- and z-components of the input vertex are updated differently. All the remaining calculations are based on the known distance w and the direction $-\mathbf{d}$, labeled $\mathbf{u}$ for convenience. The angle $\alpha = w/R$ is used, as well, to update the final position.

If $\alpha < \pi$, then the final position of the vertex lies on the semicircle and can be calculated as in Equation (3.7):

$$\mathbf{Q_{xy}} = \mathbf{E} + R \cdot \sin\,\alpha \cdot \mathbf{u}. \qquad (3.7)$$

If $\alpha \geq \pi$ instead, the updated position will just be parallel to the original plane as Equation (3.8) states:

$$\mathbf{Q_{xy}} = \mathbf{E} - (w - \pi R)\,\mathbf{u}. \qquad (3.8)$$

As for the depth component, the final z-position is calculated as $Q_z = -2w/\pi$ if the vertex lies in the semicircle and $Q_z = -2R$ otherwise.

Note that the final depth value is always in the range allowed for normalized device coordinates (this is necessary to avoid clipping after the perspective divide), since the relation in Equation (3.9) holds:

$$Q_z \in (-2R, 0) \subset (-1, 1)\,, R < 0.5. \qquad (3.9)$$

The described algorithm can be implemented in the vertex shader as shown in Listing 3.1. Note that the texture coordinates do not need to be altered since only the vertex positions change.

```
attribute highp    vec3   inVertex;
attribute medium vec2   inTexCoord;
uniform highp float Radius;
uniform highp vec2 Direction;
uniform highp vec2 Tangent;
uniform highp vec2 Point;
varying medium vec2    TexCoord;
const highp float PI = 3.141592;
const highp float INV_PI_2 = 2.0 / PI;
void main()
{
  highp vec2 vertex = inVertex.xy;
  highp vec2 v = vertex - Point;
  // w can equally be calculated with the cross product
  highp float w = -dot(v, Direction);
  if (w > 0.0)
  {
    highp vec2 E = Point + dot(v, Tangent) * Tangent;
    highp float angle = w / Radius;
    if (angle < PI) {
      gl_Position.xy = E - Radius * sin(angle) * Direction;
      gl_Position.z = -INV_PI_2 * w;
    }
    else {
      gl_Position.xy = E + (w - PI * Radius) * Direction;
      gl_Position.z = -2.0 * Radius;
    }
  }
  else
    gl_Position.xyz = vec3(vertex, 0.0);

  gl_Position.w = 1.0;

  TexCoord = inTexCoord;
}
```

Listing 3.1. OpenGL ES 2.0 vertex shader for basic page-peeling effect.

3.2.3 Taking Aspect Ratio into Account

The description above assumes that the input quad is a square. Since all devices have a rectangular aspect ratio, applying the basic algorithm will cause the image to appear stretched along the major axis and the edges of the page to look nonorthogonal. This can be solved by premultiplying the x-component of the input vertex by the aspect ratio before applying the algorithm, and dividing the x-component of the final position by the aspect ratio. Additionally, it is recommended that the relative tessellation of the input grid matches the screen aspect ratio, so that the vertices will be spaced equally in the two dimensions, once stretched to the screen.

3.3 Enabling Two Pages Side-by-Side

The presented approach illustrates the basic page-folding effect, although a representative usage case is composed of two pages side-by-side, with the additional constraint that pages cannot be folded on the inner side. The algorithm can be extended to take this into account, and only the preprocessing stage needs to be modified.

More formally, the bending axis can intersect the page either on the top or bottom edge or both. The x-coordinate of this intersection (the closest to the inner edge if two intersections are present) represents the amount by which the page is folded on either the top or bottom edge, and must be smaller than the width of the page (which is equivalent to the aspect ratio a). Such amount x depends on the folding value F, direction $\mathbf{d}$, and tangent $\mathbf{t}$ as illustrated by Equation (3.10), which is solved by Equations (3.11) and (3.12):[2]

$$F\mathbf{d} + \lambda\mathbf{t} = \begin{pmatrix} x \\ 0 \end{pmatrix},\tag{3.10}$$

$$\begin{cases} Fd_x - \lambda d_y = x \\ Fd_y + \lambda d_x = 0, \end{cases}\tag{3.11}$$

$$x = Fd_x - \left(-F\frac{d_y}{d_x}\right)d_y = F\left(d_x + \frac{d_y^2}{d_x}\right) = F\frac{d_x^2 + d_y^2}{d_x} = \frac{F}{d_x}.\tag{3.12}$$

If $x > a$, then F exceeds the maximum value given the direction $\mathbf{d}$, as shown in Figure 3.5(a). If a different angle is chosen, the page can fold in a direction that satisfies the constraint, while preserving the same folding value F.

Let θ be the angle corresponding to the direction $\mathbf{d}$. Values of $|\theta|$ close to $\pi/2$ cause x to approach the limit a quickly, since the page folds almost vertically,[3] therefore when $x > a$ it is appropriate to use a new value θ', where $|\theta'| < |\theta|$. Once the new angle is calculated, all other dependent variables can be updated and passed to the vertex shader.

---

[2]Here the corner is assumed to have coordinates $(0,0)$ and applying the two vectors $F\mathbf{d}$ and $\lambda\mathbf{t}$ corresponds to a translation of $(x,0)^T$.

[3]Since the page can fold upwards or downwards, θ can be positive or negative and the modulus operator accounts for this.

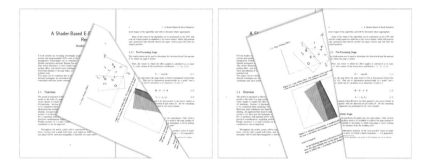

Figure 3.5. Angle correction: to prevent page tearing (left), the direction is modified in order to meet the constraint $x \leq a$ (right).

The correction $\theta_c = \theta' - \theta$ that needs to be applied in order to meet the constraint is calculated in Equation (3.13):

$$\theta_c = -\text{sign}(d_x d_y) F \frac{x - a}{x}. \tag{3.13}$$

The term $-\text{sign}(d_x d_y)$ takes into account the fact that θ can be positive or negative, ensuring that $|\theta'| < |\theta|$.[4]

The absolute value of θ_c needs to be proportional to F and the difference $(x - a)$, normalized by a factor $1/x$ to ensure small corrections for large x values (this is an heuristic that works well in practice).

```
bool PageFolded(theta, newTheta, radius, newRadius) {
  if (theta * newTheta < 0) {
    newRadius = radius - abs(newTheta);
    newTheta = 0;
    if (newRadius < 0) {
      newRadius = 0;
      return true; // page completely folded
    }
  }
  return false; // page not completely folded
}
```

Listing 3.2. Pseudo-code to enforce the additional constraint on side-by-side pages.

---

[4]The term d_x in Equation (3.13) is necessary to handle correctly the right page, where the angle correction needs to be inverted. The full example can be found in the code.

If F is large enough, it means that the user is dragging a finger across the whole screen, and the page should fold completely. In order to do this it is necessary to modify the current model so that once θ' reaches 0 (condition by which the page is parallel and almost completely covers the one underneath), the radius decreases to 0 as well to complete the peel effect. Listing 3.2 illustrates the final update stage.

Once the angle and radius are updated, all the required uniforms are calculated and passed to the vertex shader.

3.4   Improving the Look and Antialiasing Edges

Since pages are predominantly white, when a page is folded the edge is not clearly visible, and it's therefore useful to add some sort of shading to improve the general look. A simple technique to achieve this is to use a fade-to-gray gradient on the edges of the pages. This can be done efficiently by splitting the grid representing a page into two meshes (as in Figure 3.3), one representing the page content to be rendered with a standard lookup shader, and a border rendered with a shader that mixes the color of the page with a gray gradient (since a color mix is done in the fragment shader and this affects only the border of the page, the simpler shader can be used when the gradient is not necessary).

The effect highlights the border of the pages as required, but introduces some noticeable aliasing artifacts on the edges. By adding an external border that can be rendered with a similar gradient and enabling blending, a shadow-like effect is made and the aliasing problem is mitigated. Figure 3.6 shows how the borders can improve the render quality.

Even though aliasing is sensibly reduced by the introduction of the external border, it is not completely removed in cases where the destination color is not white. This is noticeable on the black title text in Figure 3.6(c), since, on the edge, the internal and external fragments have intensity 0.5 and 0.0, respectively, the latter due to the blend between the black text and the gray border. The quality can be considered acceptable and further refinements are not considered here.

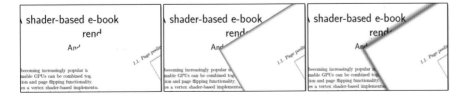

Figure 3.6. Antialiasing edges: simple shader (left), internal gradient border (center), internal and external border (right). The intensity values and widths of the borders can be tweaked to obtain the desired look.

In addition to the physical borders of the page, the area where the page bends includes an edge that can be perceived visually and could be improved by some form of shading. A gradient-based technique can be used here too, and the gradient can be calculated as a simple function of the angle α, available in the vertex shader. Since the folding direction is arbitrary, in this case it's not possible to split the original mesh in two, and this results in a more expensive fragment shader being applied to the whole page. The next section introduces an alternative rendering technique that, as a side effect, addresses this issue.

3.5 Direction-Aligned Triangle Strip

By using a screen-aligned grid, the tessellation needs to be uniform across the whole page, even though only a small part of it is folded. While in principle this can enable more complex deformation effects in the vertex shader, it is not strictly necessary for a simple page fold. A more efficient approach that exploits the nature of the problem is to tessellate only the bent part of the page, while two trapezoids can be used to render the flat areas. Since the fold is one-dimensional (i.e., it doesn't vary along the tangent) it is sufficient to generate a triangle strip aligned with the direction $\mathbf{d}$.

As Figure 3.7 shows, in the general case the page can be split into two trapezoids and a triangle strip. The intersection between the first trapezoid and the strip is delimited by the bending axis, while the length of the strip equals the length of the semicircle πR. The method in [Sutherland and Hodgman 74] can be used as a general algorithm to clip the page against the arbitrary bending

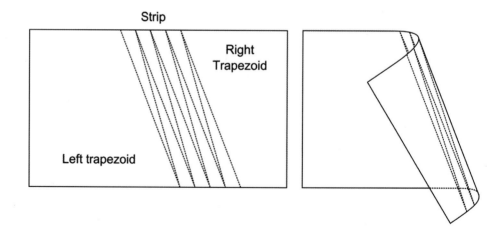

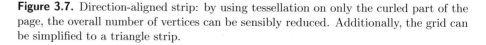

Figure 3.7. Direction-aligned strip: by using tessellation on only the curled part of the page, the overall number of vertices can be sensibly reduced. Additionally, the grid can be simplified to a triangle strip.

axis and create the two trapezoids. The triangle strip and the trapezoids can be generated procedurally on the CPU every time the input changes and can then be passed to OpenGL for rendering.

If an internal border is used as described in the previous section, the number of meshes and intersections to be determined further increases. Many subcases can be envisioned depending on how the bending axis partitions the page, and some extensive coding is necessary to cover all of them. If needed, the whole geometry can be preprocessed on the CPU and the page can be submitted already folded to the graphics renderer, allowing this technique to run on OpenGL ES 1.1-class hardware. For the purposes of this chapter only the general idea is presented and the implementation is left to the reader (though code for the tessellation-grid approach is included).

Note, separating the input quad into individual meshes further reduces the overall number of computations performed on the GPU, since a simple lookup shader can be used for most of the area (flat trapezoids), while the application of fancier shaders with gradients can be limited to the bent part of the page.

3.6 Performance Optimizations and Power Consumption

To ensure maximum battery life, render-on-demand is implemented by updating the frame only when the folding value and direction change. Although very simple to implement, this technique is critical for this kind of application, since expected battery life for eBook readers is very important. Rendering the same static image in each frame needlessly drains the battery of the device.

In typical usage the user reads a page, then folds, then reads another page and so on. Most of the time will be spent idle waiting for the next page to be folded. Drawing nonfolded pages can be done very cheaply by rendering simple quads.

When the page is actually folding and a render is required, it is preferable to use the triangle strip variant instead of the tessellated grid approach, since many fewer vertices are submitted. The cost difference between the two techniques does not apply if a page is partially folded but no render is required.

3.7 Putting it Together

The techniques illustrated so far can be used to render two pages side-by-side and fold them if required. By simply adding two more pages and keeping track of the textures to be bound to each page, it is possible to simulate a book with an arbitrary number of pages. Additional coding is necessary to limit the regions of the screen where the user can interact (pages can be folded only from the borders) and to handle page unfolding correctly. The two sides of a page can be represented by two different textures, and the page can be rendered twice, with front- and back-face cull. Figure 3.1 shows the final effect rendered on screen.

The code available in the book's web materials features a simple eBook application that allows the user to browse through a predefined set of pages and takes into account some additional practical conditions not considered in this chapter.

3.8   Future Work

The chapter has been presented with the assumption that the pages to be rendered are stored as textures, and no considerations have been made about the best way to render text. True-type fonts are common in eBook readers and a better way to display text could be to render true-type text to textures whose resolutions match the area on screen that is covered by the pages. More research could be done to ensure the best mapping of the text on screen even where the page is folded.

Procedural antialiasing techniques proved to be effective, and tweaking the blending values and gradients resulted in a neat look. Some additional improvements can be achieved, for example, by procedurally mixing the gradient in the external border with the contents underneath it, rather than using simple alpha blending.

Touchscreen interaction has been used mainly to determine the direction in which the page needs to be folded. A more advanced use could be to enable zooming and additional features based on multitouch input.

The mathematical model used to enable the page-peeling effect is simple, and some constraints like parallelism between the unfolded and folded parts of the page, and constant folding radius across the page could be relaxed. More complex models could investigate how to use multitouch to apply more folds to a single page or enable more complex types of deformation, where the tessellated-grid approach would be more suitable than the tailored triangle-strip variant.

3.9   Conclusion

Graphics hardware capable of vertex processing can exploit the problem of folding a plane in any arbitrary direction by means of a highly tessellated grid. A sample application for iPad (available in the source code release) has been developed, and approximately 17,000 faces have been used per-page without any noticeable degrade in visual quality or performance at 1024×768 resolution.

The cost per vertex is relatively low, given the optimizations introduced in this paper, and the fragment shaders are quite simple, generally consisting of a texture lookup and a sum or mix with a gradient color, making low-end OpenGL ES 2.0 devices a good target for this kind of application.

By taking a different approach, it is possible to reduce the input of the graphics renderer to two trapezoids and a triangle strip, which can be rendered on OpenGL ES 1.1-class hardware, although more coding is required to handle all the intersection subcases and pregenerate the geometry.

Render-on-demand is central in this design to maximize battery life, and some expedients can be used to minimize the cost-per-render.

3.10 Acknowledgments

The author would like to thank Kristof Beets, Sergio Tota, and the whole BizDev and DevTech teams for their work, contribution and feedback.

Bibliography

[Sutherland and Hodgman 74] Ivan E. Sutherland and Gary W. Hodgman. "Reentrant Polygon Clipping." *Communications of the ACM* 17:1 (1974), 32–42.

Post-Processing Effects on Mobile Devices

Marco Weber and Peter Quayle

Image processing on the GPU, particularly real-time post-processing, is an important aspect of modern graphical applications, and has wide and varied uses from games to user interfaces. Because of the continually improved performance levels of graphics hardware, post-processing effects are now common on the desktop and in the console space. With the current generation of OpenGL ES 2.0-enabled embedded GPUs, an increasing number of such effects are also possible on mobile devices. Bloom effects, for example, can add a vivid glow to a scene; color transforms and distortions can provide a stylistic flair; blur, and depth-of-field effects can draw attention to areas of interest, or highlight selected elements in a user interface. Figure 4.1 shows some generic examples of post-processing effects, and Figure 4.2 demonstrates the use of a blur effect in a user interface.

Post-processing is the modification and manipulation of captured or generated image data during the last stage of a graphics pipeline, resulting in the final output picture. Traditionally, these operations were performed by the host system CPU by reading back the input image data and altering it. This is a very costly operation and is not suitable for applications that require interactive frame rates on mobile platforms. Using the processing power of modern graphics hardware to do the image data manipulation is a more practical and efficient approach.

This chapter describes a general approach to post-processing and provides an example of a real-time effect that can be implemented on OpenGL ES 2.0-capable hardware, such as POWERVR SGX.

4.1 Overview

The general idea behind post-processing is to take an image as input and generate an image as output (see Figure 4.3). You are not limited to only using the provided input image data, since you can use any available data source (such as

Figure 4.1. Radial twist, sepia color transformation, depth of field, depth of field and sepia color transformation combined (clockwise from top left).

Figure 4.2. Post-processing effect on the Samsung Galaxy S. The background of the user interface is blurred and darkened to draw attention to items in the foreground.

Input Image   Output Image

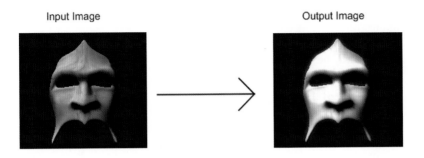

Figure 4.3. Image input and output.

depth and stencil buffers), as additional input for the post-processing step. The only requirement is that the end result has to be an image.

One direct advantage of this approach is that, due to the identical basic format of input and output, it is possible to chain post-processing techniques. As illustrated in Figure 4.4, the output of the first post-processing step is reused as input for the second step. This can be repeated with as many post-processing

Input Image   Effect   Output Image

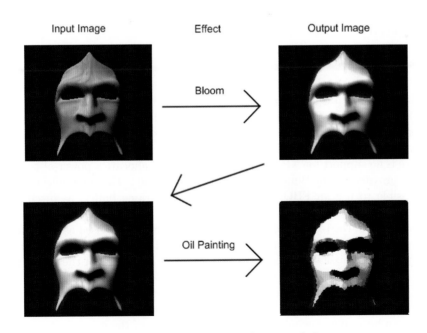

Figure 4.4. Image input and output chain.

techniques as required. Some sets of post-processing techniques can be merged to avoid the overhead of chaining, while others can exploit chaining to achieve a performance increase, as explained later.

Each step is performed by rendering to a frame buffer object (FBO). The final output image will be displayed on the screen.

4.2 Technical Details

To generate the first input image we must render our scene to a texture. As mentioned in the previous section, to do this we use FBOs. There are other ways to accomplish the same results, such as creating textures by copying data from the framebuffer, but using FBOs is better for performance (for a more detailed discussion see [Imagination Technologies 10]).

We will make use of pixel-shader support, as found in the POWERVR SGX graphics cores, since they provide a great deal of flexibility when developing post-processing effects. It is possible to implement some basic post-processing techniques with a fixed-function pipeline, but this is beyond the scope of this chapter.

The basic algorithmic steps for a post-processing effect are as follows:

1. Render the scene to a texture.

2. Render a full screen pass using a custom pixel shader, with the texture from the previous stage as input, to apply the effect.

3. Repeat step two until all effects are processed.

The first step is the most straightforward, because it simply requires setting a different render target. Instead of rendering to the back buffer, you can create an FBO of the same dimensions as your frame buffer. In the case that the frame buffer dimensions are not a power of two (e.g., 128×128, 256×256 etc.), you must check that the graphics hardware supports non-power-of-two (NPOT) textures. If there is no support for NPOT textures, you could allocate a power-of-two FBO that approximates the dimensions of the frame buffer. For some effects it may be possible to use an FBO far smaller than the frame buffer, as discussed in Section 4.4.

In step two, the texture acquired during step one can be used as input for the post-processing. In order to apply the effect, a full-screen quad is drawn using a post-processing pixel shader to apply the effect to each pixel of the final image.

All of the post-processing is executed within the pixel shader. For example, in order to apply an image convolution filter, neighboring texels have to be sampled and modulated to calculate the resulting pixel. Figure 4.5 illustrates the kernel, which can be seen as a window sliding over each line of the image and evaluating each pixel at its center by fetching neighboring pixels and combining them.

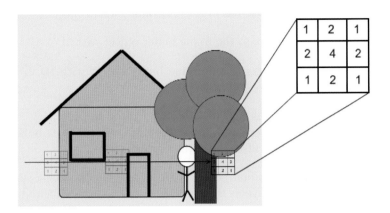

Figure 4.5. Gaussian blur filtering.

Step three describes how easy it is to build a chain of post-processing effects by simply executing one after another, using the output of the previous effect as the input for the next effect. In order to accomplish this, it is necessary to allocate more than one frame buffer object as it is not possible to simultaneously read from and write to the same texture.

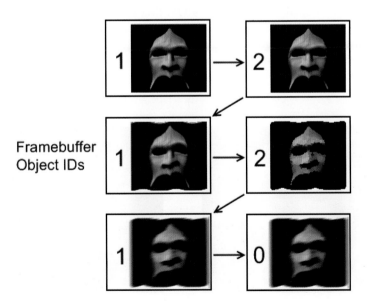

Figure 4.6. Post-processing steps and frame buffer IDs.

Figure 4.6 illustrates the re-use of several frame buffer objects:

- The initial step renders to the frame buffer object with ID 1

- The second step renders to the frame buffer object with ID 2, using the previous frame buffer object as input.

- The whole procedure is repeated for steps three and four, but instead of using frame buffer object 2 again for the last step, the back buffer is used since the final result will be displayed on the screen.

Depending on the individual effect, some of the illustrated passes may be merged into one pass. This avoids the bandwidth cost associated with processing the whole image for each effect that is merged, and reduces the total number of passes required.

4.3 Case Study: Bloom

The whole concept of post-processing, as presented in the previous section, is suitable for high-performance graphics chips in the desktop domain. In order to implement post-processing on mobile graphics chipsets, such as POWERVR SGX graphics cores, it is most important to act with caution. In this section, we illustrate an actual implementation of the bloom effect tailored for implementation on an embedded GPU, such as POWERVR SGX, at an interactive frame rate. The required optimizations and alterations to the original algorithm are explained throughout the following sections. At the beginning of this section the effect itself will be explained, followed by the actual implementation and some optimization strategies.

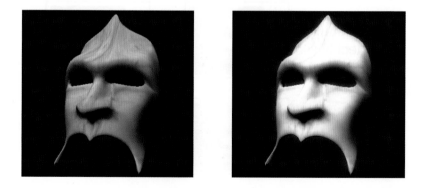

Figure 4.7. Mask without and with glow applied.

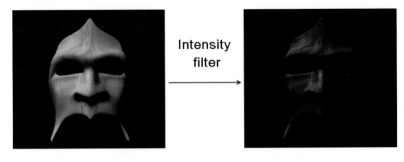

Figure 4.8. Applying an intensity filter to obtain bright parts.

The bloom effect simulates our perception of bright light by producing a pronounced glow and a halo around bright objects. Furthermore, it gives the impression of high dynamic range rendering despite being done in a low dynamic range. Another useful side effect is that it reduces aliasing artifacts due to the slight glow at the edges of objects. The whole effect and its intensity can be controlled by an artist and can be used to attract attention to objects and make them distinct (see Figure 4.7).

The bloom effect is achieved by intensifying bright parts of the image. In order to accomplish this, the bright parts of the image have to be identified and isolated. This can happen either implicitly by applying an intensity filter to the input image to extract the bright parts (see Figure 4.8), or explicitly by specifying the glowing parts through a separate data source, (e.g., the alpha channel of the individual textures).

The intensity filtered texture, which contains the bright parts of the image, will then be blurred with a convolution kernel in the next step. The weights of the kernel used in this example are chosen to resemble the weights of the Gaussian blur kernel. The kernel itself is applied by running a full shader pass over the whole texture and executing the filter for each texture element. Depending on the number of blur iterations and the size of the kernel, most of the remaining high frequencies will be eliminated and a ghostly image will remain (see Figure 4.9). Furthermore, due to the blurring, the image is consecutively smeared and thus enlarged, creating the halos when combined with the original image.

The final step is to additively blend the resulting bloom texture over the original image by doing a full screen pass. This amplifies the bright parts of the image and produces a halo around glowing objects due to the blurring of the intensity-filtered texture (see Figure 4.10).

The final amount of bloom can be controlled by changing the blend function from additive blending to an alpha-based blending function, offering even more artistic freedom. By animating the alpha value we can vary the amount of bloom and simulate a pulsing light.

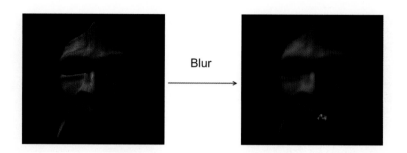

Figure 4.9. Applying Gaussian blur.

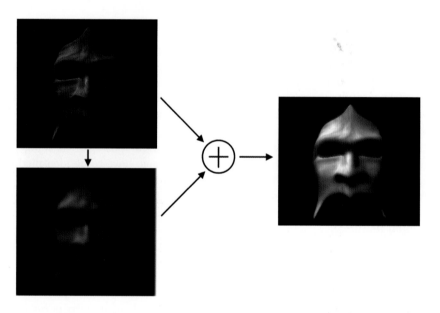

Figure 4.10. Additive blending of original and blurred intensity-filtered image.

4.4   Implementation

The bloom algorithm presented in the previous section describes the general approach one might implement when processing resources are vast. Two full screen passes for intensity filtering and final blending and several passes for the blur filter in the most naive implementation are very demanding even for the fastest graphics cards.

Due to the nature of mobile platforms, adjustments to the original algorithm have to be made in order to get it running, even when the hardware is equipped with a highly efficient POWERVR SGX core.

The end result has to look convincing and must run at interactive frame rates. Thus, most of the steps illustrated in Section 4.3 have to be modified in order to meet the resource constraints.

4.4.1 Resolution

One of the realities of mobile graphics hardware is a need for low power and long battery life, which demand lower clock frequencies. Although the POWERVR SGX cores implement a very efficient tile-based deferred rendering approach, it is still essential to optimize aggressively when implementing full screen post-processing effects.

In our implementation the resolution of the frame buffer object for the blurred texture was set to 128×128, which has shown to be sufficient for VGA (640×480) displays. Depending on the target device's screen and the content being rendered, even 64×64 may be adequate; the trade-off between visual quality and performance should be inspected by regularly testing the target device. It should be kept in mind that using half the resolution (e.g., 64×64 instead of 128×128) means a 75% reduction in the number of pixels being processed.

Since the original image data is not being reused because of the reduced resolution, the objects using the bloom effect have to be redrawn. This circumstance can be exploited for another optimization. As we are drawing only the objects which are affected by the bloom, it is possible to calculate a bounding box enclosing these objects that in turn will be reused in the following processing steps as a kind of scissor mechanism.

When initially drawing the objects to the frame buffer object, one could take the optimization even further and completely omit texture mapping (see Figure 4.11). This would mean that the vertex shader would calculate only the

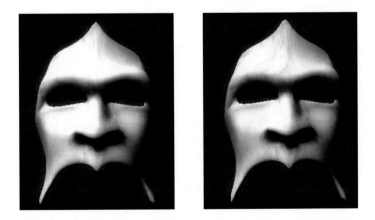

Figure 4.11. Difference between nontextured (left) and textured (right) bloom.

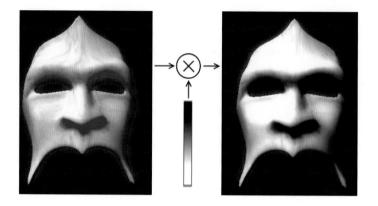

Figure 4.12. Transforming the brightness scalar by doing a texture lookup in an intensity map.

vertex transformation and the lighting equation, which would reduce the amount of data being processed in the fragment shader even further, at the expense of some detail. Each different case should be evaluated to judge whether the performance gain is worth the visual sacrifice.

When omitting texture mapping, the scalar output of the lighting equation represents the input data for the blur stage, but if we simply used scalar output for the following steps, the resulting image would be too bright, even in the darker regions of the input image, which is why the intensity filter has to be applied. Applying the intensity filter can be achieved by doing a texture lookup into a 1D texture, representing a transformation of the luminance (see Figure 4.12). This texture can be generated procedurally by specifying a mapping function, or manually, whereby the amount of bloom can be stylized to meet artistic needs. The lookup to achieve the intensity filtering can potentially be merged into the lighting equation. Other parts of the lighting equation could also be computed via the lookup table, for example, by premultiplying the values in it by a constant color.

4.4.2 Convolution

Once we've rendered our intensity-filtered objects to the frame buffer object, the resulting image can be used as input for the blur-filtering steps. This section explains the blur-filtering methods which are depicted in Figure 4.13.

Image convolution is a common operation and can be executed very efficiently on the GPU. The naive approach is to calculate the texture-coordinate offsets (e.g., 1/width and 1/height of texture image) and sample the surrounding texels. The next step is to combine these samples by applying either linear filters (Gaussian, median, etc.) or morphologic operations (dilation, erosion, etc.).

Figure 4.13. Blurring the input image in a low-resolution render target with a separated blur filter kernel.

In this case we will apply a Gaussian blur to smooth the image. Depending on the size of the filter kernel, we have to read a certain amount of texture values, multiply each of them by a weight, sum the results, and divide by a normalization factor. In the case of a 3×3 kernel this results in nine texture lookups, nine multiplications, eight additions, and one divide operation, which is a total of 27 operations to filter a single texture element. The normalization can be included in the weights, reducing the total operation count to 26.

Fortunately, the Gaussian blur is a separable filter, which means that the filter kernel can be expressed as the outer product of two vectors:

$$\begin{pmatrix} 1 & 2 & 1 \\ 2 & 4 & 2 \\ 1 & 2 & 1 \end{pmatrix} = \begin{pmatrix} 1 & 2 & 1 \end{pmatrix} \otimes \begin{pmatrix} 1 & 2 & 1 \end{pmatrix}.$$

Making use of the associativity,

$$t \cdot (v \cdot h) = (t \cdot v) \cdot h,$$

where t represents the texel, v the column, and h the row vector, we can first apply the vertical filter and, in a second pass, the horizontal filter, or vice versa. This results in three texture lookups, three multiplications, and two additions per pass, giving a total of 16 operations when applying both passes. This reduction in the number of operations is even more dramatic when increasing the kernel size (e.g., 5×5, 7×7, etc.)(see Table 4.1):

Kernel	Texture Lookups	Muls	Adds	No. Of Operations
3x3 (standard)	9	9	8	26
3x3 (separated)	6	6	4	16
5x5 (standard)	25	25	24	74
5x5 (separated)	10	10	8	28
9x9 (standard)	81	81	80	242
9x9 (separated)	18	18	17	53

Table 4.1.

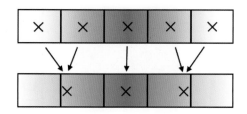

Figure 4.14. Reducing the number of texture lookups by using hardware texture filtering.

In most cases, separating the filter into horizontal and vertical passes results in a large performance increase. However, the naive single-pass version may be faster in situations in which bandwidth is severely limited. It is always worth benchmarking to ensure the best solution for a given platform or scenario.

The number of texture lookups can be decreased again by exploiting hardware texture filtering. The trick is to replace the texture lookup for the outer weights with one which is between the outer texels, as shown in Figure 4.14.

The way this works is as follows: when summing the contribution, s, of the outer texels, t_0 and t_1, in the unoptimized version, we use

$$s = t_0 w_0 + t_0 w_1. \tag{4.1}$$

When we sample between the outer texels with linear filtering enabled we have

$$s = t_0(1 - u) + t_1 u, \tag{4.2}$$

where u is the normalized position of the sample point in relation to the two texels. So by adjusting u we can blend between the two texel values. We want to blend the texels with a value for u such that the ratio of $(1 - u)$ to u is the same as the ratio of w_0 to w_1. We can calculate u using the texel weights

$$u = w_1 / (w_0 + w_1). \tag{4.3}$$

We can then substitute u into Equation (4.2). Because u must be a value between 0 and 1, we need to multiply s by the sum of the two weights. Our final equation looks like this:

$$s = (t_0 (1 - u) + t_1 u) (w_0 + w_1). \tag{4.4}$$

Although this appears to contain more operations than Equation (4.1), the cost of the term in the first set of brackets is negligible because linear texture filtering is effectively a free operation. In the case of the 5×5 filter kernel, the number of texture lookups can be reduced from ten to six, yielding the identical number of computation necessary as for the 3×3 kernel.

It is important that the texture coordinates are calculated in the vertex shader and passed to the pixel shader as varyings, rather than being calculated in the pixel shader. This will prevent dependent texture reads. Although these are supported, they incur a potentially substantial performance hit. Avoiding dependent texture reads means that the texture-sampling hardware can fetch the texels sooner and hide the latency of accessing memory.

4.4.3 Blending

The last step is to blend the blurred image over the original image to produce the final result, as shown in Figure 4.15.

Therefore, the blending modes have to be configured and blending enabled so that the blurred image is copied on top of the original one. Alternatively, you could set up an alpha-value-based modulation scheme to control the amount of bloom in the final image.

In order to increase performance and minimize power consumption, which is crucial in mobile platforms, it is best that redundant drawing be avoided as much as possible. The single most important optimization in this stage is to minimize the blended area as far as possible. Blending is a fill-rate intensive operation, especially when being done over the whole screen. When the bloom effect is applied only to a subset of the visible objects, it is possible to optimize the final blending stage:

- In the initialization stage, calculate a bounding volume for the objects which are affected.

- During runtime, transform the bounding volume into clip space and calculate a 2D bounding volume, which encompasses the projected bounding volume. Add a small margin to the bounding box for the glow.

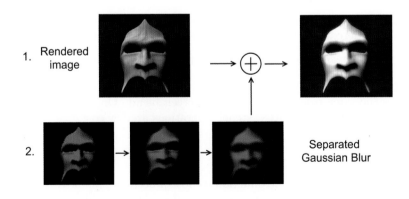

Figure 4.15. Overview of the separate bloom steps.

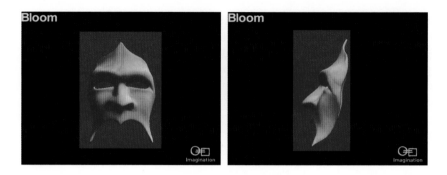

Figure 4.16. Bounding box derived rectangle (red) used for final blending.

- Draw the 2D bounding object with appropriate texture coordinates to blend the blurred texture over the original image.

Figure 4.16 shows the blending rectangle which is derived from the object's bounding box. The bounding box in this case is a simple axis-aligned bounding box which is calculated during the initialization. At runtime, the eight vertices of the bounding box are transformed into clip space and the minimum and maximum coordinate components are determined. The blended rectangle is then derived from these coordinates and the texture coordinates are adapted to the vertex positions. Depending on the shape of the object, other, more suitable, bounding volumes might be appropriate (e.g., bounding spheres).

This bounding-box-directed blending can lead to artifacts when the blending rectangles of two or more objects overlap, resulting in sharp edges and highlights that are too bright. A work-around for this overlap issue is to use the stencil buffer:

- Clear the stencil buffer to zero and enable stencil testing.

- Configure the stencil test so that only the pixels with a stencil value of zero are rendered, and the stencil value is always incremented.

- Draw all bounding volumes and disable stencil test.

Use of this algorithm prevents multiple blend operations on a single pixel and produces the same result as a single full screen blend. On a tile-based deferred renderer like POWERVR SGX, stencil operations are low cost.

4.5   Conclusion

We have presented a brief introduction to post-processing, followed by a detailed case study of a well-known post-processing effect. We have illustrated optimization techniques that make it possible to use the effect while achieving interactive framerates on mobile hardware. Many of the optimization techniques shown can be adapted and applied to other post-processing effects.

Bibliography

[Imagination Technologies 10] *PowerVR SGX OpenGL ES 2.0 Application Developer Recommendations.* 2010. http://www.imgtec.com/POWERVR/insider/POWERVR-sdk.asp.

5

Shader-Based Water Effects
Joe Davis and Ken Catterall

5.1   Introduction

Generating efficient and detailed water effects can add a great deal of realism to 3D graphics applications. In this chapter, we highlight techniques that can be used in software running on POWERVR SGX-enabled platforms to render high-quality water effects at a relatively low computational cost.

Such effects can be achieved in a variety of ways, but we will focus on the use of vertex and fragment shaders in OpenGL ES 2.0 to alter the appearance of a plane to simulate a water effect.

Although there are many examples of water effects using shaders that are readily available, they are designed mainly for high-performance graphics chips on desktop platforms. The following sections of this chapter describe how the general concepts presented in desktop implementations, in particular the technique discussed by K. Pelzer [Pelzer 04], can be tailored to run at an interactive frame rate on even low-cost POWERVR SGX platforms, including the optimizations that were made to achieve the required performance.

We refer to an example application OGLES2Water that is part of the freely available POWERVR OpenGL ES 2.0 SDK, which is included in the example code with this chapter. Up-to-date SDKs are available from the Imagination Technologies website.[1] Specific performance numbers cited refer to tests run on an OMAP3530 BeagleBoard[2] platform at VGA resolution.

5.2   Techniques

5.2.1   Geometry

In the demonstration, the plane that the water effect is applied to is a horizontal plane in world space, extending to the boundaries of the view frustum—this is

---

[1]http://www.imgtec.com/powervr/insider/powervr-sdk.asp
[2]http://www.beagleboard.org

constructed from only four or five points, as a high level of tessellation is not required. The `PVRTools` library from the POWERVR SDK contains a function, `PVRTMiscCalculateInfinitePlane()`, which obtains these points for a given set of view parameters. Because the plane is horizontal, certain calculations can be simplified by assuming the normal of the plane will always lie along the positive y-axis.

A skybox is used to encapsulate the scene. This is textured with a PVRTC-compressed 4 bits per-pixel format cubemap using bilinear filtering with nearest mipmapping to provide a good balance between performance and quality (for more information, see S. Fenney's white paper on texture compression [Fenney 03]).

5.2.2 Bump Mapping

To simulate the perturbation of the water's surface, a normal map is used to bump the plane. The normal map used in the demo is y-axis major (as opposed to many other bump maps that are z-axis major). The texture coordinate for each vertex is calculated in the vertex shader as the x- and z-values of the position attribute that has been passed into the shader. The water surface is animated by passing a time-dependent offset to the bump-map coordinates.

Since this offset amounts to a simple linear translation of the bump map, the effect on its own looks unrealistic because the perturbation travels in a single direction, rather than rippling as one would expect. For this reason it is suggested that at least two scaled and translated bump layers are applied to the plane to make the surface perturbations look much more natural (Figure 5.1).

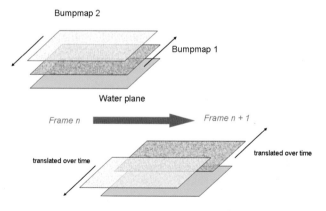

Figure 5.1. Bump map animation over two frames.

5.2.3 Reflection Render Pass

Reflection in the program is achieved through an additional render pass before the main render loop. The purpose of this is to render all of the geometry that needs to be reflected during the frame and store this information as a texture that can be applied to the water's surface during the main render. Before rendering the scene, the camera needs to be mirrored about the plane to give the correct view for the reflection.

To mirror the view matrix about the water plane, a custom transformation is required. The code in Listing 5.1 shows how this matrix is constructed (from `RenderReflectionTexture` in our example).

```
// Mirror the view matrix about the plane.
PVRTMat4 mMirrorCam(PVRTMat4::Identity());
mMirrorCam.ptr()[1]  = -m_vPlaneWater.x;
mMirrorCam.ptr()[5]  = -m_vPlaneWater.y;
mMirrorCam.ptr()[9]  = -m_vPlaneWater.z;
mMirrorCam.ptr()[13] = -(2.0f * m_vPlaneWater.w);

m_mView = m_mView * mMirrorCam;
```

Listing 5.1. Constructing the view matrix.

As the diagram in Figure 5.2 shows, mirroring the camera is not enough by itself, because it results in the inclusion of objects below the water's surface, which spoils the reflection. This issue can be avoided by utilizing a user-defined clip plane along the surface of the water to remove all objects below the water from the render (See Section 5.3.1 for information on how this can be achieved in OpenGL ES 2.0). Using this inverted camera, the entire reflected scene can be rendered. Figure 5.3 shows the clipped reflection scene rendered to texture in the demo.

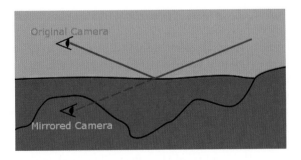

Figure 5.2. Mirrored camera for reflection.

Figure 5.3. Reflection stored as a texture.

In the main render pass, where the water plane is drawn, the reflected scene is sampled using screen-space coordinates, and then is distorted using an animated bump map normal.

The `gl_FragCoord` variable can be used to retrieve the current fragment's coordinate within the viewport, which is then normalized as follows:

```
myTexCoord = gl_FragCoord.xy * RcpWindowSize;

// where RcpWindowSize is a vec2 containing the reciprocal window
dimensions.
```

The multiply operation is used in place of a divide operation in order to reduce the required number of cycles.

To distort the reflection, an offset needs to be subtracted from these coordinates. This offset is calculated using a scaled normal sampled from a bump map. Figure 5.4 shows the perturbed result achieved from sampling the reflected scene using these distorted coordinates.

Used alone, this reflection technique results in unrealistically reflective water, since objects lying beneath the surface or coloring caused by dirt within the body of water are not considered. There are a number of steps that can be taken at this stage to improve the quality of the effect. The best option depends on the required aesthetics and performance of a particular implementation:

Figure 5.4. Water effect using only a permutated reflection texture.

- Perform another render pass to create a refraction texture (Section 5.2.4). This is expensive—reduced the performance of the effect on the development hardware by 60%, as was expected due to the extra pixel-render workload.

- Mix the color value of the fragment with a constant water color. This is good for simulating very murky water—reduced the performance by 9%, as expected due to the extra shader instructions per pixel.

- Alpha blend the water so objects below the water can be seen (Figure 5.5). This reduces the realism of the effect when rendering deep water because the edges of submerged objects will still appear sharp—reduced the performance by 11%, as expected due to the higher number of visible fragments per pixel.

It may be worth opting for one of the less intensive solutions if the required water effect is shallow, since there may be little value applying refraction in these cases. A mix between the texel color with a water color can be done in one of two ways, as discussed in Section 5.2.4.

Though introducing a new render pass comes at an additional cost, this can be reduced by adhering to the following recommendations:

1. *Render only what is necessary.* The CPU should be used to determine which objects are above the water plane and, if possible, which objects are

Figure 5.5. Water effect using a permutated reflection texture and alpha blending.

intersecting the plane since these are the only objects that will be needed during the render. If this still proves to be too expensive, the pass can be reduced to just drawing the key objects in the scene, such as a skybox and terrain.

2. *Favor FBO use over reading from the frame buffer.* Rather than using a copy function such as `glReadPixels()`, a frame buffer object with a texture bound to it should be used to store the output of the render pass in a texture [PowerVR 10]. This avoids the need to copy data from one memory location (the frame buffer) to another (texture memory), which would cost valuable cycles and bandwidth within the system. Even more important, it avoids direct access of the frame buffer that can result in a loss of parallelism, as the CPU would often be stalled, waiting for the GPU to render.

3. *Render to texture at the lowest acceptable resolution.* As the reflection texture is going to be distorted anyway, a lower resolution may be acceptable for it. A 256×256 texture has proven to be effective in the demo when running at a 640×480 display resolution, but depending on the maximum resolution of the screen on the platform being developed, this resolution could be reduced further. Keep in mind that a drop from 256×256 to 128×128 will result in a 75% lower resolution and workload.

4. *Avoid using* `discard` *to perform clipping.* Although using the discard keyword works for clipping techniques, its use decreases the efficiency of early
   order-independent depth rejection performance advantages that the POW-
   ERVR architecture offers (See Section 5.3.1 for more information).

5.2.4 Refraction Render Pass

In a case where the rendered water should appear to be fairly deep, adding refraction to the simulation can vastly improve the quality of the effect. To do this, an
approach similar to that taken during the reflection render pass should be used,
in which all objects below the water are rendered out to a texture (Figure 5.6).
Clipping (using the inverse of the water plane) can be assisted by rough culling
on the CPU beforehand. This reduces the GPU workload [PowerVR 10].

If the effect should produce very clear water, all elements of the scene below
the water should be rendered, including the skybox (or similar object) (Figure 5.7). If a murky water effect is required, a fogging effect can be used to fade
out objects at lower depths (discussed later in this section).

Once the scene has been rendered to a texture, it can then be utilized by
the water's fragment shader. The screen-space texture coordinates (as used in
Section 5.2.3) are also used to sample the refraction texture. The refraction
sample is then combined with the reflection sample, either at a constant ratio
(e.g., 50/50), or using an equation such as the Fresnel term to provide a dynamic

Figure 5.6. Refraction stored as a texture.

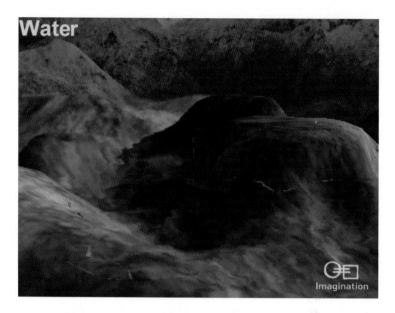

Figure 5.7. Water effect using only the refraction texture (without fogging).

Figure 5.8. Full water effect, showing edge artifact.

mixing of color, based on the current viewing angle. Figure 5.8 shows the full effect of the water, where reflection and refraction textures are mixed using the Fresnel term.

Fogging. A fogging effect to simulate water depth can be accomplished by setting a maximum fogging depth (below which objects are no longer visible) and using the value to perform a linear fade between the object's original color and the fog color based on the object's depth. To do this, the refraction pass must use the fog color as the clearing color; objects such as the skybox that should appear infinite, and therefore past the maximum fogging distance, should be omitted from the render (see Figure 5.9). Alternatively, a different fade can be used to create a more realistic fogging effect, such as an exponential fade, but this may come at an additional cost.

As the demo assumes the water plane's normal will always lie along the positive y-axis, the w-component of the water plane equation can be negated and passed into the shader as the water height (displacement from the center of the world space along the y-axis). The depth value of the vertex is then calculated in the vertex shader as an offset from this value:

```
vtx_depth=w-inVertex.y
```

The fragment shader then calculates the mixing ratio of the fog color and the object's color. This ratio is obtained using the following equation:

```
Ratio=(vtx_depth)/(max_fog_depth)
```

Figure 5.9. Water effect using only the refraction texture (with fogging).

(In practice, cycles can be saved by multiplying by the reciprocal of max_fog_depth instead of performing a division per vertex). This ratio is clamped to the range [0, 1] and then is used to determine how much of the fogging color is applied to the fragment.

On the development hardware, disabling the fogging effect gave a 3.5% increase in performance level.

The max_fog_depth value can also be used on the CPU to cull geometry below this depth. This is a good way to decrease the number of objects that need to be rendered during the refraction pass. As with the reflection pass, this rough culling reduces the amount of geometry submitted, thus saving bandwidth and unnecessary computations.

Fresnel term. The Fresnel term is used to determine how much light is reflected at the boundaries of two semitransparent materials (the rest of which is absorbed through refraction into the second material). The strongest reflection occurs when the angle of incidence of the light ray is large, and, conversely, reflection decreases as the angle of incidence decreases (Figures 5.10 and 5.11). The Fresnel term provides a ratio of transmitted-to-reflected light for a given incident light ray.

In practice, this is used to determine the correct mix between the reflected and refracted textures for any point on the water's surface from the current view position. This is the Fresnel principle in reverse, and the ratio can be obtained using an approximation derived from the same equations.

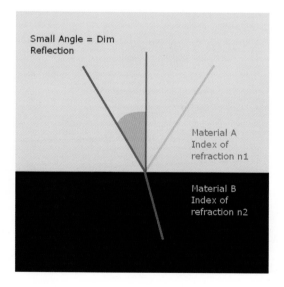

Figure 5.10. Small angle of Fresnel reflection.

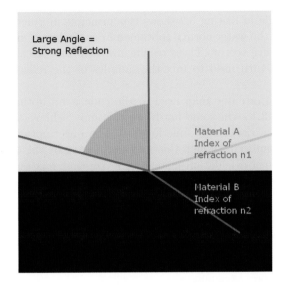

Figure 5.11. Large angle of Fresnel reflection.

The approximation of the Fresnel term used in the demo is determined using the following formulae, where n_1 and n_2 are the indices of refraction for each material [Pelzer 04]:

$$R(0) = \frac{(n_1 - n_2)^2}{(n_1 + n_2)^2},$$

$$R(\alpha) = (1 - R(0))(1 - \cos \alpha)^5 + R(0).$$

To save computation time, the result of the equation above is calculated outside of the application, using the values in Table 5.1.

Using these numbers, the constant terms in the formula can be precalculated (see Table 5.2).

n_1 (Air)	1.000293
n_2 (Water at room temperature)	1.333333

Table 5.1. Indices of refraction used in Fresnel term.

	Fresnel approximation
R(0)	0.02037
1–R(0)	0.97963

Table 5.2. Approximate values in Fresnel calculation.

The shader code in Listing 5.2 shows this principle in practice; first calculate the angle between the water normal (obtained from the bump map technique) and then the water-to-eye vector. These results are then used to calculate the Fresnel term, which is in turn used to mix the samples of the reflected and refracted scenes.

The normalization cube map used in the code is an optimization discussed later in Section 5.3.1. On some hardware this may achieve faster results than using the built-in `normalize()` functionality. The water normal here is assumed to be already normalized, though this may not always be the case.

Using the Fresnel calculation instead of a constant mix on the development hardware reduces the performance by 22%, but gives a much more realistic output.

```
// Use normalization cube map instead of normalize()
lowp vec3 vWaterToEyeCube =
    textureCube(NormalisationCubeMap,WaterToEye).rgb
        * 2.0 - 1.0;

mediump float fEyeToNormalAngle =
        clamp(dot(vWaterToEyeCube, vAccumulatedNormal), 0.0, 1.0);

// Use the approximations:
// R(0)-1 $\sim $= 0.98
// R(0) $\sim $= 0.02
mediump float fAirWaterFresnel = 1.0 - fEyeToNormalAngle;
fAirWaterFresnel = pow(fAirWaterFresnel, 5.0);
fAirWaterFresnel = (0.98 * fAirWaterFresnel) + 0.02;

// Blend reflection and refraction
lowp float fTemp = fAirWaterFresnel;
gl_FragColor = mix(vRefractionColour, vReflectionColour, fTemp);
```

Listing 5.2. Fresnel mix implementation.

5.3   Optimizations

5.3.1   User Defined Clip Planes in OpenGL ES 2.0

Although the programmability of the OpenGL ES 2.0 pipeline provides the flexibility to implement this water effect, there is a drawback in that the API does not have user-defined clip plane support, which is required to produce good quality reflections and refractions. Many OpenGL ES 2.0 text books suggest performing

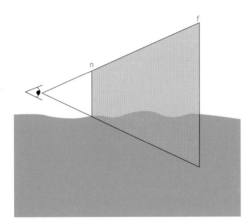

Figure 5.12. View frustum with n and f planes from original projection.

a render pass that uses a discard in the fragment shader so that fragments beyond the user-defined clip plane will be ignored. Although this method works and will produce the required output, using the `discard` keyword is highly inadvisable because it means the hardware is unable to perform early depth testing, and instead is forced to perform the full fragment shader pass. This cancels out specific performance advantages offered by some GPUs, such as those using early Z mechanisms or tile-based deferred rendering (TBDR) which include the POWERVR SGX architecture [PowerVR 10].

To solve this problem, a projection matrix modifying technique can be used [Lengyel 04]. The projection matrix (M) is used to convert all of the objects in the scene from view-space coordinates into normalized device coordinates (NDC), and part of this process is to clip objects that do not fall between the near, far, left, right, top, and bottom planes of the view frustum (Figure 5.12). By considering the function of the projection matrix in this way, it becomes apparent that there is already a built-in mechanism for clipping. Clipping along a user-defined plane can be achieved by altering the contents of the projection matrix, but this does introduce a number of problems (which will be discussed later).

The first stage of this technique requires the user-defined clip plane ($\vec{P}$) to be converted into view space. This can be done by multiplying the row vector representing the plane's coefficients (expressed in world space) by the inverse of the view matrix:

$$\vec{C} = \vec{P} \times M_{\text{view}}^{-1} = [C_x \quad C_y \quad C_z \quad C_w].$$

For this technique to work, the clipping plane must be facing away from the camera, which requires the C_w component to be negative. This does restrict the flexibility of the clipping method, but does not pose a problem for the clipping required for the water effect.

Altering the clipping planes requires operations on the rows of the projection matrix, which can be defined as

$$M = \begin{bmatrix} \vec{R}_1 \\ \vec{R}_2 \\ \vec{R}_3 \\ \vec{R}_4 \end{bmatrix}.$$

The near clipping plane ($\vec{n}$) is defined from the projection matrix M as the third row plus the fourth row, so these are the values that need to be altered:.

$$\vec{n} = \vec{R}_3 + \vec{R}_4.$$

For perspective correction to work, the fourth row must keep the values $(0, 0, -1, 0)$. For this reason, the third row has to be

$$\vec{R}_3 = [C_x \quad C_y \quad C_z + 1 \quad C_w].$$

On the other hand, the far plane ($\vec{f}$) is calculated using the projection matrix by subtracting the third row from the fourth

$$\vec{f} = \vec{R}_4 - \vec{R}_3.$$

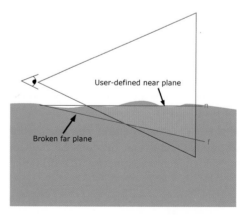

Figure 5.13. Modified view frustum with user-defined n and broken f.

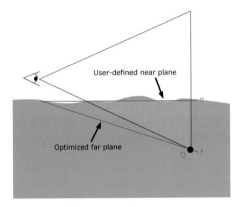

Figure 5.14. Corrected view frustum with user-defined n and optimized f.

Unfortunately, changing the near plane from its default direction along the positive z-axis results in a skewed far plane that no longer remains parallel with the near plane (Figure 5.13). This is due to the way in which the far plane is calculated in the above formula.

Although this problem cannot be corrected completely, the effect can be minimized by scaling the clip plane before the third row is set, which causes the orientation of the far clipping plane to change. Ideally, this scaling should result in an optimized far plane that produces the smallest possible view frustum that can still encapsulate the conventional view frustum (Figure 5.14).

To do this, the point $(\vec{Q})$ that lies furthest opposite the near plane within NDC must be calculated, using the following equation:

$$\vec{Q} = M^{-1} \left[\ \operatorname{sgn}(C_x) \quad \operatorname{sgn}(C_y) \quad 1 \quad 1 \ \right].$$

The result of this calculation can then be used to determine the scaling factor (a) that should be applied to the camera-space clip plane before it is used to alter the projection matrix:

$$a = \frac{2\vec{R}_4 \cdot \vec{Q}}{\vec{C} \cdot \vec{Q}}.$$

The camera-space plane can now be scaled before it is used to alter the projection matrix, using the following calculation:

$$\vec{C} = a\vec{C}.$$

Although this technique may seem more difficult to understand than the discard method of clipping, it is significantly faster because it allows the graphics hardware to perform clipping at almost no additional cost.

5.3.2   #define in GLSL

During production of this demo, it became apparent that using Booleans for
if and if-else statements in vertex and fragment shaders resulted in at least an
extra cycle for each decision point. This quickly became an issue because simple
shaders that were covering large portions of the screen, such as the skybox, were
processing needless cycles. Rolling out the code into a number of nearly identical
shader files would provide a way around this issue, but would cause a lot of code
duplication. To allow single shader files to be used repeatedly for multiple code
paths, the `#define` preprocessor directive was used with `#ifdef` and `#else` in
shader files so that code paths could be specified during compilation-time instead
of at runtime.

The SDK allows this when using the method `PVRTShaderLoadFromFile()`
by providing inputs for the additional parameters `aszDefineArray` and
`uiDefArraySize`, where `aszDefineArray` is a pointer to an array of strings hold-
ing defines the user wants to append and `uiDefArraySize` is the number of defines
in the array. This method automatically provides the `#define` and new-line character that need to be appended to the source code for each `define`, so the user
only needs to provide an array of strings for the names, e.g., `A_USEFUL_DEFINE`.

Once a number of shaders have been loaded in this way, the shader used for
an object can be changed during runtime to a shader with a different code path.
Although this method creates a shader for each decision path (which uses more
memory, but would also have been done if the code was rolled out in different
files), it allows the performance of shaders to be improved by removing redundant
cycles.

5.3.3   Further Optimizations/Improvements

Normalization cube map. On some hardware, the vector `normalize()` operation is
costly and a texture lookup may be cheaper. On such platforms, normalization on
a three-dimensional vector can be performed using a lookup to a normalization
cube map. For demonstration purposes, the method of generating the normal
map has been left in the code of this example, but time spent initializing the
application could be saved by loading a preexisting normalization map instead.

The theory behind this method is simple; take a directional vector as the
texture coordinate of the lookup and return the color at that position. This
color represents the normalized value of any directional vector that points to its
position. As the value retrieved using this technique is in texture space $[0, 1]$, a
conversion into normal-space $[-1, 1]$ is required. On the development platform,
this method approximately halved the number of cycles required to normalize a
vector.

Scale water distortion. Without scaling the amount of distortion that is applied
to each fragment, water in the distance can ultimately sample the reflection and

refraction textures at too large an offset, which gives water in the distance an unrealistic degree of distortion. Additionally, the bigger offset for distant fragments results in a higher amount of texture-read cache misses.

By scaling the amount of distortion that is applied to a given fragment, the visual quality of the effect can be improved and the number of stall cycles caused by texture cache misses can be reduced. This is done in the demo by dividing the wave's distortion value by the distance between the camera and the fragment's position (so fragments further from the camera are distorted less). The extra cycle cost has a minimal impact on performance (less than 1% on the test hardware) because, even though the texture-read stalls are reduced, they still account for the main bottleneck.

Render the water effect to a texture. Because of the heavy use of the fragment shader to produce the effect, the demo tends to be fragment limited on most hardware. To reduce this bottleneck, the water effect can be rendered to a texture at a lower resolution and then applied to the water plane during the final render pass. This technique benefits the speed of the demonstration by reducing the number of fragments that are rendered using the water effect. This can be further reduced (especially on a TBDR) by rendering objects that will obscure areas of the water in the final render pass, such as the demo's terrain. Although the introduction of numerous objects to the render can improve the speed of the water effect, the inaccuracies caused by mapping the texture to the final water plane can result in artifacts around the edges of models that were used during the low-resolution pass. Such artifacts are generally not that noticeable, provided that the shaders used for the additional objects in the low-resolution pass are the same as those used in the final render (i.e., rendering geometry without lighting during the low-resolution pass will cause highlights around dark edges of models in the final pass, so this should be avoided). One of the best ways to steer clear of the problems caused by the scaling is to avoid drawing objects that are very detailed around their edges that overlap the water because this reduces the likelihood of artifacts occurring. In the demo, the boat is omitted from the water's render pass because it is too detailed to be rendered without causing artifacts and does not afford as great a benefit as the terrain when covering areas of the water.

When rendering to a texture at a 256×256 resolution and performing the final render pass to a 640×480 screen, the reduction in quality is only slightly noticeable, but on the test hardware the performance level is increased by $\sim$18%.

Removing artifacts at the water's edge. One of the biggest problems with shader effects that perturb texture coordinates is the lack of control over the end texel that is chosen. Due to the clipping that is implemented in the reflection and refraction render passes, it is very easy for artifacts to appear along the edges of objects intersecting the water plane. The occurrence of artifacts occurs when

Figure 5.15. Full effect using artifact fix.

the sampled texel is taken from behind the object intersecting the water, which results in the texture sample being either the clear color, or geometry that ought to be obscured, resulting in visible seams near the water's edge. The edge artifact can be seen in Figure 5.8. To compensate, the clip-plane location is set slightly above the water surface (a small offset along the positive y-axis). In the case of the refraction render pass, such an offset will cause some of the geometry above the water to be included in the rendered image, which helps to hide the visible seams by sampling from this above-the-water geometry.

Although another inaccuracy is introduced because of the deliberately imperfect clipping, it is barely noticeable, and the effect of the original artifact is effectively removed for very little additional computation. The same benefit applies to the reflected scene, although in this case the offset direction is reversed, and clipping occurs slightly below the water. Figure 5.15 shows the scene with the artifact fix in place.

Another way to compensate for the artifacts, and improve the aesthetics of the effect, is to use fins or particle effects along the edges of objects intersecting the water to give the appearance of a wake where the water is colliding with the objects. The drawback of these techniques is that they both require the program to know where in the scene objects are intersecting the water, which can be very expensive if the water height is changing or objects in the water are moving dynamically.

5.4 Conclusion

We have presented a technique that allows a water effect to be augmented onto a simple plane, using several render passes, some simple distortion, and texture mixing in the fragment shader. Additionally, we have presented optimal techniques for user-defined clip planes, normalization, removing artifacts caused by texture-coordinate perturbation, and have also highlighted the benefits of utilizing low-resolution render passes to reduce the fragment shader workload. The result is a high-performance example with extremely compelling visual results. Though this example targets the current low-cost OpenGL ES 2.0 capable devices, it can be correspondingly scaled to take advantage of higher resolution displays and increased GPU power.

Bibliography

[PowerVR 10] Imagination Technologies. "POWERVR SGX OpenGL ES 2.0 Application Development Recommendations." www.imgtec.com/.../POWERVR%20SGX. OpenGL%20ES%202.0%20Application%20Development%20Recommendations, 2010.

[Feneny 03] Simon Fenney, "Texture Compression using Low-Frequency Signal Modulation." In *Proceedings Graphics Hardware*, pp. 84–91. New York: ACM, 2003.

[Lengyel 04] Eric Lengyel. "Modifying the Projection Matrix to Perform Oblique Near-plane Clipping." Terathon Software 3D Graphics Library, 2004. Available at http://www.terathon.com/code/oblique.html.

[Pelzer 04] Kurt Pelzer. "Advanced Water Effects." In *ShaderX*^{2}. Plano, TX: Wordware Publishing, Inc, 2004.

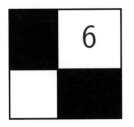

6

Realistic Real-Time Skin Rendering on Mobile

Renaldas Zioma and Ole Ciliox

6.1 Introduction

Rendering realistic human skin has always been a challenge. Skin and especially faces have many subtle properties to which our brain and eyes are very well adapted. As observers we are very quick to spot discrepancies and missing details in shading of the skin—and reject them as implausible.

Despite these challenges, the task of rendering realistic skin in real time has became possible in recent years [Jimenez 12] using the power of modern GPUs and physically based shading models. In this chapter we will discuss how to adopt the most visually important aspects of skin shading—this time on mobile GPUs.

6.2 Overview

The challenge of skin rendering lies in the fact that both aspects of light reflectance— (a) subsurface scattering and (b) surface reflectance—are more complex compared to most non-organic materials like plastic or wood.

For many uniform materials [Pharr and Humphreys 04] we can approximate subsurface scattering computation with a single diffuse term and surface reflectance with a simple calculation of specular—using Blinn-Phong, for example.

Skin, however, consists of multiple layers of translucent tissue with different light reflectance and scattering properties. In order to achieve a plausible image at real time, we have to find an effective approximation of light interacting within multiple tissue layers.

6.2.1 Skin Surface Reflectance Model

When the light hits the surface of the skin, a small fraction of it is reflected from the outermost oily layer. The oil and tissue cells of the outermost layer are dielectric materials and reflect the light without coloring it, so it can be modeled with a specular reflection function.

Most of the light enters the skin, where it is absorbed, scattered, or reflected. A significant portion of the light is reflected at the interface between subsurface layers and exits the skin again. Unsurprisingly, as demonstrated by [Donner and Jensen 05], single specular lobe is not enough to simulate this complicated process. For our implementation we have followed advice from [d'Eon and Luebke 07] and adopted two separate specular reflectance lobes.

We know from practical observations that surface reflectance is very important for how we perceive skin. Modeling specular reflectance with traditional Blinn-Phong is simply not enough. For more physically accurate surface reflectance we chose a model inspired by microfacet theory.

We use (a) Beckmann as microfacet distribution function, (b), we use a very crude approximation of the geometric term, and (c) we sacrifice correctness of the Fresnel term by measuring it from per-pixel normal instead of half-vector. Overall, our model is close to the simplification of Cook-Torrance in [Kelemen and Szirmay-Kalos 01].

6.2.2   Skin Subsurface Scattering Model

Beneath the skin's surface, light quickly becomes diffuse as it scatters and acquires color as it gets partially absorbed by the tissue. To make matters more complicated, skin consists of many layers of tissue with slightly different absorption properties—an analytical solution for such a process quickly becomes unviable.

Instead of simulating complex diffusion in subsurface skin layers, incoming light can be captured in a dedicated buffer and then blurred. Both the original article [Borshukov and Lewis 03] and the high-quality real-time implementation [d'Eon and Luebke 07] suggest using multiple gaussian blurs in texture space. However, such an approach quickly becomes impractical on mobile GPU due to high-memory bandwidth requirements.

Alternatively, incoming light can be captured in a screen-space buffer [Jimenez et al. 09], and subsurface scattering can be approximated by blurring directly in screen space. This approach has significantly lower memory bandwidth requirements with relatively small quality degradation—perfect for mobile GPUs.

6.2.3   Importance of Linear Lighting

Accurate shading of skin will fall short without gamma correction; an unrealistic yellowish tint of the skin is a typical sign [d'Eon and Luebke 07]. Since albedo textures are authored and stored in sRGB gamma, we have to *uncompress* them into the same linear space where lighting equations take place and then *compress* them back to match the sRGB gamma of display.

6.3 Power of Mobile GPU

Despite recent tremendous developments and rapid performance improvements, mobile GPUs are still at least one league behind their desktop siblings. Although programmable flexibility of mobile GPUs is quickly gaining (OpenGL ES3.0 compatible GPUs have all the features of the last generation consoles and sometimes more), computational power (ALU) and memory bandwidth are lagging behind.

Let's look at important aspects of skin rendering and discuss how viable those approaches are on mobile GPUs.

6.3.1 Skin Subsurface Scattering

Although the blurring of the screen-space buffer requires an additional rendering pass, in practice the whole subsurface scattering step takes only around 5–10% of the GPU workload in our demo, and it scales very well with the numbers of skin shaded geometry. The performance-versus-quality trade-off can easily be managed by reducing the resolution of the screen-space buffer.

6.3.2 Physically Based Shading

Even the simplest energy-conserving Blinn-Phong specular lobe is still too expensive for a real-time application on mobile GPU today. It requires too many ALU operations per-pixel. If we want to achieve a physically plausible shading beyond Blinn-Phong, then we have to rely heavily on pre-computing the BRDF using 2D textures.

Final shading of skin pixels takes around 50% of GPU workload for close-up scenes in our demo. It proved crucial to optimize this part of the algorithm.

6.3.3 Per-pixel Environment Reflections

To evaluate environment reflections a per-pixel normal sampled from normal map has to be transformed from tangent to world space. That requires three additional dot products per-pixel.

We opt to sacrifice quality and sample environment reflections using per-vertex normal instead. Because we employ extremely dense geometry for the characters, visual difference was minimal in our case.

6.3.4 Linear Lighting

Although sRGB (gamma corrected) texture reads are trivial operations for the desktop GPU, in the case of OpenGL ES2.0 such reads are only available via platform-specific extensions. Even in the case of OpenGL ES3.0 where gamma correction is part of the core API, texture reads might incur different costs depending on the GPU family. The same situation applies when writing out linear values into the final sRGB framebuffer—an extension is required in the case of

OpenGL ES2.0 and varying performance can be expected in the case of OpenGL ES3.0 depending on the device.

However, we can be smart and gamma correct only when it is absolutely necessary, i.e., only for skin pixels. The rest of scene geometry can be shaded without gamma correction.

We expect this optimization to be unnecessary in the relatively close future when OpenGL ES3.0 takes over and performance differences between GPU families become smaller.

6.4 Implementation

6.4.1 Screen-Space Light Accumulation Buffer

Our approach to subsurface scattering is to use a temporary low-resolution screen-space buffer where we accumulate all incoming light, both diffuse and ambient (see Figure 6.1). By default we use quarter resolution of the screen for the light accumulation buffer.

We start by rendering all skin shaded characters in the scene, evaluating incoming light and storing results in the buffer. Note that we want to store the light as it hits the surface and disregard albedo of the skin at this step. We mark covered pixels with alpha values to distinguish them from the background for further use in the blur step.

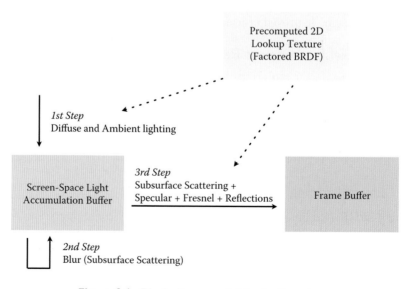

Figure 6.1. Block diagram of skin shading steps.

When rendering into the light accumulation buffer we offset geometry a little bit along normals to compensate for the low resolution of the buffer and to have more visually pleasing results on the edges of the skin shaded geometry. Possible offsets in the center of the skinned objects will be covered when we perform blur in the next step.

6.4.2 Subsurface Scattering (Screen-Space Diffusion)

As a second step, we perform a separable Gaussian blur that simulates the scattering inside the skin tissue. We use the alpha channel values to mask out the regions without skin to avoid leaking of the light. We found that one blur pass is enough to achieve visually pleasing results; however, multiple blur passes will improve the quality of the final image.

Subsequently, results of the blurred light accumulation buffer will be sampled in the final step of the skin shading to retrieve the diffuse component of the light-affecting pixels.

In practice it is rare for skin to cover a significant portion of the screen. We take advantage of that fact by generating bounding quad geometry and blurring only inside. This allows us to save on the memory bandwidth, especially when skin shaded characters are farther away.

6.4.3 Skin Layers

Many offline and online render systems model skin as a three-layer material with an oily top, an epidermal, and a subdermal layer, all employing different light absorption and scattering parameters. We, however, have opted for only a two-layer model for performance reasons. In fact we present a "fake" three-layer model to the artist because most seem more familiar with such setup (see Figure 6.2). Then we internally convert parameters to suit our two-layer model. The mixing of the layers is done in the last step of the skin shading.

6.4.4 Implementing a Physically Based Shading

As discussed earlier, we chose physically based microfacet distribution for our specular reflectance. To achieve real-time performance on mobile GPUs we precompute a single 2D lookup texture to capture the most intensive aspects of our BRDF calculation. We pre-compute the lookup texture by evaluating our custom BRDF before rendering of the scene starts.

Later, inside the pixel shader, we will address lookup texture using the angle between normal and half-vector $(N \cdot H)$ on one dimension and the angle between normal and view vector $(N \cdot V)$ on another dimension. We can store response to varying roughness parameters in the mip-chain of the lookup texture.

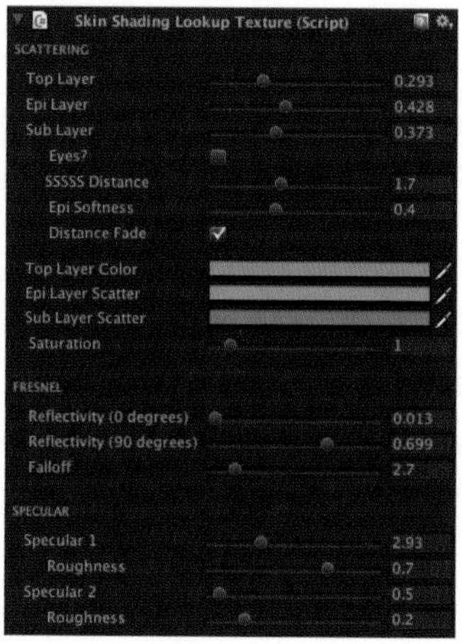

Figure 6.2. UI controls for multilayered skin and two specular lobes.

We use all four channels of pre-computed lookup texture separately to store different information:

- the first two channels contain $N \cdot H$ and $N \cdot V$ response for both specular lobes;

- the third channel contains a pre-computed Fresnel term for $N \cdot V$;

- the last channel contains an energy conservation term for the diffuse component, the integral of light reflected before it enters subsurface layers.

Because of the use of pre-computed lookup texture, overhead for the second specular lobe is negligible. Moreover, we achieve the energy conservation virtually for free.

6.4.5   GPU Workload Balance

We strive to split the workload between pre-computing and real-time evaluation of the parts of our lighting equation in such a way as to leverage the parallel nature of GPU arithmetic units and texture access units.

Note that finding an appropriate size of the lookup texture is a very important optimization step. An increase in the lookup texture size leads to better visual quality with less visible banding, but at the same time puts more stress on the texture cache and causes potential micro-stalls. For our demo we chose to use a 32×128 resolution for the lookup texture.

6.4.6 Alternative BRDF Factoring

There are other possible BRDF factoring approaches when working with the pre-computed lookup textures. One alternative is to use the angle between normal and half-vector ($N \cdot H$) and the angle between view and light vectors ($V \cdot L$)—ideal for storing different approximations of the Cook-Torrance model developed by [Schüler 11].

6.4.7 Selective Gamma Correction

As discussed earlier, linear lighting is an important aspect of skin shading and requires an inverse gamma correction of the input albedo textures and a gamma correction of the output. We use a couple of tricks to speed these steps on mobile GPUs.

First we use a gamma of 2.0, which allows us to use square (multiplication with self) and square root operations for *compression* and *decompression*. Multiplication and square root operations are significantly faster than calculating the power of 2.2 or 2.4.

Second we do gamma correction only on the most important pixels on the screen instead of doing it fullscreen as we would on a desktop or console. We implement the correction explicitly in the pixel shader.

6.4.8 Reflecting Environment

On top of the analytical specular reflections, we use a pre-rendered cube-map for reflecting light coming from all the surrounding environment. Reflected environment light is factored by both a Fresnel term and artist-defined reflectivity map and is mostly used for characteristic rim reflections on the skin.

6.4.9 Scattering for Eyes

Eyes were initially one of our biggest challenges. They seemed to "stick out" of the character shading. The solution we ended up with is to neglect simulation of the subsurface scattering inside the eyes. We simply do not render eyes into the light accumulation buffer. Possible issues are hidden by the typically very high amount of reflectivity when shading eyes (see Figure 6.3). For close ups, we added a small amount of parallax offset to model the eye lens refractions.

6.4.10 Skin Level of Detail

To avoid waxy and very flat-looking skin in the distance, the size of the scattering kernel needs to be decreased according to the distance from the viewer. However, using very small blur kernels with the accumulation buffer can result in a *low-resolution* look. Hence, along with decreasing the effect of blur at a distance, we also fade into a simpler single pass skin shader. A single pass skin shader does

Figure 6.3. Fake "scattering" and surface reflectance of the eyes.

does a very crude approximation of the subsurface scattering by rejecting the high frequency of per-pixel normals (so-called *bent normals* from [Penner and Borshukov 11] and others) while keeping the surface reflectance part identical to the main shader. As a pleasant side effect, this makes distant skin much cheaper to render.

6.5 Results

6.5.1 Issues and Limitations

Our current skin shading approach is limited to a single per-pixel light for performance reasons. We evaluate the rest of the lights per-vertex.

A comparatively expensive aspect of our approach could be that skin shaded geometry needs to be rendered twice: first into the light accumulation buffer, next into the framebuffer. However, the first pass uses a very cheap shader and renders a relatively small amount of pixels.

Due to the limitation of the screen-space scattering approach, the backscattering phenomena (such as ears flashing up in red color when in front of a light source) are difficult to model. Reasonable quality-versus-performance results can be achieved using pre-computed thickness maps along with sampling inverted normals to approximate backscatter while rendering into the light accumulation buffer.

6.5.2 Comparison

A pre-integrated approach as described by [Penner and Borshukov 11] can be used to render skin on mobile GPUs. However, we found that determining a curvature to sample pre-integrated BRDF per-pixel can be quite expensive on mobile GPUs. Pre-computing curvature offline and storing in additional texture is possible and has to be investigated, along with the applicability of using the pre-integrated approach along with per-vertex lighting.

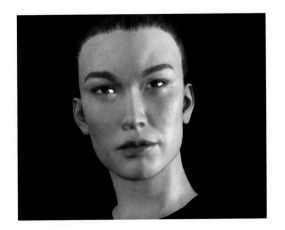

Figure 6.4. Example showing most features of the skin.

6.5.3 Shader

Our final shader (see Figure 6.4) contains four independent texture reads,

1. albedo and reflectivity map,

2. normal map,

3. environment reflection cube-map,

4. blurred irradiance texture,

and one dependent texture read for pre-calulated BRDF lookup texture. The shader executes around 40 vector operations per pixel. This amount of texture reads and arithmetic operations leads to good utilization of parallel units in modern Mobile GPU.

6.6 Summary

An average frame of our demo "The Chase" contains more than 60,000 animated polygons with the skin shaded geometry covering a significant portion of the screen. By employing the approach described in this chapter combined with optimized rendering for the rest of the scenery, we achieve smooth 30 frames per second on iPad4 at full Retina resolution (2048×1536 pixels). We achieve similar performance on a variety of modern mobile devices.

Bibliography

[Borshukov and Lewis 03] George Borshukov and J. P. Lewis. "Realistic Human Face Rendering for *The Matrix Reloaded*." In *ACM SIGGRAPH 2003 Sketches & Applications*, SIGGRAPH '03, p. Article no. 1. New York: ACM, 2003.

[d'Eon and Luebke 07] Eugene d'Eon and David Luebke. "Advanced Techniques for Realistic Real-Time Skin Rendering." In *GPU Gems 3*, edited by Hubert Nguyen, pp. 293–347. Upper Saddle River, NJ: Addison-Wesley, 2007.

[Donner and Jensen 05] Craig Donner and Henrik Wann Jensen. "Light Diffusion in Multi-layered Translucent Materials." *ACM Transactions on Graphics* 24:3 (2005), 1032–1039.

[Jimenez et al. 09] Jorge Jimenez, Veronica Sundstedt, and Diego Gutierrez. "Screen-Space Perceptual Rendering of Human Skin." *ACM Transactions on Applied Perception* 6:4 (2009), 23:1–23:15.

[Jimenez 12] Jorge Jimenez. "Practical Real-Time Strategies for Photorealistic Skin Rendering and Antialiasing." Ph.D. thesis, Universidad de Zaragoza, Zaragoza, Spain, 2012. Available online (http://diglib.eg.org/EG/DL/dissonline/doc/jimenez.pdf).

[Kelemen and Szirmay-Kalos 01] Csaba Kelemen and László Szirmay-Kalos. "A Microfacet Based Coupled Specular-Matte BRDF Model with Importance Sampling." In *Proceedings Eurographics '01*, pp. 25–34. Aire-la-Ville, Switzerland: Eurogrpahics Association, 2001.

[Penner and Borshukov 11] Eric Penner and George Borshukov. "Pre-Integrated Skin Shading." In *GPU Pro 2*, edited by Wolfgang Engel, pp. 41–55. Natick, MA: A K Peters, Ltd., 2011.

[Pharr and Humphreys 04] Matt Pharr and Greg Humphreys. *Physically Based Rendering: From Theory to Implementation*. San Francisco: Morgan Kaufmann, 2004.

[Schüler 11] Christian Schüler. "The Blinn-Phong Normalization Zoo." www.thetenthplanet.de/archives/255, 2011.

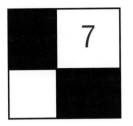

7

Deferred Rendering Techniques on Mobile Devices
Ashley Vaughan Smith

7.1 Introduction

With ongoing advances in GPU technology and the introduction of OpenGL ES 3.0, it has now become possible to utilize rendering techniques that were previously only usable on desktop GPUs. Applications that use dynamic lighting require a technique to shade the scene in an efficient way in real time. On mobile devices with a low power requirement, this is difficult to achieve.

This chapter discusses the available techniques for deferred rendering [Hargreaves and Harris 04] on mobile devices and implementation details that allow optimized rendering of these techniques. The purpose of this chapter is to give the reader an overview of the available deferred rendering techniques using OpenGL ES 2.0 and 3.0, but not an in-depth tutorial on implementing each technique. Readers unfamiliar with deferred rendering may wish to review previous literature about deferred rendering, e.g., [Calver 03, Thibieroz 04]. Also included are new opportunities to use OpenGL ES extensions to optimize these techniques even further.

7.2 Review

In review, there are two mainstream approaches to going about lighting a scene: forward rendering and deferred rendering. Forward rendering was common in fixed function pipelines, such as OpenGL ES 1.0, where there was no option to use deferred rendering. It is also possible to use forward rendering with programmable pipelines like OpenGL ES 2.0. An application that uses forward rendering requires information for a set number of lights that will be used to affect the geometry in the first pass. This usually requires some way of discarding lights when there are too many affecting a single piece of geometry or rendering the same piece of geometry multiple times and blending the results. Because of this, forward rendering is $O(\text{geometry} \cdot \text{lights})$ in processing complexity, meaning the complexity of rendering geometry is affected by the total number of lights in the scene.

7.2.1   Deferred Rendering

Deferred rendering [Hargreaves and Harris 04] is a technique whereby the application defers a scene's lighting calculations until all information required is available in a second pass. The technique decouples the lighting complexity from rendering the geometry and also allows the application to move these lights dynamically without needing to discard lights. This technique also helps the application to reduce the number of light calculations to a minimum by considering lighting on a per-fragment basis instead of a per piece-of-geometry basis. Deferred rendering is $O(\text{lights})$ in processing complexity, therefore this allows the application to render many more lights in the scene compared to the forward rendering approach.

Deferred rendering comes at a cost because the information to shade geometry in screen space requires that each pixel have all lighting information required available in G-buffers. With screens larger than 1920×1080 on some recent mobile devices, this can reach into tens of MBs, which needs to be written and read each frame. This increases memory usage and memory bandwidth, which could be utilized better.

7.3   Overview of Techniques

The techniques covered in this chapter are

- deferred rendering [Hargreaves and Harris 04],

- light pre-pass rendering [Engel 08],

- light indexed rendering [Treblico 09].

Also covered are how each of these techniques applies to both OpenGL ES 2.0 and OpenGL ES 3.0; as each API now has different features available and OpenGL ES extensions, these are features that are available on different mobile devices that are not present in the core OpenGL ES API. Applications can utilize these features but some mobile devices will not expose them.

7.3.1   Deferred Rendering

Deferred rendering [Hargreaves and Harris 04] is the traditional way of deferring the light calculations until a second pass. This technique involves writing out at least albedo, normals and depth to the G-buffer in one pass. Then in a separate pass, render each of the lights with geometry representing the volumes of the

```
glGenTexture( 1, &m_uiAlbedoTexture );
glBindTexture( GL_TEXTURE_2D, m_uiAlbedoTexture );
glTexImage2D( GL_TEXTURE_2D, 0, GL_RGBA, 1920, 1080, 0, GL_RGBA,
 GL_UNSIGNED_BYTE, 0 );
// Create other textures

glGenFramebuffers( 1, &m_uiGBufferFBO );
glBindFramebuffer( GL_FRAMEBUFFER, m_uiGBufferFBO );
glFramebufferRenderbuffer( GL_FRAMEBUFFER,
 GL_DEPTH_STENCIL_ATTACHMENT, GL_RENDERBUFFER,
 m_uiGBufferRenderBuffer );
glFramebufferTexture2D( GL_FRAMEBUFFER, GL_COLOR_ATTACHMENT0,
 GL_TEXTURE_2D, m_uiAlbedoTexture, 0 );
glFramebufferTexture2D( GL_FRAMEBUFFER, GL_COLOR_ATTACHMENT1,
 GL_TEXTURE_2D, m_uiNormalsTexture, 0 );
// Bind other textures to attachments

GLenum bufs [] = { GL_COLOR_ATTACHMENT0, GL_COLOR_ATTACHMENT1 };
glDrawBuffers( 2, bufs );
```

Listing 7.1. An example of how to create a G-buffer for deferred rendering in OpenGL ES 3.0.

lights. i.e., a sphere for a point light, a fullscreen quad for a directional light. This pass reads the information from the G-buffer and additively calculates the lighting for the scene.

OpenGL ES 2.0. Deferred rendering in OpenGL ES 2.0 is not optimal because applications do not have access to multiple render targets. The application would need to render the geometry once for each render target with this technique unless the extension GL_EXT_draw_buffers, described later in this chapter, is used.

OpenGL ES 3.0. In OpenGL ES 3.0 deferred rendering can be used much like in desktop OpenGL (Listing 7.1).

OpenGL ES 3.0 uses out variables in the fragment shader to implement multiple render targets. Each of these may have a layout specifier that binds that fragment output to an attached texture. For example,

```
layout( location = 0 ) out lowp vec4 albedoOutput;
layout( location = 1 ) out lowp vec4 normalsOutput;
```

Encoding. Utilizing deferred rendering requires a way of encoding diffuse albedo color, normal information, and either depth or world position into textures. These are the minimum requirements for the G-buffer in deferred rendering. Albedo color and normals can be encoded without any further changes. However, as world position encoding requires three times the memory bandwidth of writing

```
precision highp float; // Requires highp
vec4 packFloatToVec4( const float value ) {
 vec4 bitSh = vec4( 256.0*256.0*256.0, 256.0*256.0, 256.0, 1.0 );
 vec4 bitMsk = vec4( 0.0, 1.0/256.0, 1.0/256.0, 1.0/256.0 );
 vec4 res = fract( value * bitSh );
 res -= res.xxyz * bitMsk;
 return res;
}
float unpackFloatFromVec4( const vec4 value ) {
 const vec4 bitSh = vec4( 1.0/( 256.0*256.0*256.0 ),
  1.0/( 256.0*256.0 ), 1.0/256.0 , 1.0 );
 return dot( value, bitSh );
}
```

Listing 7.2. Encoding and decoding a single floating point value into 32 bits of an RGBA8 texture.

depth only, applications that are memory bandwidth limited should consider encoding depth instead and reconstruct the world position in the light volume pass. Reconstructing the world position from depth in both OpenGL ES 2.0 and 3.0 is recommended, as these APIs do not have floating point render target support as a core feature.

To encode depth to a texture in OpenGL ES 2.0 requires the extension GL_OES_depth_texture. If this extension is not available, the application can instead encode the depth into 32 bits of a separate RGBA8 texture. An example of how to encode the depth into 32 bits of the texture is shown in Listing 7.2. This method may also be used to encode world position.

To reconstruct the position from this depth, the application can use the following code (Listing 7.3). This code applies when rendering the light volumes and takes the world position of the current view frustum as input uniforms to the shader.

```
gl_Position = mvpMatrix * inVertex;
vec2 textureCoord = gl_Position.xy / gl_Position.w;
textureCoord = ( textureCoord + 1.0 ) * 0.5;

// Interpolate the far frustum so that we have a point in world
// space. Multiply by w as gl will do this for us while
// interpolating varyings, noperspective is not available
farWorldPos = mix(
 mix( farFrustumBL, farFrustumTL, textureCoord.y ),
 mix( farFrustumBR, farFrustumTR, textureCoord.y ),
  textureCoord.x ) * gl_Position.w;
nearWorldPos = mix(
 mix( nearFrustumBL, nearFrustumTL, textureCoord.y ),
 mix( nearFrustumBR, nearFrustumTR, textureCoord.y ),
  textureCoord.x ) * gl_Position.w;
```

Listing 7.3. Reconstructing the world position from a linear depth.

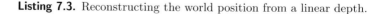

Then in the fragment shader the world position can be acquired.

```
float depth = unpackFloatFromVec4(
  texture( depthTexture, textureCoord ) );
// Multiply by w to negate the implicit divide by w
vec3 world = mix( nearWorldPos * gl_FragCoord.w,
  farWorldPos * gl_FragCoord.w, depth );
```

In OpenGL ES 3.0 depth textures are a core feature.

As shown above, a common practice in deferred rendering is reconstructing the world position from a depth value. When using an RGBA8 texture to encode depth, the application can linearize the depth value it writes out. Therefore reconstructing world position by using a depth texture is different from using an RGBA8 texture, as the depth texture value is not linearized. Listing 7.4 [Reinheart 13] is an example that will reconstruct the world position from a depth texture and the GL_OES_depth_texture extension.

Utilizing deferred rendering in both OpenGL ES APIs has been described above, giving the application the flexibility to use either a depth texture or a separate render to texture to encode the depth value. Limitations with deferred rendering include the memory usage required for the G-buffers and the memory bandwidth of writing this information. This leaves the application less bandwidth to use for more detailed texturing. If the application requires more intensive texturing it can use a different technique, light pre-pass. Figure 7.1 shows the intermediate render targets for this technique.

7.3.2 Light Pre-pass Rendering

Light pre-pass rendering [Engel 08] differs from deferred rendering by storing only the lighting information per pixel instead of the geometry information. The advantage here is reduced memory required by the application and therefore reduced memory bandwidth usage. It involves rendering the (light color)·(light direction×

```
uniform vec2 pixelSize; // 1.0/viewportSize
vec3 ndcSpace = vec3( gl_FragCoord.xy * pixelSize,
  texture( depthTexture, textureCoord ).x ) * 2.0 - 1.0;

vec4 clipSpace;
clipSpace.w = projMatrix[3][2] /
  (ndcSpace.z - (projMatrix[2][2] / projMatrix[2][3]));
clipSpace.xyz = ndcSpace * clipSpace.w;

vec4 worldPos = inverseViewProjMatrix * clipSpace;
```

Listing 7.4. An example of how to reconstruct world position from a depth texture.

Figure 7.1. The render targets for deferred rendering: from left to right, final image, normals, encoded depth, and albedo color.

normal) information to a texture and then doing a second pass of geometry with the diffuse textures to produce the final image. As this technique processes the geometry twice, if the application is limited by vertex processing then this technique may not be the best option. However, if the application is limited by fragment operations, then this technique may be a good option because it uses less memory and therefore less memory bandwidth than other techniques.

OpenGL ES 2.0 and 3.0. Light pre-pass rendering can be performed in both OpenGL ES 2.0 and 3.0.

Limitations of both deferred and light pre-pass rendering include the inability to do hardware antialiasing. A technique that allows this possibility is called light indexed rendering. When using a depth texture, the application can avoid using multiple render targets. Figure 7.2 shows the intermediate render targets for this technique.

7.3.3 Light Indexed Rendering

Light indexed rendering [Treblico 09] is so-called because instead of storing the required lighting information such as normals and color per pixel, we store an index to the light affecting each pixel. We then use this index to sample separate one-dimensional textures, each with a different property, i.e., light position and light color. This acts like forward rendering; however, there is much more control

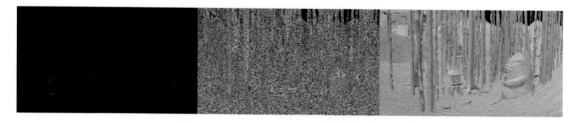

Figure 7.2. Render targets for light pre-pass rendering: lighting texture (left), encoded depth (center), and normals (right).

over how many lights can affect each pixel and the number of light sources is still decoupled from the rendering complexity.

Another advantage of light indexed rendering is that it allows the user to turn on hardware antialiasing. This is not possible with the previous two techniques because the APIs do not expose multisampled multiple render targets.

OpenGL ES 2.0 and 3.0. Light indexed rendering can be applied in both OpenGL ES 2.0 and 3.0. In this technique the application first renders the light volumes in the scene to a fullscreen texture. Each of these volumes has a unique index. This index is written to the texture in a specific channel using `glColorMask()` allowing up to four lights (one for each channel of the texture) and up to 256 different lights in the scene (the maximum index that can be stored in one channel of an RGBA8 texture). If the application determines that some pixels will be affected by more than four lights, it can render the extra light volumes to a different texture. This allows the application in reality to have any number of lights per pixel.

In the second pass the application renders the scene geometry passing in diffuse textures and information to shade the scene. It then looks up the index from the light index texture in screen space and uses that index to look up the light properties. An example of this lighting calculation is shown in Listing 7.5.

```
uniform sampler2D lightIndexTex, lightPositions,
  lightScales, lightColors, diffuseTex;

varying vec3 worldPosition;
varying vec2 diffuseTexCoord;
varying vec3 vertexWorldNormals;

vec3 doLightCalc(float lightId, vec3 worldNormal)
{
  // very simple lighting
  float lightScale = texture2D(lightScales, vec2(0.0, lightId)).x;
  vec3 lightPosition = texture2D(lightPositions, vec2(0.0,
      lightId)).rgb;
  vec3 lightColor = texture2D(lightColors, vec2(0.0,
      lightId)).rgb;

  vec3 lightDirection = normalize(lightPosition - worldPosition);
  float lightDist = distance(lightPosition, worldPosition);
  float invLightDist = max(lightScale - lightDist * 0.5, 0.0);

  float attenuation = 1.0 / lightDist;

  float ndl = clamp(dot(worldNormal, lightDirection), 0.0, 1.0);
  float attenuation2 = ndl * invLightDist * attenuation;

  return attenuation2 * lightColor;
}
```

Listing 7.5. Lighting calculations in light indexed deferred rendering.

```
void main()
{
  vec3 worldNormal = vertexWorldNormals;
  vec2 texCoord = gl_FragCoord.xy * pixelSize;

  vec3 diffuse = texture2D(diffuseTex, diffuseTexCoord).rgb;

  vec4 lightIndices = texture2D(lightIndexTex, texCoord);

  // Do a lighting calculation for each channel in the texture(s)
  // Not checking if a light index is valid means calculating some
  //   useless lighting calculations
  vec3 lightIntensity = doLightCalc(lightIndices.r, worldNormal);
  lightIntensity += doLightCalc(lightIndices.g, worldNormal);
  lightIntensity += doLightCalc(lightIndices.b, worldNormal);
  lightIntensity += doLightCalc(lightIndices.a, worldNormal);
  gl_FragColor = vec4(diffuse * lightIntensity, 0.0);
}
```

Listing 7.6. Scene rendering in light indexed deferred rendering.

The lighting is calculated for each channel in the current texture. With some GPU architectures it is often more optimal to do the lighting calculation for each channel even if it is not used. This is because branches in the shader will cause stalls in the pipeline. An example of calculating the lighting for a given pixel is shown in Listing 7.6.

Sorting lights. Light indexed rendering has a maximum number of lights per pixel that can be shown. If the number of lights per pixel exceeds this then the application needs to decide what to do. The application can have a maximum of as many lights per pixel as we can render to multiple textures. However, if this maximum is reached during execution, then lights will need to be discarded, throwing away the light influence of one or more lights from one frame to the next. In order to make this as un-noticeable as possible, the lights should be sorted so that the lights that take up the least screen space or are smallest in contribution to the final image are discarded first. There is also a possibility of joining multiple small lights into one larger one to reduce the number of lights per pixel.

This section has described how to use light indexed rendering in OpenGL ES 2.0 and 3.0; the next section describes how to optimize each of the techniques using OpenGL ES extensions.

7.4   OpenGL ES Extensions

This chapter has covered various deferred rendering techniques and how to implement them using OpenGL ES 2.0 and 3.0. Each of these APIs has various OpenGL ES extensions that may be utilized to optimize the techniques. This section describes how to utilize these extensions with some new techniques for deferred rendering. The extensions are

- `GL_EXT_draw_buffers`

- `GL_EXT_shader_framebuffer_fetch`

7.4.1 Draw Buffers

The draw buffers extension enables the ability to use multiple render targets in OpenGL ES 2.0. The API does not provide this functionality without the extension. The extension entry point `glDrawBuffersEXT()` works the same as `glDrawBuffers()` in OpenGL ES 3.0 and provides the same attachment indices. GLSL shaders that use this extension must declare so at the top of the GLSL source files:

```
#extension GL_EXT_draw_buffers : require
```

7.4.2 Framebuffer Fetch

The framebuffer fetch extension provides the contents of the framebuffer to GLSL using `gl_LastFragData[0]`, or by using the `inout` specifier when using OpenGL ES 3.0. Also named programmable blending, it allows the application to do custom blending equations to merge the incoming fragment color with the framebuffer color.

When using light indexed rendering the extension allows the application to avoid calling `glColorMask()` between rendering each set of lights. Instead, the application can perform custom blending in the fragment shader and avoid state changes.

```
gl_FragData[0] = vec4( lightIndex, gl_LastFragData[0].xyz );
```

Or, in OpenGL ES 3.0:

```
layout(location = 0) inout highp vec4 ioLightIndex;
void main() {
  ioLightIndex = vec4( lightIndex, ioLightIndex.xyz );
}
```

Technique	OpenGL ES 2.0	OpenGL ES 3.0	MSAA available
Deferred	N (Y with extensions)	Y	N
Light-pre pass	N (Y with extensions)	Y	N
Light indexed	Y	Y	Y

Table 7.1. Overview of which techniques are applicable to each API.

This is the equivalent of rendering the first set of lights in the red channel only, then the blue channel, etc. It assumes that none of the pixels rendered in each set overlap.

7.5 Conclusion and Future Work

This chapter has covered various techniques of rendering multiple, dynamic lights efficiently in OpenGL ES 2.0 and 3.0. Each technique has advantages and use-cases and this chapter has discussed the possibilities for using these techniques, allowing the reader to choose which techniques to utilize. Table 7.1 gives an overview of which techniques work with which APIs.

The framebuffer fetch extension is relatively new to the mobile graphics space. Further work on how to utilize this extension would be of use in future deferred rendering work. For example, this functionality could allow the use of alpha-blended objects in deferred rendering. There is also the possibility of using the currently unused alpha channels in both deferred and light pre-pass rendering for specular highlights.

Bibliography

[Calver 03] Dean Calver. "Photo-Realistic Deferred Lighting." White paper, http://www.beyond3d.com/content/articles/19, 2003.

[Engel 08] Wolfgang Engel. "Light Pre-Pass Renderer." http://diaryofa graphicsprogrammer.blogspot.co.uk/2008/03/light-pre-pass-renderer.html, March 16, 2008.

[Hargreaves and Harris 04] Shawn Hargreaves and Mark Harris. "Deferred Shading." Presentation, NVIDIA Developer Conference: 6800 Leagues Under the Sea, London, UK, June 29, 2004. Available online (https://developer.nvidia.com/sites/default/files/akamai/gamedev/docs/6800_Leagues_Deferred_Shading.pdf).

[Reinheart 13] Alfonse Reinheart. "Compute Eye Space from Window Space." Preprint, http://www.opengl.org/wiki/Compute_eye_space_from_window_space, 2013.

[Thibieroz 04] Nicolas Thibieroz. "Deferred Shading with Multiple Render Targets." In *ShaderX2: Shader Programming Tips & Tricks with DirectX 9*, edited by Wolfgang Engel, pp. 251–269. Plano, TX: Wordware Publishing, 2004.

[Treblico 09] Damian Treblico. "Light Indexed Deferred Rendering." In *ShaderX7: Advanced Rendering Techniques*, edited by Wolfgang Engel, Chapter 2.9. Boston: Charles River Media, 2009.

Bandwidth Efficient Graphics with the ARM® Mali™ GPUs

Marius Bjørge

8.1 Introduction

GPUs in mobile devices today are becoming increasingly powerful. The biggest concern in the mobile space is battery life and one of the biggest consumers of battery is external memory access. Modern mobile games use post-processing effects in various ways and while the GPU itself is capable of doing this, the bandwidth available to the GPU is typically not.

A major strength of Mali and other tile-based architectures is that a lot of operations can be performed on-chip without having to access external memory. For an application to run efficiently on such architectures it is beneficial to try and keep the processing on-chip for as long as possible. Flushing tile-buffer data to a framebuffer that is subsequently read by sampling a texture can be expensive and consume a lot of bandwidth.

ARM have implemented extensions for OpenGL ES 2.0 and OpenGL ES 3.0 to reduce the requirement of accessing external memory for doing post-processing and other operations. This chapter introduces these extensions as well as use-cases for them.

8.2 Shader Framebuffer Fetch Extensions

The Mali-T600 series and Mali-400 series of GPUs support a fragment shader extension that allows applications to read existing framebuffer color, depth, and stencil of the current pixel being processed. Since the data is in the tile buffer, reading it is practically free and you avoid the bandwidth consuming write-read loop that otherwise would be required.

This section will introduce two extensions:

- GL_ARM_shader_framebuffer_fetch

- GL_ARM_shader_framebuffer_fetch_depth_stencil

8.2.1 GL_ARM_shader_framebuffer_fetch

This extension enables reading of the existing framebuffer color. This enables use-cases such as programmable blending and other operations that may not be possible to implement using fixed-function blending.

The extension is enabled by adding

```
#extension GL_ARM_shader_framebuffer_fetch : enable
```

to the very start of a fragment shader.

See Table 8.1 for a list of the built-in variables added by the extension and Listing 8.1 for a simple programmable blending example using the extension.

Variable	Type	Description
gl_LastFragColorARM	vec4	Reads the existing framebuffer color.

Table 8.1. New built-in variables introduced with the GL_ARM_shader_frame buffer_fetch extension.

```
#extension GL_ARM_shader_framebuffer_fetch : enable
precision mediump float;

uniform vec4 uBlend0;
uniform vec4 uBlend1;

void main(void)
{
  vec4 Color = gl_LastFragColorARM;

  Color = lerp(Color, uBlend0, Color.w * uBlend0.w);
  Color *= uBlend1;

  gl_FragColor = Color;
}
```

Listing 8.1. Programmable blending using GL_ARM_shader_framebuffer_fetch.

8.2.2 GL_ARM_shader_framebuffer_fetch_depth_stencil

This extension enables reading of the existing framebuffer depth and stencil values. This enables use-cases such as programmable depth/stencil testing, soft particles, and modulating shadows. It also offers applications a very convenient method of reconstructing 3D positions of any pixel on the screen.

The extension is enabled by adding

```
#extension GL_ARM_shader_framebuffer_fetch_depth_stencil : enable
```

to the very start of a fragment shader.

See Table 8.2 for a list of the built-in variables added by the extension and Listings 8.2 and 8.3 for example use-cases for this extension.

```
#extension GL_ARM_shader_framebuffer_fetch_depth_stencil : enable
precision mediump float;

uniform float uTwoXNear;        // 2.0 * near
uniform float uFarPlusNear;     // far + near
uniform float uFarMinusNear;    // far - near
uniform float uInvParticleSize;

uniform sampler2D uParticleTexture;

varying float vLinearDepth;
varying vec2 vTexCoord;

void main(void)
{
  vec4 ParticleColor = texture2D(uParticleTexture, vTexCoord);

  // convert from exponential depth to linear
  float LinearDepth = uTwoXNear / (uFarPlusNear - ↩
      gl_LastFragDepthARM *
      uFarMinusNear);

  // compute blend weight by subtracting current fragment depth ↩
      with depth in depth buffer
  float Weight = clamp((LinearDepth - vLinearDepth) * ↩
      uInvParticleSize, 0.0, 1.0);

  // modulate with particle alpha
  ParticleColor.w *= Weight;

  gl_FragColor = ParticleColor;
}
```

Listing 8.2. Sample that uses depth read-back to render soft particles.

Variable	Type	Description
gl_LastFragDepthARM	float	Reads the existing framebuffer depth value.[a]
gl_LastFragStencilARM	int	Reads the existing framebuffer stencil value.

[a] The returned depth value is in window coordinate space.

Table 8.2. New built-in variables introduced with the GL_ARM_shader_framebuffer_fetch_depth _stencil extension.

```
#extension GL_ARM_shader_framebuffer_fetch_depth_stencil : enable
precision highp float;

uniform float uTwoXNear;     // 2.0 * near
uniform float uFarPlusNear;  // far + near
uniform float uFarMinusNear; // far - near

vec2 pack16(float x)
{
  vec2 p;
  p.y = fract(x * 255.0);
  p.x = x - p.y / 255.0;
  return p;
}

void main(void)
{
  // convert from exponential depth to linear
  float Depth = uTwoXNear / (uFarPlusNear - gl_LastFragDepthARM *
      uFarMinusNear);

  // compute moments
  float m1 = Depth;
  float m2 = Depth * Depth;

  // store and pack for RGBA8 texture format
  gl_FragColor = vec4(pack16(m1), pack16(m2));
}
```

Listing 8.3. Sample that creates a variance shadow map [Donnelly and Lauritzen 06] in a single pass. The benefit of this approach is that there's no need to invoke the fragment shader while writing geometry to depth. This fragment shader is used as a final resolve shader to convert the depth into variance moments.

8.2.3 Limitations

These extensions have a couple of limitations:

- When multisampling is enabled the gl_LastFragColorARM, gl_LastFragDepth ARM, and gl_LastFragStencilARM built-in variables will return a value that is between the minimum and maximum of the samples values.

- The GL_ARM_shader_framebuffer_fetch extension does not work with multiple render targets.

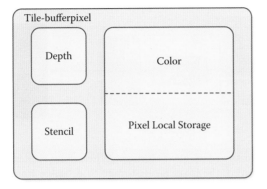

Figure 8.1. A pixel in the tile buffer. Note that color and pixel local storage are physically stored at the same location, so writing to one will overwrite the other. Also note that depth and stencil are separate from the pixel local storage data.

8.3   Shader Pixel Local Storage

The Mali-T600 series of GPUs support a fragment shader extension that can completely change how applications and games construct pixel data. The extension, which is only available for OpenGL ES 3.0, provides a mechanism for applications to pass information between fragment shader invocations covering the same pixel. This persistent data is stored in a format that is independent of the currently attached framebuffer. On the Mali-T600 series the pixel local storage size is 128 bits, which can be freely partitioned by the application. (See Figure 8.1.)

With Shader Pixel Local Storage an application can freely control the per fragment dataflow throughout the lifetime of a framebuffer. Figure 8.2 illustrates normal rendering behavior without pixel local storage.

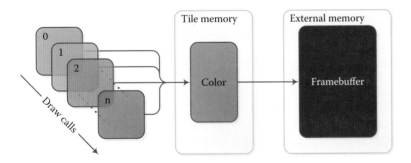

Figure 8.2. The rendered geometry overwrites the existing color value. This is what the pipeline normally looks like when rendering opaque geometry.

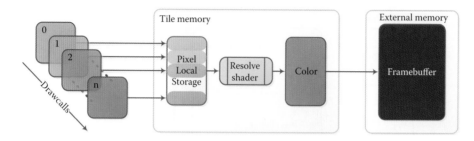

Figure 8.3. Each draw call adds data to the pixel local storage. When done rendering, the application must use a custom resolve shader to convert the pixel local storage to a usable framebuffer color. This needs to be done before end of frame.

Shader Pixel Local Storage changes this by allowing the application to store more data at each pixel fragment. With Shader Pixel Local Storage you no longer generate a pixel per fragment shader invocation. Instead, each pixel is the product of a queue of fragment shaders, which build up the result progressively, and rasterization is the means for describing the queue of fragment work. Figure 8.3 illustrates this by having multiple draw calls read and write to the pixel local storage.

8.3.1   Extension Usage

Shader Pixel Local Storage can be enabled and disabled by calling `glEnable` and `glDisable` with `GL_SHADER_PIXEL_LOCAL_STORAGE_EXT`.

The extension can be enabled in a fragment shader with

```
#extension GL_EXT_shader_pixel_local_storage : enable
```

Before disabling the pixel local storage, the application must ensure that the contents of the pixel local storage is resolved to a native framebuffer. Not doing so will lead to undefined data being written to the framebuffer.

8.3.2   Pixel Local Storage

The Shader Pixel Local Storage extension introduces new qualifiers for declaring the pixel local storage. These are the `__pixel_localEXT`, `__pixel_local_inEXT`, and `__pixel_local_outEXT` qualifiers, as outlined in Table 8.3. Listing 8.4 shows an example of how the pixel local storage can be declared in a shader.

Mixing `pixel_local_inEXT` and `pixel_local_outEXT` in the same fragment shader allows applications to process, reinterpret, and convert data between fragment shader invocations.

`__pixel_localEXT`	Storage can be read and written to.
`__pixel_local_inEXT`	Storage can be read from.
`__pixel_local_outEXT`	Storage can be written to.

Table 8.3. Qualifiers for declaring the pixel local storage.

```
__pixel_localEXT FragLocalData
{
  highp uint v0;
  highp uint v1;
  highp uint v2;
  highp uint v3;
} Storage;
```

Listing 8.4. Declaring a pixel local storage.

8.3.3 Layout Qualifiers

Layout qualifiers describe how the variable data is laid out in the underlying storage. Currently supported layout qualifiers are listed in Table 8.4. For a complete list of supported qualifiers, please see the extension specification [Khronos 14].

An implicit data conversion occurs when reading from or writing to a pixel local variable. When declaring a variable with a layout qualifier, the variable base type and number of components must match that of the qualifier; otherwise, a compiler error is produced.

Listings 8.5, 8.6, and 8.7 show some sample declarations using different data types.

Layout	Base Type
r32ui	uint (default)
r11f_g11f_b10f	vec3
r32f	float
rg16f	vec2
rgb10_a2	vec4
rgba8	vec4
rg16	vec2
rgba8i	ivec4
rg16i	ivec2
rgb10_a2ui	uvec4
rgba8ui	uvec4
rg16ui	uvec2

Table 8.4. Supported layout qualifiers.

```
__pixel_localEXT FragLocalData
{
  highp uint v0; // all of these will use the
  highp uint v1; // default r32ui layout.
  highp uint v2;
} Storage;
```

Listing 8.5. All variables will use the default **r32ui** storage layout.

```
layout(r32f) __pixel_localEXT FragLocalData
{
  highp float v0; // all of these will inherit the r32f layout
  highp float v1; // from the local storage declaration.
  highp float v2;
} Storage;
```

Listing 8.6. All variables will inherit the **r32f** storage layout.

```
__pixel_localEXT FragLocalData
{
  layout(r11f_g11f_b10f) vec3 v0;
  layout(r32ui) uint v1;
  layout(rg16) vec2 v2;
             vec2 v3; // v3 will inherit from the previously
                      // defined layout qualifier (rg16).
} Storage;
```

Listing 8.7. Multiple storage layouts used together.

8.3.4   Usage Patterns

There are multiple ways to use this extension.

Pixel local storage. This example uses the Shader Pixel Local Storage to do all
the rendering.

1. Clear framebuffer to 0.

2. Call glEnable(GL_SHADER_PIXEL_LOCAL_STORAGE_EXT).

3. Do operations on the pixel local storage by rendering geometry, etc.

4. Resolve from pixel local storage to one or more user-defined fragment shader
   outputs.

5. Call glDisable(GL_SHADER_PIXEL_LOCAL_STORAGE_EXT).

6. Call eglSwapbuffer.

Combined rendering. This example shows how an application can combine the use of pixel local storage with a normal rendering pipeline.

1. Begin frame with normal rendering by just writing color to a user-defined fragment shader output.

2. Call `glEnable(GL_SHADER_PIXEL_LOCAL_STORAGE_EXT)`.

3. Get the current framebuffer color by using the `GL_ARM_shader_framebuffer_fetch` extension and store value in the pixel local storage.

4. Do more operations on the pixel local storage by rendering geometry, etc.

5. Resolve from the pixel local storage to a user-defined fragment shader output.

6. Call `glDisable(GL_SHADER_PIXEL_LOCAL_STORAGE_EXT)`.

7. Continue rendering with shaders that write to one or more user-defined fragment shader outputs. Render alpha-blended geometry, GUI, etc.

8. Call `eglSwapbuffer`.

8.3.5 Limitations

The extension has the following limitations:

- When writing to pixel local storage, the value of the framebuffer pixel covered by that fragment becomes undefined.

- When writing to any user-defined fragment output, the pixel local storage values for that fragment become undefined.

- Multiple render targets is not supported while pixel local storage is enabled.

- Multisampling is not supported.

- Blending is not supported.

8.4 Deferred Shading Example

Techniques such as deferred shading [Hargreaves and Harris 04] are typically implemented using multiple render targets by rendering the required intermediate data and then sampling from this data using textures. While flexible, this approach consumes a large amount of external memory bandwidth.

Since the deferred shading data is often only written to and read by shaders executing on the same pixel position, the Shader Pixel Local Storage extension can offer a more efficient alternative by keeping the data on-chip. This allows large amounts of data to be kept per-pixel, with zero external memory bandwidth impact.

The Shader Pixel Local Storage extension can be used to implement deferred shading in a way very similar to the classic multiple render target based approach. In this section we look at what such an implementation might look like.

The implementation can be split up into three rendering steps:

1. render geometry,

2. light accumulation,

3. resolve.

8.4.1   Step 1: Render Geometry

This step is implemented almost the same way as the classic approach using multiple render targets. The only difference is that we write everything to the pixel local storage. This means that existing code can often be easily ported to make use of this extension. (See Listing 8.8.)

```
#version 300 es
#extension GL_EXT_shader_pixel_local_storage : enable

precision mediump float;

__pixel_local_outEXT FragData
{
  layout(r11f_g11f_b10f) mediump vec3 Color;
  layout(rgb10_a2) mediump vec4 Normal;
  layout(r11f_g11f_b10f) mediump vec3 Lighting;
} gbuf;

in mediump vec2 vTexCoord;
in mediump vec3 vNormal;
uniform mediump sampler2D uDiffuse;

void main(void)
{
  // store diffuse color
  gbuf.Color = texture(uDiffuse, vTexCoord).xyz;

  // store normal vector
  gbuf.Normal = vec4(normalize(vNormal) * 0.5 + 0.5, 0.0);

  // reserve and set lighting to 0
  gbuf.Lighting = vec3(0.0);
}
```

Listing 8.8. Example code that initializes the pixel local storage with G-buffer data.

8.4.2   Step 2: Light Accumulation

This step makes use of both the Shader Pixel Local Storage extension and the depth/stencil fetch extension to compute the light contribution of each light. The lights are rendered with depth test enabled and depth writes off. (See Listing 8.9.)

```
#version 300 es
#extension GL_EXT_shader_pixel_local_storage : enable
#extension GL_ARM_shader_framebuffer_fetch_depth_stencil : enable

precision mediump float;

__pixel_localEXT FragData
{
  layout(r11f_g11f_b10f) mediump vec3 Color;
  layout(rgb10_a2) mediump vec4 Normal;
  layout(r11f_g11f_b10f) mediump vec3 Lighting;
} gbuf;

uniform mat4 uInvViewProj;
uniform vec2 uInvViewport;
uniform vec3 uLightPos;
uniform vec3 uLightColor;
uniform float uInvLightRadius;

void main(void)
{
  vec4 ClipCoord;
  ClipCoord.xy = gl_FragCoord.xy * uInvViewport;
  ClipCoord.z = gl_LastFragDepthARM;
  ClipCoord.w = 1.0;
  ClipCoord = ClipCoord * 2.0 - 1.0;

  // Transform to world space
  vec4 WorldPos = ClipCoord * uInvViewProj;
  WorldPos /= WorldPos.w;

  vec3 LightVec = WorldPos.xyz - uLightPos;
  float fDist = length(LightVec);
  LightVec /= fDist;

  // unpack normal from pixel local storage
  vec3 normal = gbuf.Normal.xyz * 2.0 - 1.0;

  // Compute light attenuation factor
  float fAtt = clamp(1.0 - fDist * uInvLightRadius, 0.0, 1.0);
  float NdotL = clamp(dot(LightVec, normal), 0.0, 1.0);

  // compute and add light value back to pixel local gbuf storage
  gbuf.Lighting += uLightColor * NdotL * fAtt;
}
```

Listing 8.9. Accumulate light contribution by rendering light geometry.

```
#version 300 es
#extension GL_EXT_shader_pixel_local_storage : enable

precision mediump float;

__pixel_local_inEXT FragData
{
  layout(r11f_g11f_b10f) mediump vec3 Color;
  layout(rgb10_a2) mediump vec4 Normal;
  layout(r11f_g11f_b10f) mediump vec3 Lighting;
} gbuf;

// Declare fragment shader output.
// Writing to it effectively clears the contents of
// the pixel local  storage.
out vec4 FragColor;

void main(void)
{
  // read diffuse and lighting values from pixel local gbuf storage
  vec3 diffuse = gbuf.Color;
  vec3 lighting = gbuf.Lighting;

  // write contents to FragColor. This will effectively write
  // the color data to the native framebuffer format of the
  // currently attached color attachment
  FragColor = diffuse * lighting;
}
```

Listing 8.10. This example code resolves the contents of the pixel local storage to the native framebuffer format. This is a very simple shader that modulates the data in the pixel local storage and writes it to a fragment shader output.

8.4.3   Step 3: Resolve Everything

This step is similar to classic deferred shading implementations we also need to resolve the pixel local storage to store the color data in the native framebuffer format. (See Listing 8.10.)

8.4.4   Bandwidth Numbers

The example deferred shading implementation has very different bandwidth usage when compared to a conventional multiple render target implementation. As Figure 8.4 shows, using the extensions saves as much as $9\times$ total read and write bandwidth per frame. This also translates into reduced power consumption and longer battery life, which is very important in mobile devices. Table 8.5 shows a further breakdown of the graph. The multiple render target implementation is set up as follows:

- RGBA10_A2 for albedo with D24S8 depth/stencil,

- RGBA10_A2 for normals,

- RGBA10_A2 for lighting.

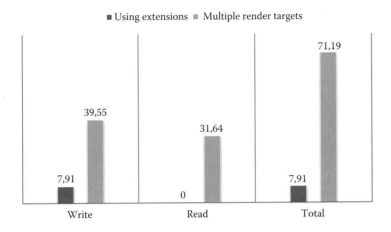

Figure 8.4. External bandwidth comparison for deferred shading implementations. Assuming 1080p resolution with 32-bit framebuffer and D24S8 depth/stencil.

	Extensions		MRT	
	Read	Write	Read	Write
Fill G-buffer	0 MB	0 MB	0 MB	23.73 MB
Light accumulation	0 MB	0 MB	15.82 MB	7.91 MB
Resolve	0 MB	7.91 MB	15.82 MB	7.91 MB
Totals	0 MB	7.91 MB	31.64 MB	39.55 MB

Table 8.5. Breakdown of graph data showing a 9× bandwidth reduction.

Note: Read data for lighting is approximated since this depends on coverage and overdraw. This is isolated to only framebuffer bandwidth and does not take into account texture lookups for diffuse and normal when filling the G-buffer. It does not take into account bandwidth consumed by vertex shader reads/writes and fragment shader varying reads since that will be similar on both implementations.

8.5 Conclusion

We introduced extensions that allow applications to reduce the need to access external memory. Reducing external memory access can not only increase performance, but also increase battery life. Use-cases such as programmable blending and reading of depth/stencil can enable applications to allow more work to be done in on-chip memory. The novel Shader Pixel Local Storage extension gives applications even more control of the per-pixel data in tile-enabling use-cases such as deferred shading.

Experiments with other use-cases such as limited order independent transparency, volume rendering, Lightstack rendering [Martin et al. 13], and Forward+ [Harada et al. 12] rendering just show the potential of this technology.

For more detailed information please see the Khronos OpenGL ES Registry [Khronos 14] website for the extension specifications.

Bibliography

[Donnelly and Lauritzen 06] William Donnelly and Andrew Lauritzen. "Variance Shadow Maps." http://www.punkuser.net/vsm/vsm_paper.pdf, 2006.

[Harada et al. 12] Takahiro Harada, Jay McKee, and Jason C. Yang. "Forward+: Bringing Deferred Lighting to the Next Level ." In *Proceedings of Eurographics 2012*, pp. 5–8. Geneva, Switzerland: Eurographics Association, 2012.

[Hargreaves and Harris 04] Shawn Hargreaves and Mark Harris. "Deferred Shading." Presentation, NVIDIA Developer Conference: 6800 Leagues Under the Sea, London, UK, June 29, 2004. Available online (http://http.download.nvidia.com/developer/presentations/2004/6800_Leagues/6800_Leagues_Deferred_Shading.pdf).

[Khronos 14] Khronos. "OpenGL ES Registry." http://www.khronos.org/registry/gles/, 2014.

[Martin et al. 13] Sam Martin, Marius Bjorge, Sandeep Kakalapudi, and Jan-Harald Fredriksen. "Challenges with High Quality Mobile Graphics ." In *ACM SIGGRAPH 2013 Mobile*, p. Article no. 7. New York: ACM, 2013.

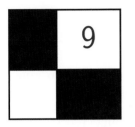

9

Efficient Morph Target Animation Using OpenGL ES 3.0

James L. Jones

9.1 Introduction

Demand for impressive graphics in mobile apps has given rise to ever-more powerful GPUs and new graphics APIs such as OpenGL ES 3.0. These advances enable programmers to write cleaner and more efficient implementations of computer graphics algorithms than ever before. One particular area that stands to benefit is the facial animation of characters in mobile games, a technique that is commonly implemented using morph targets.

Morph target animation requires artists to pre-create multiple poses of a model offline. Later on, during application execution, these poses are mixed together in varying quantities to create animation sequences such as blinking eyes or a frowning face. When used in conjunction with skinning, the technique can serve as the foundation of a feature-rich character animation system. Historically, morph target animation has seen heavy use in PC and console games but a lack of flexibility in earlier graphics APIs has led to complicated or expensive implementations on mobile platforms. This chapter describes an efficient implementation of morph target animation that makes use of the transform-feedback API introduced in OpenGL ES 3.0. The application in this chapter is a continuation of the Gremlin demo, which was first introduced in a previous article [Senior 09]. The demo has been entirely rewritten and has been updated to take advantage of OpenGL ES 3.0 on PowerVR Series6 mobile GPUs.

9.2 Previous Work

An interesting geometry texturing approach was suggested for mobile GPUs that made use of the OpenGL ES 2.0 API [Senior 09]. This approach used a vertex encoding scheme to store vertex displacements between target poses in textures.

The morphing procedure would be performed entirely on textures bound to frame-buffer objects, with the final texture then being used to displace mesh vertices using vertex texture fetch operations. There are problems with this approach, most notably the fact that the maximum number of texture units provided by a platform is allowed to be zero [Munshi and Leech, pp. 40–41]. This means that on some platforms an alternative approach would need to be used. Transform-feedback functionality, which is standardized in OpenGL ES 3.0, allows for a simpler implementation and removes the need for wasteful vertex texture encoding and decoding operations.

9.3 Morph Targets

Morph target animation is used in cases where many small, per-vertex changes need to be applied to a model. This is in contrast to large, sweeping motions normally handled by skeletal animation systems. A good use-case for morph targets is the animation of facial muscles required to create believable facial expressions for video game characters. (See Figure 9.1.)

An implementation typically operates on multiple versions of a stored mesh, known as target poses or key poses. These poses are stored in conjunction with a base pose, which serves as a representation of the animation in a neutral state. To create different animation sequences, the position of each mesh vertex is blended with one or more target poses using a weight vector. The components of this vector are associated with a corresponding target pose and denote how much this target pose influences the result.

To be able to blend between target poses, a difference mesh is used. This is a mesh that is created for each target pose that gives the per-vertex difference between the target pose and the base pose [Senior 09, Lorach 08]. These difference

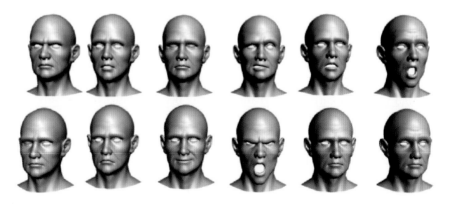

Figure 9.1. Multiple target poses showing a range of facial expressions.

vectors are used as bases in a vector space (i.e., each vertex in an output mesh can be constructed by taking a linear combination of these bases using a weight vector). More precisely, for each output vertex v_i at time t in N morph targets with base target vertex b_i, weight vector w, and target pose vertex p_i, we have

$$v_i(t) = b_i + \sum_{k=0}^{N} w_k(t) \cdot (p_{k,i} - b_i).$$

The formula above summarizes all that is necessary for a morph target implementation. However, for many scenes, it is often the case that only some of the total possible weights change every frame. Because of this, we want to avoid wastefully re-calculating the entire contribution from all target poses every frame. A better idea is to instead keep track of the changes in the weight vector along with the current pose in memory. For a change in frame time h, the new position is equal to the current pose position plus the change in this position:

$$v_i(t + h) = v_i(t) + \Delta_h[v_i](t).$$

We also see that the per-frame change in the position depends only on the per-frame changes in the weights:

$$\Delta_h[v_i](t) = \sum_{k=0}^{N} \Delta_h[w_k](t) \cdot (p_{k,i} - b_i).$$

Using this information, we develop an approach where we only need to compute and update the pose with the per-frame contribution for weights that have changed, i.e., when $\Delta_h[w_k](t) \neq 0$.

9.4 Implementation

This implementation uses vertex buffers that are bound to a transform feedback object to store and update the current pose across frames. Unfortunately, OpenGL ES 3.0 prevents reading and writing to the same buffer simultaneously so a secondary vertex buffer is used to ping-pong the current pose (i.e., the output buffer is swapped with the input buffer every frame). The difference meshes are computed in a pre-processing pass by iterating through the vertices and subtracting the base pose. Sensible starting values are loaded into the feedback vertex buffers (in this case the base pose is used). Every frame, we update the current pose in the vertex buffers using the changes in the weights. This update can be performed with or without batching. Finally, we render the contents of the updated vertex buffer as usual. We perform the computation on vertex normals in the same fashion as vertex positions; this gives us correctly animated normals for rendering. (See Figure 9.2.)

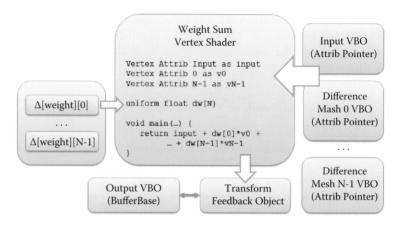

Figure 9.2. Technique overview.

9.4.1 Pose Update

Before we update the pose, we must first compute the changes in the weights. The following pseudo code illustrates how this can be done.

```
// Inputs:
// w[] : current frame weight vector
// p[] : previous frame weight vector
// dw[] : delta weight vector

// Per-Frame Weight Update:
animate(w)
for i = 0 to length(w):
    dw[i] = w[i] - p[i]
    p[i] = w[i]
```

Using the delta weights we can now check to see what components of the weight vector have changed. For those weights that have changed, do a transform feedback pass using the key-pose.

```
// Inputs:
// q[] : array of difference mesh VBOs
// dw[] : delta weight vector
// vbo[] : array of vertex buffer objects for storing current
//         pose
// tfo : transform feedback object
// shader : shader program for accumulation

// Per-Frame Pose Update:
glBindTransformFeedback(tfo)
glEnable(RASTERIZER_DISCARD)
```

```
glUseProgram(shader)
for(i = 0, i < length(q), i++):
    // Only for weights that have changed...
    if (abs(dw[i]) != 0):
        // Set the weight uniform
        glUniform1f(...,dw[i])
        // Bind the output VBO to TBO
        glBindBufferBase(GL_TRANSFORM_FEEDBACK_BUFFER,0,vbo[1])
        // Bind the inputs to vertex shader
        glBindBuffer(GL_ARRAY_BUFFER,vbo[0])
        glVertexAttribPointer(ATTRIBUTE_STREAM_0,...)
        glBindBuffer(GL_ARRAY_BUFFER,q[i])
        glVertexAttribPointer(ATTRIBUTE_STREAM_1,...)
        // Draw call performs per-vertex accumulation in vertex
        // shader.
        glEnableTransformFeedback()
        glDrawArrays(...)
        glDisableTransformFeedback()
        // Vertices for rendering are referenced with vbo[0]
        swap(vbo[0],vbo[1])
```

9.4.2 Batching

For efficiency, further improvements can be made. In this version, updates are batched together into fewer passes. Instead of passing in the attributes and weight uniform for one pose at a time, we can instead use a vertex shader that processes multiple key-poses per update pass. We then perform the update with as few passes as possible.

```
// Inputs:
// q[] : difference mesh VBOs, where corresponding dw != 0
// vbo[] : array of vertex buffer objects for storing current
//         pose
// dw[] : delta weight vector
// shader[] : shader programs for each batch size up to b
// b : max batch size

// Per-Frame Batched Pose Update:
// ... Similar setup as before ...
for(i = 0, i < length(q), ):
    k = min(length(q),i+b) - i
    glUseProgram(shader[k])
    glBindBufferBase(GL_TRANSFORM_FEEDBACK_BUFFER,0,vbo[1])
    // Bind attributes for pass
    for(j = 0, j < b, j++):
        if (j < k):
            glEnableVertexAttribArray(ATTRIBUTE_STREAM_1+j)
            glBindBuffer(GL_ARRAY_BUFFER,q[i+j])
            glVertexAttribPointer(ATTRIBUTE_STREAM_1+j,...)
        else:
            glDisableVertexAttribArray(ATTRIBUTE_STREAM_1+j)
    // Set the delta weights
    glUniform1fv(...)
    // Bind current pose as input and draw
    glEnableVertexAttribArray(ATTRIBUTE_STREAM_0)
    glBindBuffer(GL_ARRAY_BUFFER,vbo[0])
```

```
glVertexAttribPointer(ATTRIBUTE_STREAM_0,...)
glEnableTransformFeedback()
glDrawArrays(...)
glDisableTransformFeedback()
swap(vbo[0],vbo[1])
i = i + k
```

This technique requires multiple versions of the shader where each version executes the summation on incrementally more input attributes up until the maximum batch size. It is important to note that the maximum number of input attributes available is limited by the API. This value (which must be at least 16) can be retrieved by querying `glGetIntegerv` with the argument `GL_MAX_VERTEX_ATTRIBS`.

9.4.3   Results

While gathering the data for the graph in Figure 9.3, a maximum batch size of seven targets was used (batch size indicates the number of additions being performed in the vertex shader). The demo was executed multiple times for varying batch sizes. For each run the average frame rate was taken.

These results show that batching the passes reduces the overhead cost of redrawing the geometry during the animation update. Depending on the number of targets used during a given frame, an adequately large batch size should be chosen to reduce this cost.

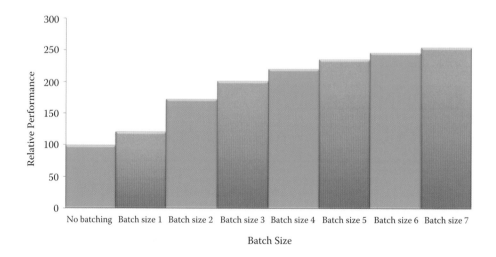

Figure 9.3. Relative performance against batch size when running the demo app.

9.5 Conclusion

This chapter has demonstrated an efficient morph target animation system using transform-feedback. The technique can be computed as a separate pass before rendering, and additional techniques such as skinning can be easily implemented on top of this system.

9.6 Acknowledgments

I would like to thank my colleagues Ken Catterall, Kristof Beets, and Peter Quayle of Imagination Technologies for their consistent support and encouragement.

Bibliography

[Lorach 08] Tristan Lorach. "DirectX 10 Blend Shapes: Breaking the Limits." In *GPU Gems 3*, edited by Hubert Nguyen, pp. 53–67. Upper Saddle River, NJ: Addison-Wesley, 2008.

[Munshi and Leech] Aaftab Munshi and Jon Leech, editors. *OpenGL ES Common Profile Specification*. Khronos Group Inc.

[Senior 09] Andrew Senior. "Facial Animation for Mobile GPUs." In *ShaderX7: Advanced Rendering Techniques*, edited by Wolfgang Engel, pp. 561–569. Boston: Charles River Media, 2009.

Tiled Deferred Blending

Ramses Ladlani

10.1 Introduction

Desktop and mobile GPUs are designed with very different goals in mind. While the former mainly focuses on performance, the latter must strive for controlled power consumption. This directly impacts the memory bandwidth, which often constitutes the main performance bottleneck on mobile devices, especially when using fillrate intensive effects such as alpha blending.

Some GPU manufacturers have come up with designs centered around a tile-based architecture (e.g., Imagination Technologies PowerVR, ARM Mali, Qualcomm Adreno) allowing for a fraction of the original bandwidth to be used. On those *tile-based renderers* (TBR), the blending operation in itself is very cheap because it is entirely performed using the on-chip memory [Merry 12].

Other manufacturers, such as NVIDIA and its Tegra family of SoCs, have opted for a more traditional *immediate mode rendering* (IMR). On those systems, the read-modify-write cycle to the framebuffer required by alpha blending places a significant additional burden on the memory system, and it is of critical importance to use it sparingly while trying to minimize overdraw [NVIDIA 13].

This discrepancy between platform capabilities provides an extra challenge for developers to offer a similar and interesting experience to the end users.

This chapter describes a technique that has been developed at Fishing Cactus while porting *After Burner Climax* from Xbox360/PS3 onto mobile (iOS and Android) to efficiently support effects with lots of alpha blending (e.g., the clouds seen during level transitions) on all the target platforms. Figure 10.1 shows some screenshots showcasing this effect.

The basic idea behind the technique is to leverage the programmability of OpenGL ES 2 and the multiple texture units available on those devices to render several layers of transparency at once with minimal overdraw. The grouping scheme is somewhat inspired by *tiled shading techniques* where lights affecting a scene are bucketed into screen-space tiles [Pranckevičius 12, Olsson and Assarsson 11] so that they can be rendered more efficiently later. This tech-

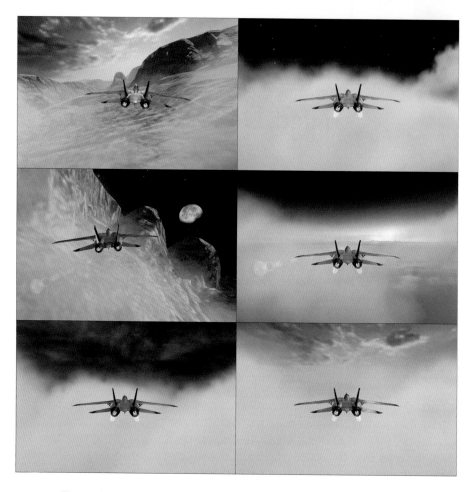

Figure 10.1. Cloud level transitions in *After Burner Climax* (iOS).

nique is essentially the application of the "use multi-texturing instead of multiple passes" [Apple 13b] recommendation to the blending problem.

While being a natural fit for rendering particle systems, this method is generic enough to be used for rendering any combination of transparent textured quads (e.g., sprites, interface elements). The main goal of the technique is to optimize memory bandwidth consumed by blending operations, but it also provides a good opportunity to reduce the number of batches sent to the GPU.

In the following sections, we will briefly outline the algorithm before peeking into more details about its implementation. This will be followed by a section focusing on some optimizations and we will end with a discussion around the results obtained with the proposed solution.

10.2 Algorithm

The algorithm is based on a division of the rendering area into smaller screen-space tiles. Tile layouts are discussed in Section 10.3.1.

Once a layout has been defined, the general algorithm can be summarized in the following steps (see Figure 10.2).

1. Project vertices on CPU to find the screen-space extent of each sprite quad.

2. For each quad, find intersecting tiles and store their ID in each affected cell.

3. (optional) Optimize grid by grouping compatible cells (see Section 10.4.1).

4. For each tile, compute required information to render aggregated sprites.

5. For each non empty tile, for each fragment use interpolated texture coordinates to sample bound textures and blend results manually.

First, the sprites vertices are transformed on the CPU to figure out where they will land on screen after projection. Once the screen-space positions are known, we can compute, for each tile, the list of sprites affecting it. The lack of compute shader on OpenGL ES forces us to make all those computations on CPU.

For complex scenes containing lots of sprites to blend together, SIMD instructions (e.g., ARM NEON[1] Instruction Set) provide a good opportunity to reduce the extra CPU overhead induced by the technique. Libraries[2] are available to get you started quickly.

After having computed the list of sprites affecting each tile, we can, for each cell and for each sprite, compute the texture coordinate transform that will transform the tile texture coordinates into those of each sprite it aggregates. Those 3×2 transform matrices (2D rotation + translation) will be passed later as uniforms to the vertex shader.

Finally, the render phase itself simply consists in rendering the tiles, one at a time, using the interpolated texture coordinates to sample each texture (the same texture can be bound to several samplers if desired) and to blend the intermediate results manually, respecting the transparency order.

An optional optimization phase (step 3) can take place after building the per-tile sprite lists and before computing the extrapolated texture coordinates; this optimization consists in merging together cells that share the exact same sprites, thus lowering the number of primitives sent to the GPU.

---

[1]ARM is a registered trademark of ARM Limited (or its subsidiaries) in the EU and/or elsewhere. NEON is a trademark of ARM Limited (or its subsidiaries) in the EU and/or elsewhere. All rights reserved.

[2]https://code.google.com/p/math-neon/

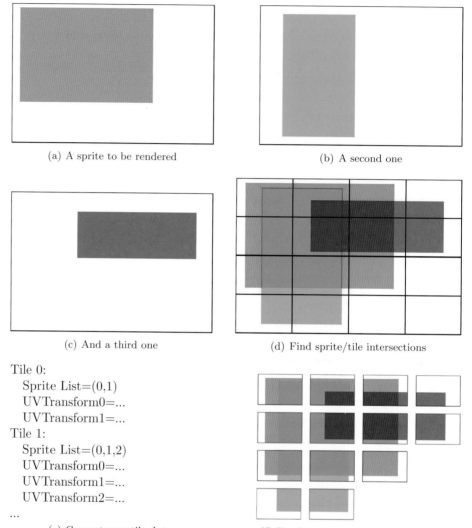

(a) A sprite to be rendered   (b) A second one

(c) And a third one   (d) Find sprite/tile intersections

Tile 0:
    Sprite List=(0,1)
    UVTransform0=...
    UVTransform1=...
Tile 1:
    Sprite List=(0,1,2)
    UVTransform0=...
    UVTransform1=...
    UVTransform2=...
...

(e) Compute per tile data   (f) Render non empty tiles one at a time

Figure 10.2. Algorithm overview.

10.3   Implementation

10.3.1   Tile Layout

Choosing the right tile layout is crucial for achieving good performance; a good choice depends heavily on the positioning and size of the sprites to be rendered.

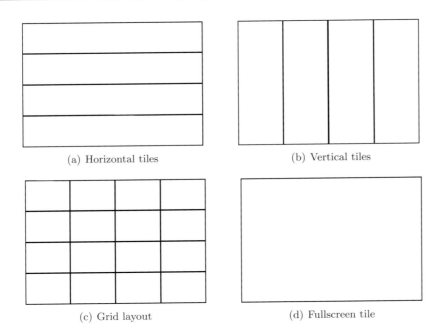

(a) Horizontal tiles

(b) Vertical tiles

(c) Grid layout

(d) Fullscreen tile

Figure 10.3. Different tile layouts.

Make the tiles too big compared to the underlying geometry and too many fragments will unnecessarily be shaded (using a stencil can come in handy here as described in Section 10.4.3).

A good layout is a layout that minimizes partially covered tiles (fully transparent fragments) and that keeps the number of draw calls as low as possible. Depending on the number of sprites to be rendered, a well-chosen layout can even help reduce the total draw call count considerably (in the best case, up to eight times fewer draw calls on current gen mobile GPUs).

Simple useful common layouts include vertical slices, horizontal slices, the grid, or even the single fullscreen tile as demonstrated in Figure 10.3.

In Section 10.4.1, we describe a simple approach to dynamically reduce the number of tiles to be rendered.

10.3.2 Supporting More Layers

When the number of sprites to blend in a single tile is above the maximum it can hold (see Section 10.3.4), new screen-space tiles can be instantiated as required at the exact same position to support the extra layers to blend. Figure 10.4 shows how a second tile layer was added to support the example scene if each tile could only blend two layers.

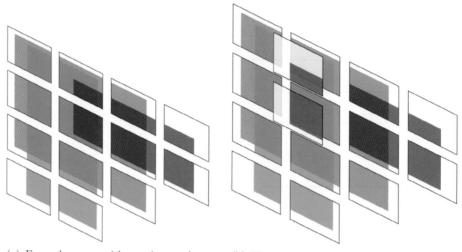

(a) Example scene with maximum three layers per tile

(b) The same scene with maximum two layers per tile

Figure 10.4. Tiles can be layered to support more blended layers.

10.3.3 Sprite-Tile intersection

The relatively low complexity of our tile layout in *After Burner Climax* (eight vertical tiles) and the small amount of clouds to render (a few dozens) allowed us to use a simple (SIMD) axis aligned rectangle-rectangle intersection test on CPU with no performance problem.

When using a higher density grid, it could prove to be useful to use a rasterization strategy as suggested by [Olsson and Assarsson 11] in the context of tiled shading. This would also allow for arbitrary shapes to be used instead of just regular quads.

10.3.4 Rendering

The number of layers aggregated by each tile is only limited by the number of texture units and the number of interpolators supported by the device.[3] For the sake of the example, we will consider a maximum of eight varyings and eight texture units for the rest of this chapter (these values match current generation devices such as the iPhone5 equipped with a PowerVR SGX 543 [Apple 13a]).

To reduce unnecessary work when not all possible layers are being used, we select among eight different programs (one for each number of blended layers

---

[3]Calling `glGet()` with `GL_MAX_VARYING_VECTORS` and `GL_MAX_TEXTURE_IMAGE_UNITS` retrieves those values.

supported by the tile). This not only lowers the amount of computations to perform, it also diminishes the number of texture fetches as well as the number of interpolators being used.

The rendering phase uses a single static vertex buffer object (VBO) and performs a draw call for each non empty tile to be rendered.

By first sorting the tiles by the number of aggregated layers (1 to 8), we also minimize the number of `glUseProgram()` calls.

1. Sort tiles by number of layers being used.

2. For $i = 1$ to 8,

    (a) enable program corresponding to i blended layers;

    (b) for each tile,

        i. set uniforms,

        ii. bind textures,

        iii. render tile quad.

The uniforms being used by the program are the following as follows:

- `uPositionTransform`: A `vec4` containing the scaling and offset to apply to the positions in the VBO to properly position the tile on screen.

- `uCoordinateTransformX/Y`: Two tables of eight `vec3`, each pair representing a 3×2 matrix (2D rotation followed by a translation) used to transform the tile "unit" texture coordinates into layer coordinates.

The vertex shader is shown in Listing 10.1 and uses the aforementioned uniforms to transform the (static) attributes of the VBO and pass them as varyings to the fragment shader. A preprocessor define directive is used to ease the management of the multiple programs; each program is compiled with `LAYER_COUNT` being defined to a value ranging from 1 to 8.[4]

The fragment shader shown in Listing 10.2 is not a lot more complex. It basically samples all textures, carefully avoiding dependent texture reads by not using `.zw` components to fetch texture data [Imagination Technologies 12], and performs the blending manually. This manual blending offers the possibility, if desired, to implement more exotic blending modes than the regular lerp.

Again, `LAYER_COUNT` is used for controlling the number of layers blended by the program.

You might have noticed that the blending formula assumes premultiplied alpha. Premultiplied textures provide lots of desirable properties (e.g., blending

---

[4]To keep reasonable performances on the iPhone 4S (iOS 6.0.1), we had to unroll the fragment shader loop manually.

```
multiple_draw_call_VS]
attribute vec2
  Position,
  TextureCoordinates;

uniform mediump vec4
  uPositionTransform;
uniform mediump vec3
  uCoordinateTransformX[LAYER_COUNT],
  uCoordinateTransformY[LAYER_COUNT];

varying mediump vec2
  vTextureCoordinates[LAYER_COUNT];

void main()
{
  gl_Position.xy =
    Position.xy * uPositionTransform.xy + uPositionTransform.zw;
  gl_Position.zw = vec2( 0.0, 1.0 );
  mediump vec3 texcoord = vec3( TextureCoordinates, 1.0 );
  for( int i = 0; i < LAYER_COUNT; i++ )
  {
    vTextureCoordinates[i].x =
      dot( uCoordinateTransformX[i], texcoord );
    vTextureCoordinates[i].y =
      dot( uCoordinateTransformY[i], texcoord );
  }
}
```

Listing 10.1. The vertex shader.

associativity) [Forsyth 06], but care must still be taken to preserve transparency order. The previous shader assumes that we have sorted the transparent layers back to front.

```
varying mediump vec2
  vTextureCoordinates[LAYER_COUNT];

uniform sampler2D
  Textures[LAYER_COUNT];

void main()
{
  mediump vec4 result = vec4( 0.0, 0.0, 0.0, 0.0 );

  for( int i = 0; i < LAYER_COUNT; i++ )
  {
    mediump vec4 contribution =
      texture2D( Textures[i], vTextureCoordinates[i] );
    result = contribution + ( 1.0 - contribution.a ) * result;
  }

  gl_FragColor = result;
}
```

Listing 10.2. Multiple draw call fragment shader.

10.3.5 Sampler Configuration

The above shader works fine when setting the samplers' wrap modes to `GL_CLAMP`
`_TO_EDGE` and when using textures that have a fully transparent border. If this
is not the case (or if repeat mode is required), the shader must take care of
discarding the layer contribution if it falls out of the accepted range. The following
is an example on how to discard values outside the $[0.0, 1.0]$ range.

```
contribution =
  texture2D( Textures[i], vTextureCoordinates[i] );
result = contribution + ( 1.0 - contribution.a ) * result;
result *= step( 0.0, vTextureCoordinates[i].x );
result *= step( vTextureCoordinates[i].x, 1.0 );
result *= step( 0.0, vTextureCoordinates[i].y );
result *= step( vTextureCoordinates[i].y, 1.0 );
```

10.3.6 Simulating Depth

If depth testing is required, it needs to be handled manually because we are now
rendering screen-space tiles. After binding the depth texture and sampling it in
the fragment shader, it is now possible to compare the depth value to each tile's
depth (passed in as an extra vertex attribute) in order to modulate the intermediate results using a call to `step()`. Compared to regular blending, the depth
buffer needs to be sampled only once per pixel (per screen-space tile affecting it)
instead of once per primitive.

```
mediump float depth;
depth = texture2D( DepthTexture, tileTextureCoordinates.xy );

// ...

contribution =
  texture2D( Textures[ i ], vTextureCoordinates[i] );
result = contribution + ( 1.0 - contribution.a ) * result;
result *= step( vTextureCoordinates[i].z, depth );
```

Using `gl_FragCoord` to compute the coordinates to sample the depth textures
would result in a dependent texture fetch; a better solution consists of passing
the screen-space coordinates as varyings.

From here, we can get soft particles almost for free by using an alpha ramp
instead of the previous `step()` function.

For all this to work, the device must of course support depth textures (`OES_`
`depth_texture` extension).

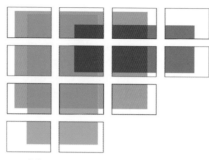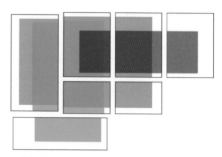

(a) Regular grid without merging   (b) The same grid after merging phase

Figure 10.5. Adaptive tile layout.

10.4   Optimizations

10.4.1   Minimize Number of Batches

Adaptive tile layout. The initial tile layout can be optimized dynamically by analyzing it to merge adjacent compatible cells together (see Figure 10.5). Two tiles are compatible if they share the same list of aggregated sprites.

This merging operation results in fewer primitives being sent down to the GPU. Fewer primitives means less memory traffic (lighter vertex buffer and smaller Parameter Buffer usage) and also less vertex shader work.

Single draw call. When using the same texture for all layers (e.g., when rendering a particle system) or when all tiles are using the same textures in the same order, we can drastically reduce the number of batches by constructing a single dynamic VBO to render the whole grid at once.

For each tile, and for each transparent layer it aggregates, the sprite texture coordinates are extrapolated to the corners of each cell. This computation is performed on CPU and the values are appended into the vertex buffer. Thus, each vertex now contains one `vec2` position and eight `vec2` texture coordinates; no uniforms are required anymore.

The vertex shader being used is a simple pass-through, which will allow all attributes to be interpolated and passed to the fragment shader (see Listing 10.3). We can notice that, even when all eight layers that can be rendered by a tile are not used, this shader will still consume eight interpolators. That many varyings can affect performance negatively as the large amount of memory required to store the interpolated values might lower the number of fragments in flight and could also trash the post-transform cache [McCaffrey 12].

When the maximum number of layers is not being used in a given tile, a solution can be found through dynamic branching to early out and not take the

```
attribute vec2
  Position,
  TextureCoordinates[LAYER_COUNT];

varying mediump vec2
  vTextureCoordinates[LAYER_COUNT];

void main()
{
  gl_Position = vec4( Position.xy, 0.0, 1.0 );

  for( int i = 0; i < LAYER_COUNT; i++ )
  {
    vTextureCoordinates[i] = TextureCoordinates[i];
  }
}
```

Listing 10.3. Single draw call vertex shader.

superfluous layers into account; this solution requires packing an extra attribute containing the number of layers aggregated by the current primitive.

We did not need to implement this, but it should be possible to address the texture limitation mentioned before (one texture or same textures in same order for all tiles) by using texture atlases at the cost of a more complex handling of texture coordinates and wrap modes. A better solution would have been to use *Array Textures* if they were available on all platforms [OpenGLWiki 13]. Starting with OpenGL ES 3.0, this will become a valid option [Khronos 13].

The fragment shader is the same as the one of the multiple draw calls approach.

Table 10.1 summarizes the main differences between the two approaches. The main argument for choosing one or the other is related to the number of tiles to render. When using a high number of tiles (e.g., 64 or more) or if your application is already sending too many batches, the single draw call approach should perform better (provided your scene fits its limitations). When using a relatively low number of tiles, we would recommend using the multiple draw calls approach, as it is much more flexible, easier to implement and provides more opportunities to lower memory traffic.

10.4.2 Render Target Resolution

For effects such as clouds and smoke, which use textures of relatively low frequencies, a commonly used optimization consists in rendering the effect to a lower resolution offscreen render target before upsampling it to the final framebuffer.

	Single Draw Call	Multiple Draw Calls
Draw calls	1	1 per tile
VS data	dynamic VBO	static VBO + uniforms
Texcoord transforms	on CPU	on GPU
Number of textures	1 (up to 8 for whole grid)	8 per tile
Unused layers	dynamic branching	different programs
Interpolators usage	high	low to high depending on aggregated layer count

Table 10.1. Single versus multiple draw calls summary.

10.4.3 Stencil

Stencil test is another common optimization for effects that affect only portions of the screen [Weber and Quayle 11].

10.5   Results

The savings achieved with this technique depend greatly on the scene complexity, the tile layout and, first and foremost, the underlying architecture. We can, however, estimate a best case scenario by comparing the cost of rendering several fullscreen quads using regular blending versus rendering the same amount of fullscreen quads using deferred tile blending. The results are presented in Figure 10.6 and in Table 10.2.

We can observe a linear relationship between the number of fullscreen layers to blend and the time it takes to render the frame. As expected, we did not notice any improvement on TBR architectures and the technique was even a bit slower than simple blending on some devices. However, on IMR GPUs such as the Tegra 3 equipping the Nexus 7, rendering time was approximately 35% shorter than without using tile-based blending.

Fullscreen layer count	SB (Nexus7)	TDB (Nexus7)	SB (iPhone4S)	TDB (iPhone4S)
8	23	16	7	8
16	45	30	13	14
24	66	44	19	21
32	87.5	58	24	28
40	109	72	32	34

Table 10.2. Tiled deferred blending (TDB) and simple blending (SB) rendering times (in ms).

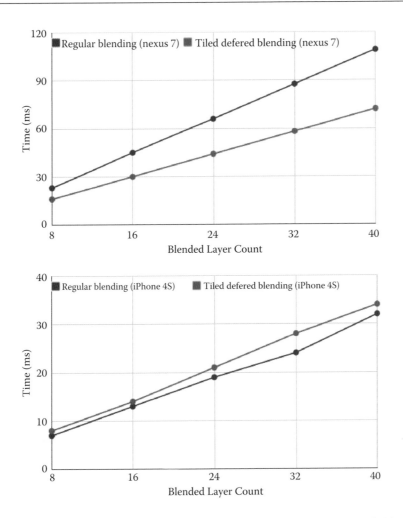

Figure 10.6. Comparing rendering time for tiled deferred blending and simple blending for Nexus 7 (top) and iPone 4S (bottom).

10.6 Conclusion

This chapter has presented a technique based on tile bucketing to reduce the memory bandwidth consumed by blending operations.

This technique is not a "one solution fits all" and should not be used blindly. For example, we would not recommend using it to render all your particle systems, as it would quickly become too expensive when the number of particles increases. However, a hybrid approach combining regular blending for small sprites and tiled deferred blending for those covering a screen area above a given threshold, à la *contribution culling*, could show some substantial gains.

Actually, the technique only works for screen-aligned quads, but, by passing depth information to the GPU, it could be extended to support arbitrary oriented sprites with perspective correct interpolation of the texture coordinates (at the price of using dependent texture fetches).

It is my hope that this technique will serve others in developing better looking effects while achieving their target performance on all devices.

Bibliography

[Apple 13a] Apple. "OpenGL ES Hardware Platform Guide for iOS." http://developer.apple.com/library/ios/documentation/OpenGLES/ Conceptual/OpenGLESHardwarePlatformGuide_iOS/OpenGLESHardware PlatformGuide_iOS.pdf, 2013.

[Apple 13b] Apple. "OpenGL ES Programming Guide for iOS." http:// developer.apple.com/library/ios/documentation/3DDrawing/Conceptual/ OpenGLES_ProgrammingGuide/OpenGLES_ProgrammingGuide.pdf, 2013.

[Forsyth 06] Tom Forsyth. "Premultiplied Alpha." http://home.comcast.net/ ~tom_forsyth/blog.wiki.html#%5B%5BPremultiplied%20alpha%5D%5D, 2006.

[Imagination Technologies 12] Imagination Technologies. "PowerVR Performance Recommendations." http://www.imgtec.com/powervr/insider/docs/ PowerVR.Performance%20Recommendations.1.0.28.External.pdf, 2012.

[Khronos 13] Khronos. "OpenGL ES 3.0.2 Specification." http://www.khronos. org/registry/gles/specs/3.0/es_spec_3.0.2.pdf, 2013.

[McCaffrey 12] Jon McCaffrey. "Exploring Mobile vs. Desktop OpenGL Performance." In *OpenGL Insights*, edited by Patrick Cozzi and Christophe Riccio, Chapter 24, pp. 337–352. Boca Raton, FL: A K Peters/CRC Press, 2012.

[Merry 12] Bruce Merry. "Performance Tuning for Tile-Based Architectures." In *OpenGL Insights*, edited by Patrick Cozzi and Christophe Riccio, pp. 323– 336. Boca Raton, Fl: A K Peters/CRC Press, 2012.

[NVIDIA 13] NVIDIA. "Optimize OpenGL ES 2.0 Performance for Tegra." http://docs.nvidia.com/tegra/data/Optimize_OpenGL_ES_2_0_ Performance_for_Tegra.html, 2013.

[Olsson and Assarsson 11] Ola Olsson and Ulf Assarsson. "Tiled Shading." *Journal of Graphics, GPU, and Game Tools* 15:4 (2011), 235–251.

[OpenGLWiki 13] OpenGLWiki. "Array Texture." http://www.opengl.org/wiki/Array_Texture, 2013.

[Pranckevičius 12] Aras Pranckevičius. "Tiled Forward Shading Links." http://aras-p.info/blog/2012/03/27/tiled-forward-shading-links/, 2012.

[Weber and Quayle 11] Marco Weber and Peter Quayle. "Post-Processing Effects on Mobile Devices." In *GPU Pro 2*, edited by Wolfgang Engel, pp. 291–305. Natick, MA: A K Peters, Ltd., 2011.

11

Adaptive Scalable
Texture Compression
Stacy Smith

11.1 Introduction

Adaptative Scalable Texture Compression (ASTC) is a new texture compression format that is set to take the world by storm. Having been accepted as a new Khronos standard, this compression format is already available in some hardware platforms. This chapter shows how it works, how to use it, and how to get the most out of it. For more in-depth information, there is a full specification provided with the encoder [Mali 14a].

11.2 Background

ASTC was developed by ARM Limited as the flexible solution to the sparsely populated list of texture compression formats previously available. In the past, texture compression methods were tuned for one or more specific "sweet spot" combinations of data channels and related bit rates. Worsening the situation was the proprietary nature of many of these formats, limiting availability to specific vendors, and leading to the current situation where applications have to fetch an additional asset archive over the internet after installation, based on the detected available formats. The central foundation of ASTC is that it can compress an input image in every commonly used format (Table 11.1) and output that image in any user selected bit rate, from 8 bpp to 0.89 bpp, or 0.59 bpp for 3D textures (Table 11.2).

Bitrates below 1 bpp are achieved by a clever system of variable block sizes. Whereas most block-based texture compression methods have a single fixed block size, ASTC can store an image with a regular grid of blocks of any size from 4×4 to 12×12 (including nonsquare block sizes). ASTC can also store 3D textures, with block sizes ranging from $3 \times 3 \times 3$ to $6 \times 6 \times 6$.

Raw Input Format	Bits per Pixel
HDR RGB+A	64
HDR RGBA	64
HDR RGB	48
HDR XY+Z	48
HDR X+Y	32
RGB+A	32
RGBA	32
XY+Z	24
RGB	24
HDR L	16
X+Y	16
LA	16
L	8

Table 11.1. Bitrates of raw image formats.

Output Block Size[a]	Bits per Pixel
4×4	8.000
5×5	5.120
6×6	3.556
8×8	2.000
10×10	1.280
12×12	0.889
$3 \times 3 \times 3$	4.741
$4 \times 4 \times 4$	2.000
$5 \times 5 \times 5$	1.024
$6 \times 6 \times 6$	0.593
4×6	5.333
8×10	1.600
12×10	1.067

[a] This is by no means an exhaustive list of available block sizes, merely the square/cube block sizes to show data rates, with a few nonsquare examples.

Table 11.2. Bitrates of ASTC output.

Regardless of the blocks' dimensions, they are always stored in 128 bits, hence the sliding scale of bit rates.

11.3 Algorithm

Each pixel in these blocks is defined as a quantized point on a linear gradient between a pair of boundary colors. This allows for fairly smooth areas of shading. For blocks containing boundaries between areas of completely different colors, the block can use one of 2048 color partitioning patterns, which split the block into different designs of 1–4 color gradients. (See Figure 11.1.)

These blocks are algorithmically generated, and selecting the right one is where the majority of the compression time goes. This technique allows a block to contain areas of completely different hues with arbitrary shading or multiple intersecting hard-edged patches of different tones. Each block defines up to four pairs of colors and a distribution pattern ID, so that each pixel knows which of those pairs it uses to define its own color. The individual pixels then have a quantized value from 0 to 1 to state where they are on the gradient between the given pair of colors.[1] Due to the variable number of bounding colors and individual pixels in each 128 bit block, the precision of each pixel within the block is quantized to fit in the available remaining data size.

---

[1] Indices are encoded at variable resolution using a scheme developed by researchers at Advanced Micro Devices, Inc.

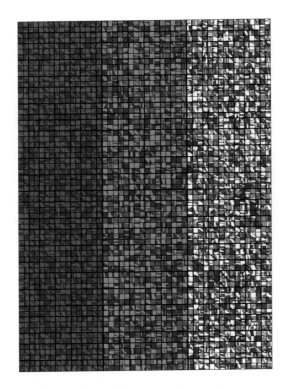

Figure 11.1. Different partition patterns.

During compression, the algorithm must select the correct distribution pattern and boundary color pairs, then generate the quantized value for each pixel. There is a certain degree of trial and error involved in the selection of patterns and boundary colors, and when compressing, there is a trade-off between compression time and final image quality. The higher the quality, the more alternatives the algorithm will try before deciding which is best. However long the compression takes, the decompression time is fixed, as the image data can always be re-extrapolated from the pattern and boundary colors in a single pass.

The compression algorithm can also use different metrics to judge the quality of different attempts, from pure value ratios of signal to noise, to a perceptual judgement weighted toward human visual acuity. The algorithm can also judge the channels individually rather than as a whole, to preserve detail for textures where the individual channels may be used as a data source for a shader program, or to reduce angular noise, which is important for tangent-space normal maps.

Overall, correct usage of these options can give a marked improvement over existing compression algorithms, as shown in Figure 11.2.

Figure 11.2. From top to bottom on the right we see a close up of the original image, the 2 bpp PVRTC [Fenney 03] compressed image, then the 2 bpp ASTC image at the bottom.

11.4 Getting Started

After downloading the evaluation compression program [Mali 14a], the command line interface can be used to compress textures. This program supports input images in PNG, Targa, JPEG, GIF(non-animated only), BMP, Radiance HDR, Khronos Texture KTX, DirectDraw Surface DDS, and Half-Float-TGA. There is also limited support for OpenEXR.

The `astcenc` application provides a full list of available command line arguments. The most basic commands are

```
astcenc -c <input.file> <output.file> <rate> [options]
```

The `-c` tells the program to compress the first file and save the compressed form into the second file. The rate is used to decide a block size. A block size can either be directly chosen as block size, such as 5×4 or $3 \times 3 \times 3$, or the algorithm can be given the bpp to aim for and it will choose automatically. The bit rate must always have one decimal place, in the range 8.0 to 0.8 (or as low as 0.6 for 3D textures).

When wishing to decompress a texture to view, use the following command:

```
astcenc -d <input.file> <output.file> [options]
```

In this case, the -d denotes a decompression, the input file is a texture that has already been compressed, and the output file is one of the uncompressed formats.

To see what a texture would look like compressed with a given set of options, use the command

```
astcenc -t <input.file> <output.file> <rate> [options]
```

The -t option compresses the file with the given options then immediately decompresses it into the output file. The interim compressed image is not saved, and the input and output files are both in a decompressed file format.

The options can be left blank, but to get a good result, there are a few useful ones to remember.

The most useful arguments are the quality presets:

```
-veryfast
-fast
-medium
-thorough
-exhaustive
```

Many options are available to set various compression quality factors, including

- the number and scope of block partition patterns to attempt,

- the various signal-to-noise cutoff levels to early out of the individual decision-making stages,

- the maximum iterations of different bounding color tests.

Most users won't explore all of these to find the best mix for their own needs. Therefore, the quality presets can be used to give a high-level hint to the compressor, from which individual quality factors are derived.

It should be noted that veryfast, although almost instantaneous, gives good results only for a small subset of input images. Conversely, the exhaustive quality level (which does exactly what it says and attempts every possible bounding pattern combination for every block) takes a very much longer time, but it will often have very little visible difference to a file compressed in thorough mode.

11.5 Using ASTC Textures

ASTC capability is a new hardware feature available starting in late 2013. To get started with ASTC right away, the ARM Mali OpenGL ES 3.0 Emulator [Mali 14b] is available from ARM's website, and this is compatible with ASTC

```
struct astc_header
{
  uint8_t magic[4];
  uint8_t blockdim_x;
  uint8_t blockdim_y;
  uint8_t blockdim_z;
  uint8_t xsize[3];
  uint8_t ysize[3];
  uint8_t zsize[3];
};
```

Listing 11.1. ASTC header structure.

texture formats and as such can be used to test ASTC-based programs on a standard desktop GPU.

Loading a texture in ASTC format is no different from loading other compressed texture formats, but the correct internal format must be used. Files output by the compressor have a data header containing everything needed to load the compressed texture.

Using the data structure in Listing 11.1, the application can detect the important information needed to load an ASTC texture. Please see the Mali Developer Center website for source code examples.

11.6   Quality Settings

This chapter has already mentioned some of the high-level quality settings, but there are far more precisely targeted ways to tweak the quality of the compressor's output. The command line compressor has two main categories of argument, search parameters and quality metrics.

The algorithm for compressing a texture relies heavily on trial and error. Many combinations of block partition and boundary colors are compared and the best one is used for that block. Widening search parameters will compare more combinations to find the right one, enabling the algorithm to find a better match but also lengthening search time (and therefore compression time).

- plimit is the maximum number of partitions tested for each block before it takes the best one found so far.

- dblimit is the perceptual signal-to-noise ratio (PSNR) cutoff for a block in dB. If the PSNR of a block attempt exceeds this, the algorithm considers it good enough and uses that combination. This PSNR may not be reached, since the algorithm may hit the other limits first.

- oplimit implements a cutoff based on comparing errors between single and dual partitioning. That is, if the dual partition errors are much worse than the single partition errors, it's probably not worth trying three or four partitions. The `oplimit` defines how much worse this error must be to give up at this point.

- `mincorrel` defines the similarity of color coefficients that the algorithm will try to fit in a single color plane. The smaller this number, the more varied colors on the same plane can be; therefore, the block will not be tested with higher numbers of partitions.

- `bmc` is a cutoff for the count of block modes to attempt. The block mode defines how the individual color values are precision weighted using different binary modes for each partition.

- `maxiters` is the maximum cutoff for the number of refining iterations to colors and weights for any given partition attempt.

These values can be set individually to extend searching in specific directions: for example,

- A texture that has lots of subtle detail should probably have a high `oplimit` to ensure subtle color variations don't get bundled into the same partition plane.

- A texture that has very busy randomized patterns should probably search more partition types to find the right one.

Usually, however, these are set to default levels based on the general quality setting, as seen in Table 11.3.

Improving quality with these factors is a trade-off between compression time and quality. The greater the search limits and the less willing the algorithm is to accept a block as "good enough" the more time is spent looking for a better match. There is another way to get a better match, though, and that is to adjust the quality metrics, altering the factors by which the compressor judges the quality of a block.

preset	plimit	dblimit[a]	oplimit	Mincorrel	bmc	maxiters
veryfast	2	18.68	1.0	0.5	25	1
fast	4	28.68	1.0	0.5	50	1
medium	25	35.68	1.2	0.75	75	2
thorough	100	42.68	2.5	0.95	95	4
exhaustive	1024	999	1000.0	0.99	100	4

[a] dblimit defaults for levels other than exhaustive are defined by an equation based on the number of texels per block.

Table 11.3. Preset quality factors.

11.6.1 Channel Weighting

The simplest quality factors are channel weighting, using the command line argument:

```
-ch <red-weight> <green-weight> <blue-weight> <alpha-weight>
```

This defines weighting values for the noise calculations. For example, the argument -ch 1 4 1 1 makes error on the green channel four times more important than noise on any other given channel. The argument -ch 0.25 1 0.25 0.25 would appear to give the same effect, but that assumption is only partly correct. This would still make errors in the green channel four times more prevalent, but the total error would be lower, and therefore more likely to be accepted by a "good enough" early out.

Channel weighting works well when combined with swizzling, using the -esw argument. For textures without alpha, for example, the swizzle -esw rgb1 saturates the alpha channel and subsequently doesn't count it in noise calculations.

11.6.2 Block Weighting

Though human eyesight is more sensitive to variations in green and less sensitive to variations in red, channel weighting has limited usefulness. Other weights can also improve a compressed texture in a number of use cases. One of these is block error checking, particularly on textures with compound gradients over large areas. By default there is no error weight based on inter-block errors. The texels at the boundary of two adjacent blocks may be within error bounds for their own texels, but with noise in opposing directions, meaning that the step between the blocks is noticeably large. This can be countered with the command line argument:

```
-b <weight>
```

The equation to judge block suitability takes into account the edges of any adjacent blocks already processed. Figures 11.3 and 11.4 show this in action. However, this simply makes the search algorithm accept blocks with better matching edges more readily than others, so it may increase noise in other ways. Awareness of adjacent smooth blocks can be particularly helpful for normal maps.

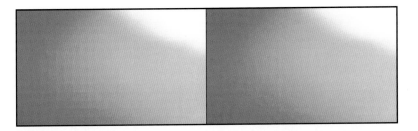

Figure 11.3. An example of block weighting. The left image shows block errors, the right image is recompressed with `-b 10`.

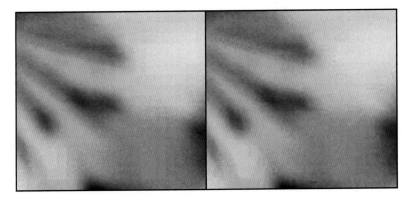

Figure 11.4. A second example of improvements from block weighting, using the same settings as Figure 11.3.

11.6.3 Normal Weighting

When compressing normal maps or maps used as a data source rather than color information, there are arguments that implement a number of additional settings all in one. These are `-normal_psnr`, `-normal_percep`, and `-mask`. Only one of these should be used at a time, as they override each other.

The first two of these are geared toward the compression of two-channel normal maps, swizzling the X and Y into luminance and alpha, overriding the default oplimit and mincorrel, and adding weight on angular error, which is far more important in normal maps. `-normal_percep` is similar but has subtly different weighting for better perceptual results. These can be seen in Figure 11.5.

.5 Both of these functions swizzle the X and Y into luminance and alpha, with an implied `-esw rrrg` argument, and also have an internal decode swizzle of `-dsw raz1` placing the luminance into X, placing the alpha into Y, and reconstructing Z using

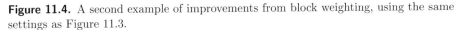

$$z = \sqrt{1 - r^2 - a^2}.$$

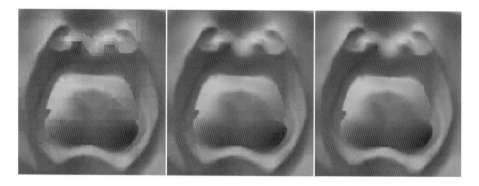

Figure 11.5. The leftmost normal map is compressed with default settings, the center uses `-normal_psnr`, and the normal map on the right uses `-normal_percep`.

The argument `-rn`, adds an error metric for angular noise. Other texture compression methodologies have lacked this option. Normal maps traditionally have been a problem to compress, as the minor variations in the angular component implied by the X and Y value can get ignored in pure signal to noise calculations.

11.6.4 Masking Channel Errors

The argument `-mask` tells the compressor to assume that the input texture has entirely unrelated content in each channel, and as such it is undesirable for errors in one channel to affect other channels.

This is shown in Figure 11.6, an example of a bitmap font where the red channel represents the characters, the blue is a rear glow, and the green is a drop shadow.

The perceptual and mask filters are based on combinations of the `-v` and `-va` arguments. These two arguments give low-level access to the way an error value for a block is collected from its individual texel differences. The full syntax is

Figure 11.6. The left image is the uncompressed data, the center is compressed with default settings, and the right image uses the `-mask` argument.

```
-v <radius> <power> <baseweight> <avgscale> <stdevscale>
   <mixing-factor>
```

The radius is the area of neighboring texels for which the average and standard deviations in error are combined using the equation

$$weight = \frac{1}{baseweight + avgscale * average^2 + stdevscale * stdev^2}.$$

The individual error values are raised to power before average and standard deviation values are calculated. The mixing factor is used to decide if the individual channel errors are combined before or after averaging. If the mixing factor is 0, each color channel has its own average and standard deviation calculated, which are then combined in the equation above. If the mixing factor is 1, the errors of each channel are combined before a single average is calculated. A value between 1 and 0 provides a combination of these two values.

The result is an erratic error value that, if just averaged over a block, can lead to a fairly noisy output being accepted. Using the standard deviation over a given radius gives the error calculations visibility of any added noise between texels, in much the same way that step changes between blocks can be checked with the block weighting (see Section 11.6.2) argument.

This equation of average noise works on the color channels, the alpha channel is controlled separately, with a similar set of values in the command line arguments:

```
-va <baseweight> <power> <avgscale> <stdevscale>
-a <radius>
```

The alpha channel is controlled separately as, particularly with punch through textures, a little bit of quantization noise may be preferable to softening of edges.[2]

11.7   Other Color Formats

ASTC supports images with one to four channels, from luminance only all the way to RGBA. Additionally, the algorithm has support for different color-space encodings:

---

[2]It's worth reassuring the reader that yes, that is quite a lot of powers and coefficients to throw at a somewhat chaotic system, so manual adjustments can often feel like a stab in the dark—hence the presets.

- Linear RGBA,[3]

- sRGB + linear A,

- HDR RGB + A,[4]

- HDR RGBA.

11.7.1   sRGB

ASTC supports nonlinear sRGB color-space conversion both at compression and decompression time.

To keep images in sRGB color space until the point that they are used, simply compress them in the usual way. Then when they're loaded, instead of the regular texture formats, use the sRGB texture formats. These are the ones that contain `SRGB8_ALPHA8` in the name. There's an sRGB equivalent of every RGBA format.

Helpfully the constants for the sRGB formats are always `0x0020` greater than the RGBA constants, allowing an easy switch in code between the two.

As an alternative to using sRGB texture types at runtime, there is also a command line argument for the compressor to transform them to linear RGBA prior to compression. The `-srgb` argument will convert the color space and compress the texture in linear space, to be loaded with the usual RGBA texture formats.

11.7.2   HDR

ASTC also supports HDR image formats. Using these requires no additional effort in code and the same loading function detailed above can be used. When encoding an image in a HDR format, the encoder doesn't use HDR encoding by default. For this, one of two arguments must be used:

```
-forcehdr_rgb
-forcehdr_rgba
```

In this mode, the encoder will use a HDR or LDR as appropriate on a per-block basis. In `-forcehdr_rgb` mode, the alpha channel (if present) is always encoded LDR. There are also the simpler arguments:

```
-hdr
-hdra
```

---

[3]The most commonly understood and supported color space.
[4]HDR RGB channels with an LDR alpha.

which are equivalent to `-forcehdr_rgb` and `-forcehdr_rgba` but with additional alterations to the evaluation of block suitability (a preset `-v` and `-va`) better suited for HDR images. Also available are

```
-hdr_log
-hdra_log
```

These are similar but base their suitability on logarithmic error. Images encoded with this setting typically give better results from a mathematical perspective but don't hold up as well in terms of perceptual artifacts.

11.8 3D Textures

The compression algorithm can also handle 3D textures at a block level. Although other image compression algorithms can be used to store and access 3D textures, they are compressed in 2D space as a series of single texel layers, whereas ASTC compresses 3D blocks of texture data, improving the cache hit rate of serial texture reads along the Z axis. Currently there are no suitably prolific 3D image formats to accept as inputs, as such encoding a of 3D texture has a special syntax:

```
-array <size>
```

With this command line argument, the input file is assumed to be a prefix pattern for the actual inputs and decorates the file name with `_0`, `_1`, and so on all the way up to `_<size-1>`. So, for example, if the input file was "slice.png" with the argument `-array 4`, the compression algorithm would attempt to load files named "slice_0.png," "slice_1.png," "slice_2.png," and "slice_3.png." The presence of multiple texture layers would then be taken as a signal to use a 3D block encoding for the requested rate (see Table 11.2).

11.9 Summary

This chapter shows the advantages of ASTC over other currently available texture compression methodologies and provides code to easily use ASTC texture files in an arbitrary graphics project, as well as a detailed explanation of the command line arguments to get the most out of the evaluation codec.

Additionally, ARM provides a free Texture Compression Tool [ARM 14] that automates the ASTC command line arguments explained in this chapter via a Graphical User Interface (GUI) to simplify the compression process and provide visual feedback on compression quality.

Bibliography

[ARM 14] ARM. "Mali GPU Texture Compression Tool." http://malideveloper
.arm.com/develop-for-mali/mali-gpu-texture-compression-tool/, 2014.

[Fenney 03] Simon Fenney. "Texture Compression Using Low-Frequency Signal
Modulation." In *Proceedings of the ACM SIGGRAPH/EUROGRAPHICS
Conference on Graphics Hardware*, pp. 84–91. Aire-la-Ville, Switzerland: Eu-
rographics Association, 2003.

[Mali 14a] Mali. "ASTC Evaluation Codec." http://malideveloper.arm.com/
develop-for-mali/tools/astc-evaluation-codec/, 2014.

[Mali 14b] Mali. "OpenGL ES SDK Emulator." http://malideveloper.arm.com/
develop-for-mali/sdks/opengl-es-sdk-for-linux/, 2014.

[Nystad et al. 12] J. Nystad, A. Lassen, A. Pomianowski, S. Ellis, and T. Olson.
"Adaptive Scalable Texture Compression." In *Proceedings of the Fourth
ACM SIGGRAPH/Eurographics Conference on High-Performance Graph-
ics*, pp. 105–114. Aire-la-Ville, Switzerland: Eurographics Association, 2012.

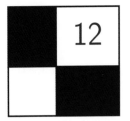

Optimizing OpenCL Kernels for the ARM® Mali™-T600 GPUs

Johan Gronqvist and Anton Lokhmotov

12.1 Introduction

OpenCL is a relatively young industry-backed standard API that aims to provide *functional portability* across systems equipped with computational accelerators such as GPUs: a standard-conforming OpenCL program can be executed on any standard-conforming OpenCL implementation.

OpenCL, however, does not address the issue of *performance portability*: transforming an OpenCL program to achieve higher performance on one device may actually lead to lower performance on another device, since performance may depend significantly on low-level details, such as iteration space mapping and data layout [Howes et al. 10, Ryoo et al. 08].

Due to the popularity of certain GPU architectures, some optimizations have become hallmarks of GPU computing, e.g., coalescing global memory accesses or using local memory. Emerging mobile and embedded OpenCL-capable GPUs, however, have rather different organization. Therefore, even seasoned GPU developers may need to forgo their instincts and learn new techniques when optimizing for battery-powered GPU brethren.

In this chapter, we introduce the ARM Mali-T600 GPU series (Section 12.3) and discuss performance characteristics of several versions of the Sobel edge detection filter (Section 12.4) and the general matrix multiplication (Section 12.5).[1]

We make no claim that the presented versions are the fastest possible implementations of the selected algorithms. Rather, we aim to provide an insight into

---

[1]Source code for some versions is available in the Mali OpenCL SDK [ARM 13].

which transformations should be considered when optimizing kernel code for the Mali-T600 GPUs. Therefore, the described behavior may differ from the actual behavior for expository purposes.

We perform our experiments on an Arndale development board[2] powered by the Samsung Exynos 5250 chip. Exynos 5250 comprises a dual-core Cortex-A15 CPU at 1.7 GHz and a quad-core Mali-T604 GPU at 533 MHz. The OpenCL driver is of version 3.0 Beta.

12.2   Overview of the OpenCL Programming Model

In the OpenCL programming model, the host (e.g., a CPU) manages one or more devices (e.g., a GPU) through calls to the OpenCL API. A call to the `clEnqueueND Range()` API function submits a job that executes on a selected device the same program (*kernel*)[3] as a collection of *work-items*.

Each work-item has a unique index (*global ID*) in a multidimensional iteration space (*ND-range*), specified as the *global work size* argument to `clEnqueueND Range()`. The *local work size* argument to `clEnqueueNDRange()` determines how the ND-range is partitioned into uniformly sized *work-groups*. Work-items within the same work-group can synchronize using the `barrier()` built-in function, which must be executed by all work-items in the work-group before any work-item continues execution past the barrier.

In our examples, the ND-range is two-dimensional: work-items iterate over the pixels of the output image (Section 12.4) or the elements of the output matrix (Section 12.5), while work-groups iterate over partitions (or *tiles*) of the same. For example, the local work size of $(4, 16)$ would result in 64 work-items per work-group, with the first work-group having global IDs (x, y), where $0 \leq x < 4$ and $0 \leq y < 16$.

12.3   ARM Mali-T600 GPU Series

The ARM Mali-T600 GPU series based on the Midgard architecture is designed to meet the growing needs of graphics and compute applications for a wide range of consumer electronics, from phones and tablets to TVs and beyond. The Mali-T604 GPU, the first implementation of the Mali-T600 series, was the first mobile and embedded class GPU to pass the OpenCL v1.1 Full Profile conformance tests.

---

[2] http://www.arndaleboard.org
[3] The kernel is typically written in the OpenCL C language, which is a superset of a subset of the C99 language standard.

12.3.1 Architecture Overview

The Mali-T604 GPU is formed of four identical cores, each supporting up to 256 concurrently executing (*active*) threads.[4]

Each core contains a tri-pipe containing two arithmetic (A) pipelines, one load-store (LS) pipeline, and one texture (T) pipeline. Thus, the peak throughput of each core is two A instruction words, one LS instruction word, and one T instruction word per cycle. Midgard is a VLIW (Very Long Instruction Word) architecture, so that each pipe contains multiple units and most instruction words contain instructions for multiple units. In addition, Midgard is a SIMD (Single Instruction Multiple Data) architecture, so that most instructions operate on multiple data elements packed in 128-bit vector registers.

12.3.2 Execution Constraints

The architectural maximum number of work-items active on a single core is $\max(I) = 256$. The actual maximum number of active work-items I is determined by the number of registers R that the kernel code uses

$$I = \begin{cases} 256, & 0 < R \leq 4, \\ 128, & 4 < R \leq 8, \\ 64, & 8 < R \leq 16. \end{cases}$$

For example, kernel A that uses $R_A = 5$ registers and kernel B that uses $R_B = 8$ registers can both be executed by *no more than* 128 work-items.[5]

12.3.3 Thread Scheduling

The GPU schedules work-groups onto cores in batches, whose size is chosen by the driver depending on the characteristics of the job. The hardware schedules batches onto cores in a round-robin fashion. A batch consists of a number of "adjacent" work-groups.[6]

Each core first creates threads for the first scheduled work-group and then continues to create threads for the other scheduled work-groups until either the maximum number of active threads has been reached or all threads for the scheduled work-groups have been created. When a thread terminates, a new thread can be scheduled in its place.

---

[4]In what follows, we assume that a single hardware thread executes a single work-item. A program transformation known as *thread coarsening* can result in a single hardware thread executing multiple work-items, e.g., in different vector lanes.

[5]Therefore, the compiler may prefer to spill a value to memory rather than use an extra register when the number of used registers approaches 4, 8, or 16.

[6]In our examples using 2D ND-ranges, two "adjacent" work-groups have work-items that are adjacent in the 2D space of global IDs (see Section 12.5.6 for a more detailed description).

Created threads enter the tri-pipe in a round-robin order. A core switches between threads on every cycle: when a thread has executed one instruction, it then waits while all other threads execute one instruction.[7] Sometimes a thread can stall waiting for a cache miss and another thread will overtake it, changing the ordering between threads. (We will discuss this aspect later in Section 12.5.)

12.3.4 Guidelines for Optimizing Performance

A compute program (kernel) typically consists of a mix of A and LS instruction words.[8] Achieving high performance on the Mali-T604 involves the following:

- Using a sufficient number of active threads to hide the execution latency of instructions (pipeline depth). The number of active threads depends on the number of registers used by kernel code and so may be limited for complex kernels.

- Using vector operations in kernel code to allow for straightforward mapping to vector instructions by the compiler.

- Having sufficient instruction level parallelism in kernel code to allow for dense packing of instructions into instruction words by the compiler.

- Having a balance between A and LS instruction words. Without cache misses, the ratio of 2:1 of A-words to LS-words would be optimal; with cache misses, a higher ratio is desirable. For example, a kernel consisting of 15 A-words and 7 LS-words is still likely to be bound by the LS-pipe.

In several respects, programming for the Mali-T604 GPU embedded on a System-on-Chip (SoC) is easier than programming for desktop class GPUs:

- The `global` and `local` OpenCL address spaces get mapped to the same physical memory (the system RAM), backed by caches transparent to the programmer. This often removes the need for explicit data copying and associated barrier synchronization.

- All threads have individual program counters. This means that branch divergence is less of an issue than for warp-based architectures.

---

[7]There is more parallelism in the hardware than this sentence mentions, but the description here suffices for the current discussion.

[8]The texture (T) pipeline is rarely used for compute kernels, with a notable exception of executing barrier operations (see Section 12.5). The main reason is that when performing memory accesses using vector instructions in the LS pipeline results in higher memory bandwidth (bytes per cycle) than using instructions in the T pipeline for kernels requiring no sampling.

12.3.5 A Note on Power

We discuss performance in terms of the time it takes to complete a computation. When analyzing the performance of an OpenCL kernel running on a mobile device, it is also important to consider the power and energy required for the execution. Often, the mobile device's thermal dissipation capacity will determine the maximum DVFS operating point (voltage and frequency) at which the GPU can be run. On Mali-T600 GPUs, it is often sufficient to characterize the performance of the *kernel* in terms of the number of cycles required for the execution. To determine the overall performance, one also has to factor in the GPU clock rate.

We focus on the cycle count of kernel execution and consider this sufficient for our optimization purposes. We posit that GPU power is (to a broad approximation) constant across sustained GPGPU workloads at a fixed operating point.[9] Energy consumed for a given workload is therefore determined by performance—both the number of cycles for that workload and the operating point required to meet the required performance target.

12.4 Optimizing the Sobel Image Filter

12.4.1 Algorithm

Our first example is the Sobel 3×3 image filter used within edge-detection algorithms. Technically speaking, the Sobel filter is a $(2K+1) \times (2K+1)$ convolution of an input image $\mathbf{I}$ with a constant mask $\mathbf{C}$:

$$\mathbf{O}_{y,x} = \sum_{u=-K}^{K} \sum_{v=-K}^{K} \mathbf{I}_{y+u,x+v} \cdot \mathbf{C}_{u,v},$$

taking an image containing the luminosity values and producing two images containing the discretized gradient values along the horizontal and vertical directions:

$$\mathbf{O}_{y,x}^{\mathbf{dx}} = \sum_{u=-1}^{1} \sum_{v=-1}^{1} \mathbf{I}_{y+u,x+v} \cdot \mathbf{C}_{u,v}^{\mathbf{dx}}, \quad \text{where} \quad \mathbf{C}^{\mathbf{dx}} = \begin{pmatrix} -1 & 0 & 1 \\ -2 & 0 & 2 \\ -1 & 0 & 1 \end{pmatrix},$$

$$\mathbf{O}_{y,x}^{\mathbf{dy}} = \sum_{u=-1}^{1} \sum_{v=-1}^{1} \mathbf{I}_{y+u,x+v} \cdot \mathbf{C}_{u,v}^{\mathbf{dy}}, \quad \text{where} \quad \mathbf{C}^{\mathbf{dy}} = \begin{pmatrix} 1 & 2 & 1 \\ 0 & 0 & 0 \\ -1 & -2 & -1 \end{pmatrix}.$$

---

[9]This assumption holds broadly on the Mali-T600 GPU series, as a result of the pipeline architecture, aggressive clock gating, and the GPU's ability to hide memory latency effectively.

12.4.2 Implementation Details

In our implementation, the input image $\mathbf{I}$ is an $H \times W$ array of unsigned 8-bit integers (uchar's) and the output images $\mathbf{O^{dx}}$ and $\mathbf{O^{dy}}$ are $H \times W$ arrays of signed 8-bit integers (char's). The results are computed as signed 16-bit integers (short's) and are normalized by dividing by 8 (i.e., shifting right by 3). The results are only computed for $(H - 2) \times (W - 2)$ inner pixels of the output images, leaving pixels on the one-pixel wide border intact.[10]

12.4.3 Performance Characteristics

Table 12.1 shows the results for all the kernel versions discussed in this section on a 512×512 input image. We present the following numbers for each kernel version:

- the number of input pixels per work-item,

- the maximal local work size, max(LWS), i.e., the maximal number of active work-items per core,

- the number of arithmetic and load-store instruction words per work-item,

- the number of arithmetic and load-store instruction words per cycle,

- the number of pixels processed per cycle.

Achieving a high proportion of the peak numbers of A-words and LS-words executed per cycle (8 and 4, respectively, for the Mali-T604) may be challenging due to memory and other effects.

12.4.4 Using Scalars

The char kernel in Listing 12.1 is a naïve, scalar version. Each work-item reads a 3×3 square of input pixels around its coordinate. The computation is performed using 16-bit integer arithmetic to avoid overflow. No vector operations are used.

Table 12.1 shows that each work-item has to pass 13 times through an A-pipe, and at least 7 times through a LS-pipe (possibly more due to cache misses). Having 256 active work-items ensures good utilization: indeed, this version reaches the highest number of LS-words per cycle. However, the overall performance is poor (0.3 pixels per cycle) due to not using vector operations.

---

[10]Our test image has a size of 512×512, which means that the interior has a size of only 510×510. We have vectorized versions that handle 8 or 16 pixels per work-item, and for those implementations, we have an (interior) image size that is not a multiple of the number of pixels per work-item. In a real application, we would have to take care to handle the border separately, but as this affects only a small percentage of the image, we will instead ignore that discussion, as it is not important for our qualitative performance considerations.

```
kernel void sobel_char(
  global const uchar * restrict in,  //< Input.
  global char * restrict dx,         //< X gradient.
  global char * restrict dy,         //< Y gradient.
  const int width)
{
  // X and Y gradient accumulators.
  short _dx, _dy;

  // Left, middle and right pixels: loaded as
  // unsigned 8-bit, converted to signed 16-bit.
  uchar lLoad, mLoad, rLoad;
  short lData, mData, rData;

  // Compute (column,row) position and offset.
  const int column = get_global_id(0);
  const int row    = get_global_id(1);
  const int offset = row * width + column;

  // Compute contribution from first row.
  lLoad = *(in + (offset + width * 0 + 0));
  mLoad = *(in + (offset + width * 0 + 1));
  rLoad = *(in + (offset + width * 0 + 2));

  lData = convert_short(lLoad);
  mData = convert_short(mLoad);
  rData = convert_short(rLoad);

  _dx = rData - lData;
  _dy = rData + lData + mData * (short)2;

  // Compute contribution from second row.
  lLoad = *(in + (offset + width * 1 + 0));
  rLoad = *(in + (offset + width * 1 + 2));

  lData = convert_short(lLoad);
  rData = convert_short(rLoad);

  _dx += (rData - lData) * (short)2;

  // Compute contribution from third row.
  lLoad = *(in + (offset + width * 2 + 0));
  mLoad = *(in + (offset + width * 2 + 1));
  rLoad = *(in + (offset + width * 2 + 2));

  lData = convert_short(lLoad);
  mData = convert_short(mLoad);
  rData = convert_short(rLoad);

  _dx += rData - lData;
  _dy -= rData + lData + mData * (short)2;

  // Store the results.
  *(dx + offset + width + 1) = convert_char(_dx >> 3);
  *(dy + offset + width + 1) = convert_char(_dy >> 3);
}
```

Listing 12.1. Initial scalar implementation: char.

Version Name	Pixels/WI	max(LWS)	A-words/WI	LS-words/WI	A-words/Cycle	LS-words/Cycle	Pixels/Cycle
char	1	256	13	7	3.9	2.1	0.3
char8	8	128	17	9	3.8	2	1.8
char16	16	64	21	7	2.3	0.8	1.8
char8_load16	8	128	18	5	5	1.4	2.2
char16_swizzle	16	128	32	8	5.1	1.3	2.6
2xchar8	16	128	29	14	3.8	1.9	2.1
2xchar8_load16	16	128	32	7	4.9	1.1	2.5
3xchar8	24	64	39	19	2.2	1.1	1.4

Table 12.1. Performance characteristics of all Sobel versions running on a 512×512 image (see Section 12.4.3 for a description of the columns). Note that our implementations compute two output pixels for each input pixel (i.e., double the output of a standard 3×3 convolution filter), but we only count the number of input pixels per work-item (WI).

12.4.5   Using Vectors

Eight components. Each work-item of the char8 kernel in Listing 12.2 performs eight char8 load operations to read a 3×10 region of input pixels and computes two char8 vectors of output pixels. The conversion and compute instructions operate on short8 data in 128-bit registers.

Table 12.1 shows that while the char8 kernel computes eight times more data, it performs only about 30% more arithmetic and memory instructions than the char kernel, resulting in a six times increase in performance (1.8 pixels per cycle). The ratio between the arithmetic and memory instructions is close to the 2:1, optimal for cases with few cache misses. Due to the increase in complexity, the kernel max(LWS) is 128, limiting the number of simultaneously active work-items per core to 128. Still, the number of instruction words executed per cycle is nearly the same as for the scalar version, which shows that we can accept a max(LWS) of 128 without significant performance problems for this kind of workload.

Sixteen components. The number of operations per pixel is reduced even further by using char16 memory operations (full vector register width) and short16 arithmetic operations (broken into short8 operations by the compiler) in the char16 kernel partially shown in Listing 12.3. Performance, however, does not increase, because this kernel can only be executed with up to 64 simultaneous work-items per core (max(LWS) = 64), which introduces bubbles into the pipelines due to reduced latency-hiding capability.

```
kernel void sobel_char8(
  global const uchar * restrict in,  //< Input.
  global char * restrict dx,         //< X gradient.
  global char * restrict dy,         //< Y gradient.
  const int width)
{
  // X and Y gradient accumulators.
  short8 _dx, _dy;

  // Left, middle and right pixels: loaded as
  // unsigned 8-bit, converted to signed 16-bit.
  uchar8 lLoad, mLoad, rLoad;
  short8 lData, mData, rData;

  // Compute (column,row) position and offset.
  const int column = get_global_id(0) * 8;
  const int row    = get_global_id(1) * 1;
  const int offset = row * width + column;

  // Compute contribution from first row.
  lLoad = vload8(0, in + (offset + width * 0 + 0));
  mLoad = vload8(0, in + (offset + width * 0 + 1));
  rLoad = vload8(0, in + (offset + width * 0 + 2));

  lData = convert_short8(lLoad);
  mData = convert_short8(mLoad);
  rData = convert_short8(rLoad);

  _dx = rData - lData;
  _dy = rData + lData + mData * (short8)2;

  // Compute contribution from second row.
  lLoad = vload8(0, in + (offset + width * 1 + 0));
  rLoad = vload8(0, in + (offset + width * 1 + 2));

  lData = convert_short8(lLoad);
  rData = convert_short8(rLoad);

  _dx += (rData - lData) * (short8)2;

  // Compute contribution from third row.
  lLoad = vload8(0, in + (offset + width * 2 + 0));
  mLoad = vload8(0, in + (offset + width * 2 + 1));
  rLoad = vload8(0, in + (offset + width * 2 + 2));

  lData = convert_short8(lLoad);
  mData = convert_short8(mLoad);
  rData = convert_short8(rLoad);

  _dx += rData - lData;
  _dy -= rData + lData + mData * (short8)2;

  // Store the results.
  vstore8(convert_char8(_dx >> 3), 0, dx + offset + width + 1);
  vstore8(convert_char8(_dy >> 3), 0, dy + offset + width + 1);
}
```

Listing 12.2. Initial vector implementation: char8.

```
41    // Compute contribution from third row.
42    lLoad = vload16(0, in + (offset + width * 2 + 0));
43    mLoad = vload16(0, in + (offset + width * 2 + 1));
44    rLoad = vload16(0, in + (offset + width * 2 + 2));
45
46    lData = convert_short16(lLoad);
47    mData = convert_short16(mLoad);
48    rData = convert_short16(rLoad);
49
50    _dx += rData - lData;
51    _dy -= rData + lData + mData * (short16)2;
52
53    // Store the results.
54    vstore16(convert_char16(_dx >> 3), 0, dx + offset + width + 1);
55    vstore16(convert_char16(_dy >> 3), 0, dy + offset + width + 1);
```

Listing 12.3. Computing contribution from the third row: `char16`.

12.4.6   Reusing Loaded Data

Larger load operations. The `char8` kernel performed eight `char8` load operations. The `char8_load16` kernel, partially shown in Listing 12.4, performs only three `char16` load operations: the required subcomponents are extracted by swizzle operations, which are often free on the Midgard architecture. Table 12.1 confirms that the number of memory operations per pixel is decreased, while still allowing the kernel to be launched with up to 128 simultaneous work-items per core.

Eliminating redundant loads. The `char16` kernel performed three `char16` load operations to read 18 bytes for the first and third rows. The `char16_swizzle` kernel, partially shown in Listing 12.5, performs two `char16` load operations for the leftmost and rightmost vectors and reconstructs the middle vector by swizzle operations.

```
41    // Compute contribution from third row.
42    load = vload16(0, in + (offset + width * 2 + 0));
43
44    lData = convert_short8(load.s01234567);
45    mData = convert_short8(load.s12345678);
46    rData = convert_short8(load.s23456789);
47
48    _dx += rData - lData;
49    _dy -= rData + lData + mData * (short8)2;
50
51    // Store the results.
52    vstore8(convert_char8(_dx >> 3), 0, dx + offset + width + 1);
53    vstore8(convert_char8(_dy >> 3), 0, dy + offset + width + 1);
```

Listing 12.4. Computing contribution from the third row: `char8_load16`.

```
41    // Compute contribution from third row.
42    lLoad = vload16(0, in + (offset + width * 2 + 0));
43    rLoad = vload16(0, in + (offset + width * 2 + 2));
44
45    lData = convert_short16(lLoad);
46    mData = convert_short16(
47      (uchar16)(lLoad.s12345678, rLoad.s789abcde));
48    rData = convert_short16(rLoad);
49
50    _dx += rData - lData;
51    _dy -= rData + lData + mData * (short16)2;
52
53    // Store the results.
54    vstore16(convert_char16(_dx >> 3), 0, dx + offset + width + 1);
55    vstore16(convert_char16(_dy >> 3), 0, dy + offset + width + 1);
```

Listing 12.5. Computing contribution from the third row: `char16_swizzle`.

While the number of instruction words increases in comparison to the `char16` kernel (by nearly 50% for A-words and even slightly for LS-words due to instruction scheduling effects), this kernel can be launched with 128 simultaneous work-items per core. This leads to the highest utilization of the A-pipes of all the versions in this study, as well as the best overall performance.

12.4.7   Processing Multiple Rows

The kernels presented so far have loaded pixels from three input rows to compute pixels in a single output row. In general, to compute pixels in n output rows, $n + 2$ input rows are needed.

```
43    // Compute contribution from third row.
44    lLoad = vload8(0, in + (offset + width*2 + 0));
45    mLoad = vload8(0, in + (offset + width*2 + 1));
46    rLoad = vload8(0, in + (offset + width*2 + 2));
47
48    lData = convert_short8(lLoad);
49    mData = convert_short8(mLoad);
50    rData = convert_short8(rLoad);
51
52    _dx1 += rData - lData;
53    _dy1 -= rData + lData + mData * (short8)2;
54    _dx2 += (rData - lData) * (short8)2;
```

```
68    // Store the results.
69    vstore8(convert_char8(_dx1 >> 3), 0, dx1 + offset + width + 1);
70    vstore8(convert_char8(_dy1 >> 3), 0, dy1 + offset + width + 1);
71    vstore8(convert_char8(_dx2 >> 3), 0, dx2 + offset + width*2 + 1);
72    vstore8(convert_char8(_dy2 >> 3), 0, dy2 + offset + width*2 + 1);
```

Listing 12.6. Computing contribution from the third row: 2xchar8.

```
41    // Compute contribution from third row.
42    load = vload16(0, in + (offset + width*2 + 0));
43
44    lData = convert_short8(load.s01234567);
45    mData = convert_short8(load.s12345678);
46    rData = convert_short8(load.s23456789);
47
48    _dx1 += rData - lData;
49    _dy1 -= rData + lData + mData * (short8)2;
50    _dx2 += (rData - lData) * (short8)2;
```

```
62    // Store the results.
63    vstore8(convert_char8(_dx1 >> 3), 0, dx1 + offset + width + 1);
64    vstore8(convert_char8(_dy1 >> 3), 0, dy1 + offset + width + 1);
65    vstore8(convert_char8(_dx2 >> 3), 0, dx2 + offset + width*2 + 1);
66    vstore8(convert_char8(_dy2 >> 3), 0, dy2 + offset + width*2 + 1);
```

Listing 12.7. Computing contribution from the third row: `2xchar8_load16`.

Computing two rows of output. The `2xchar8` and `2xchar8_load16` kernels load from four input rows to compute results for two output rows ($n = 2$). They are partially shown in Listing 12.6 and Listing 12.7 and are modifications of the `char8` and `char8_load16` kernels, respectively. Both kernels can be launched with up to 128 simultaneous work-items per core and both kernels perform better than the single-row variants. As before, the `load16` version is faster, and indeed achieves the second best performance in this study.

Computing three rows of output. The `3xchar8` kernel, partially shown in Listing 12.8, has grown too complex and can only be launched with up to 64 simultaneous work-items per core. Therefore, exploiting data reuse by keeping more than two rows in registers is suboptimal on the Mali-T604.

12.4.8 Summary

We have presented several versions of the Sobel filter, and discussed their performance characteristics on the Mali-T604 GPU. Vectorizing kernel code and exploiting data reuse are the two principal optimization techniques explored in this study. The fastest kernel, `char16_swizzle`, is nearly nine times faster than the slowest kernel, `char`, which reiterates the importance of target-specific optimizations for OpenCL code.

To summarize, we note that although the theoretical peak performance is at the ratio of two arithmetic instruction words for every load-store instruction word, the best performance was obtained in the versions with the highest number of arithmetic words executed per cycle. Restructuring the program to trade load-store operations for arithmetic operations has thus been successful, as long as the kernel could still be launched with 128 simultaneous work-items per core.

```
43   // Compute contribution from third row.
44   lLoad = vload8(0, in + (offset + width*2 + 0));
45   mLoad = vload8(0, in + (offset + width*2 + 1));
46   rLoad = vload8(0, in + (offset + width*2 + 2));
47
48   lData = convert_short8(lLoad);
49   mData = convert_short8(mLoad);
50   rData = convert_short8(rLoad);
51
52   _dx1 += rData - lData;
53   _dy1 -= rData + lData + mData * (short8)2;
54   _dx2 += (rData - lData) * (short8)2;
55   _dx3 = rData - lData;
56   _dy3 = rData + lData + mData * (short8)2;
```

```
83   // Store the results.
84   vstore8(convert_char8(_dx1 >> 3), 0, dx1 + offset + width + 1);
85   vstore8(convert_char8(_dy1 >> 3), 0, dy1 + offset + width + 1);
86   vstore8(convert_char8(_dx2 >> 3), 0, dx2 + offset + width*2 + 1);
87   vstore8(convert_char8(_dy2 >> 3), 0, dy2 + offset + width*2 + 1);
88   vstore8(convert_char8(_dx3 >> 3), 0, dx3 + offset + width*3 + 1);
89   vstore8(convert_char8(_dy3 >> 3), 0, dy3 + offset + width*3 + 1);
```

Listing 12.8. Computing contribution from the third row: `3xchar8`.

12.5 Optimizing the General Matrix Multiplication

The Sobel filter implementations have hightlighted the importance of using vector instructions and a high number of active work-items. We next study implementations of the general matrix multiplication (GEMM) to elucidate the importance of using caches effectively. We first discuss aspects of the caches and how we optimize for them. At the end, we look at the runtimes on an Arndale development board and compare to our discussions.

12.5.1 Algorithm

The general matrix multiplication is a function of the Basic Linear Algebra Subprograms (BLAS) API[11] that computes

$$C = \alpha AB + \beta C,$$

where A, B, C are matrices of floating-point numbers and α, β are scalars.

12.5.2 Implementation Details

In our implementation, the matrices are $N \times N$ arrays of single-precision floating-point numbers (SGEMM). We consider two common SGEMM variants:

---

[11]http://www.netlib.org/blas

- NN: A is non-transposed, B is non-transposed:

$$C[i,j] = \alpha \sum_{k=0}^{N-1} A[i,k] \times B[k,j] + \beta C[i,j].$$

- NT: A is non-transposed, B is transposed:

$$C[i,j] = \alpha \sum_{k=0}^{N-1} A[i,k] \times B[j,k] + \beta C[i,j],$$

where $i = 0, \ldots, N-1$ and $j = 0, \ldots, N-1$.

CPU implementations of the NN variant often first transpose B and then perform the NT variant, which has a more cache-friendly memory access pattern, as we show in Section 12.5.4.

12.5.3 Scalar Implementations

We first consider scalar implementations with an $N \times N$ ND-range covering all elements of C. From our experience with optimizing the Sobel filter, these versions are clearly suboptimal as they do not use any vector operations. We will (due to their simplicity) use them to introduce our notation for describing memory access patterns of kernels, and we will also use them as examples in some qualitative discussions later.

Non-transposed. Each work-item of the `scalarNN` version in Listing 12.9 produces one element of C by computing the dot product of a row of A and a column of B.

```
kernel void
sgemm(global float const *A, global float const *B,
      global float *C, float alpha, float beta, uint n)
{
  uint j = get_global_id(0);
  uint i = get_global_id(1);

  float ABij = 0.0f;
  for (uint k = 0; k < n; ++k)
  {
    ABij += A[i*n + k] * B[k*n + j];
  }
  C[i*n + j] = alpha * ABij + beta * C[i*n + j];
}
```

Listing 12.9. Initial scalar implementation: `scalarNN`.

```
kernel void
sgemm(global float const *A, global float const *B,
      global float *C, float alpha, float beta, uint n)
{
  uint j = get_global_id(0);
  uint i = get_global_id(1);

  float ABij = 0.0f;
  for (uint k = 0; k < n; ++k)
  {
    ABij += A[i*n + k] * B[j*n + k];
  }
  C[i*n + j] = alpha * ABij + beta * C[i*n + j];
}
```

Listing 12.10. Initial scalar implementation: `scalarNT`.

Transposed. Each work-item of the `scalarNT` version in Listing 12.10 produces one element of C by computing the dot product of a row of A and a column of B^T (or equivalently a row of B).

12.5.4 Memory Access Patterns of Scalar Implementations

A single work-item of the `scalarNN` version sequentially reads (within the `k` loop) from pairs of locations $(A[i,0], B[0,j])$, $(A[i,1], B[1,j])$, ..., $(A[i, N-1], B[N-1, j])$. We will abbreviate this access pattern to

$$\overset{N-1}{\underset{k=0}{;}}(A[i,k], B[k,j]),$$

which denotes that the accesses happen sequentially for $0 \le k < N$.

Similarly, the access pattern of a single work-item of the `scalarNT` version is

$$\overset{N-1}{\underset{k=0}{;}}(A[i,k], B[j,k]).$$

With the row-major array layout used in the C language, the `scalarNT` variant reads both A and B with stride 1, while the `scalarNN` variant reads B with stride N.

Let us assume a core executes a single work-group of dimensions (λ_0, λ_1). Since work-items execute in an interleaved order (Section 12.3.3), the actual memory access pattern of the `scalarNN` variant on the core will be

$$\overset{N-1}{\underset{k=0}{;}}\left[\left(\overset{\lambda_1-1}{\underset{i=0}{;}}\overset{\lambda_0-1}{\underset{j=0}{;}} A[i,k]\right), \left(\overset{\lambda_1-1}{\underset{i=0}{;}}\overset{\lambda_0-1}{\underset{j=0}{;}} B[k,j]\right)\right],$$

which means that on each iteration $0 \leq k < N$ all work-items first read from A and then from B. The $,$ operator for $0 \leq j < \lambda_0$ is the innermost one, due to the order in which threads are created by the device.[12]

12.5.5 Blocking

As a first step towards better implementations, we will introduce *blocking*, a program transformation that will allow us to use vector operations for memory accesses and arithmetic operations. We will later exploit blocking to improve cache usage.

Let us assume that matrix order N is divisible by blocking factors ΔI, ΔJ and $\Delta K_{\text{reg.}}$. Imagine that

- matrix A consists of $\frac{N}{\Delta I} \times \frac{N}{\Delta K_{\text{reg.}}}$ submatrices of $\Delta I \times \Delta K_{\text{reg.}}$ elements each,

- matrix B consists of $\frac{N}{\Delta K_{\text{reg.}}} \times \frac{N}{\Delta J}$ submatrices of $\Delta K_{\text{reg.}} \times \Delta J$ elements each,

- matrix C consists of $\frac{N}{\Delta I} \times \frac{N}{\Delta J}$ submatrices of $\Delta I \times \Delta J$ elements each.

Now, instead of writing the SGEMM NN algorithm as

$$C[i,j] = \alpha \sum_{i,j} A[i,k] \times B[k,j] + \beta C[i,j],$$

where $A[i,k]$, $B[k,j]$ and $C[i,j]$ were individual elements, we can write it as

$$C[I,J] = \alpha \sum_{I,J} A[I,K] \times B[K,J] + \beta C[I,J],$$

where $A[I,K]$, $B[K,J]$ and $C[I,J]$ are submatrices as above and $\times$ is the matrix multiplication operation.

Our kernels will still have the same structure, but each work-item will now compute one $\Delta I \times \Delta J$ submatrix of $C[I,J]$. Each iteration of the k loop will multiply a $\Delta I \times \Delta K_{\text{reg.}}$ matrix by a $\Delta K_{\text{reg.}} \times \Delta J$ matrix.

For the NN variant, where both A and B use normal matrix layout, we implement the matrix multiplication between a 1×4 block from A and the 4×4 block from B as[13]

---

[12]The GPU increments the ID associated with λ_0 as the innermost index, and by assigning `get_global_id(0)` to j, we have chosen j as the innermost index in our implementation. This choice will be discussed in Section 12.5.6

[13]In code snippets such as these, we gloss over some details, such as the fact that we need $4k$ instead of k as the offset in the reads from B.

```
float4 a  = A[i,    k];
float4 b0 = B[k+0, j];
float4 b1 = B[k+1, j];
float4 b2 = B[k+2, j];
float4 b3 = B[k+3, j];
ab += a.s0*b0 + a.s1*b1 + a.s2*b2 + a.s3*b3;
```

where `ab` (of type `float4`) is the accumulator for the 1×4 block of C and all operations are vector operations. The kernel is shown in Listing 12.11.

For the NT variant, we instead select ($\Delta I = 2$, $\Delta J = 2$, $\Delta K_{\text{reg.}} = 4$) and implement the multiplication between the 2×4 block of A and the 2×4 block of the transposed B as

```
float4 a0 = A[i  , k];
float4 a1 = A[i+1, k];
float4 b0 = B[j  , k];
float4 b1 = B[j+1, k];
ab.s01 += (float2) (dot(a0, b0), dot(a0, b1));
ab.s23 += (float2) (dot(a1, b0), dot(a1, b1));
```

where `ab` is an accumulator variable of type `float4` for the 2×2 block of the matrix C.[14] The full kernel is shown in Listing 12.12.

```
kernel void
sgemm(global float4 const *A, global float4 const *B,
      global float4 *C, float alpha, float beta, uint n)
{
  uint j = get_global_id(0);
  uint i = get_global_id(1);
  uint nv4 = n >> 2;

  float4 accum = (float4) 0.0f;
  for (uint k = 0; k < nv4; ++k)
  {
    float4 a = A[i*nv4 + k];

    float4 b0 = B[(4*k+0)*nv4 + j];
    float4 b1 = B[(4*k+1)*nv4 + j];
    float4 b2 = B[(4*k+2)*nv4 + j];
    float4 b3 = B[(4*k+3)*nv4 + j];

    accum += a.s0*b0+a.s1*b1+a.s2*b2+a.s3*b3;
  }
  C[i*nv4 + j] = alpha * accum + beta * C[i*nv4 + j];
}
```

Listing 12.11. Vectorized implementation: `blockedNN`.

---

[14]The components `ab.s01` accumulate the top row and the components `ab.s23` accumulate the bottom row of the 2×2 block.

```
kernel void
sgemm(global float4 * const A, global float4 * const B,
    global float2 *C, float alpha, float beta, uint n)
{
  uint i = get_global_id(0);
  uint j = get_global_id(1);
  uint nv4 = n >> 2;

  float4 ab = (float4)(0.0f);
  for (uint k = 0; k < nv4; ++k)
  {
    float4 a0 = A[ 2*i    *nv4 + k];
    float4 a1 = A[(2*i+1)*nv4 + k];

    float4 b0 = B[ 2*j    *nv4 + k];
    float4 b1 = B[(2*j+1)*nv4 + k];

    ab += (float4)(dot(a0, b0), dot(a0, b1),
                   dot(a1, b0), dot(a1, b1));

  }
  uint ix = 2*i*(n>>1) + j;
  C[ix]         = alpha * ab.s01 + beta * C[ix];
  C[ix + (n>>1)] = alpha * ab.s23 + beta * C[ix + (n>>1)];
}
```

Listing 12.12. Vectorized implementation: `blockedNT`.

We saw the need to introduce blocking to enable the use of vector operations, but register blocking also decreases the number of loads necessary. Our scalar implementations (both the NN and NT variants) loaded N elements of A and N elements of B to compute one element of C, so we needed to load $(N + N)N^2 = 2N^3$ elements from A and B. in general, we need to load one $\Delta I \times \Delta K_{\text{reg.}}$ block from A and one $\Delta K_{\text{reg.}} \times \Delta J$ block from B per iteration, and we need $N/\Delta K_{\text{reg.}}$ iterations. We need one work-item for each of the $(N/\Delta I)(N/\Delta J)$ blocks in C, which gives us a total of

$$(\Delta I \Delta K_{\text{reg.}} + \Delta K_{\text{reg.}} \Delta J)\frac{N}{\Delta K_{\text{reg.}}}\frac{N}{\Delta I}\frac{N}{\Delta J} = N^3\left(\frac{1}{\Delta J} + \frac{1}{\Delta I}\right)$$

elements to be loaded into registers.

The above result tells us that we should want to choose ΔI and ΔJ large and similar, while the choice of $\Delta K_{\text{reg.}}$ is less important. We always set $\Delta K_{\text{reg.}}$ to 4, as this is the smallest value that allows us to use vector operations.[15]

In NN implementations, we have to also choose ΔJ as a multiple of 4, to allow for the use of vector operations, whereas $\Delta I = \Delta J = 2$ is one option we may choose in the NT case. We can compute the difference in load requirements between the $1 \times 4 \times 4$ and $2 \times 4 \times 2$ implementations[16] by computing $1/\Delta I + 1/\Delta J$

---

[15]We note that the scalar version corresponds to $\Delta I = \Delta J = \Delta K_{\text{reg.}} = 1$.

[16]We will sometimes refer to a blocking by writing it $\Delta I \times \Delta K_{\text{reg.}} \times \Delta J$.

for them, and we find 1.25 and 1, respectively, showing that the second blocking needs fewer load operations. We see that the added flexibility we are given to choose blocking widths in the NT version can help us decrease the number of memory operations, and this is one reason to expect that the NT variants will perform better on the GPU.

In both cases, however, we perform $O(N^3)$ load operations from data of size $O(N^2)$, which means that each datum is reloaded into registers $O(N)$ times. Effective cache usage will clearly be important, as it allows us to access data from caches rather than from main memory.

12.5.6 L1 Cache Analysis of the $1 \times 4 \times 4$ Blocked NN SGEMM

Overview. To estimate the cache usage of our kernels, we have to take into account the order of reads within a work-item, as well as the fact that many work-items are active at the same time. We will first look at one specific choice of program and local work size and then try to extend the analysis to be able to compare the cache usage of different implementations and local work sizes.

In the program we choose to analyze first, the $1 \times 4 \times 4$ blocked NN implementation, every work-item performs five memory operations per iteration in its loop, and we will assume that the memory operations take place in the same order as they appear in the program (i.e., the compiler does not change their order), and that, for a given work-item, memory operations never execute in parallel. Another restriction that we will also make in our analysis, and which is important, is that we are able to perfectly predict the order in which work-items execute on the GPU. Finally, this section will only focus on the L1 cache, which allows us to restrict the analysis to a single core, as each core has its own L1 cache.

Thread order. A single work-item loops over the variable k, and for every value of k, it performs one memory load from A and four memory loads from B. With our assumptions, we know that the work-item[17] will enter the load-store pipeline once for each of those instructions, in the order they appear in the program source. We also know that we schedule one work-group of work-items at a time, that those work-items execute their memory operations in an interleaved fashion one after the other, and that they always do this in the order they were spawned by the GPU. We will now see what how we can use that knowledge to analyze the L1 data cache that we need to use.

---

[17]From a hardware point of view, we of course discuss the behavior and order of threads, but we continue to use the term work-item, remembering that one work-item in OpenCL corresponds to one thread in the GPU.

Fixed local work size. Using our notation introduced previously, work-item (j, i) performs the following reads in loop iteration k:

$$A[i, k], B[4k + 0, j], B[4k + 1, j], B[4k + 2, j], B[4k + 3, j],$$

where each memory access now loads a `float4` vector. With many active threads, we will first see all threads performing their first reads from A, and thereafter we will see all threads performing their first read from B, etc. This implies that reads that are executed after each other correspond to different threads executing the same instruction in the program code. With a local work size of $(4,32)$, the GPU initiates the work-items for work-group (m, n) by incrementing the first index first, i.e., in the order

$$(4m, 32n), (4m + 1, 32n), (4m + 2, 32n), (4m + 3, 32n),$$
$$(4m, 32n + 1), (4m + 1, 32n + 1), (4m + 2, 32n + 1), (4m + 3, 32n + 1),$$
$$(4m, 32n + 2), (4m + 1, 32n + 2), (4m + 2, 32n + 2), (4m + 3, 32n + 2),$$
$$\dots,$$
$$(4m, 32n + 31), (4m + 1, 32n + 31), (4m + 2, 32n + 31), (4m + 3, 32n + 31),$$

where we have again used the comma as a sequencing operation to describe the ordering of `global_id` values of the work-items.

This means that the memory reads for loop iteration k will execute in the following order:

$$\left(\underset{i=32n}{\overset{32n+31}{,}} \underset{j=4m}{\overset{4m+3}{,}} A[i, k] \right),$$

$$\left(\underset{i=32n}{\overset{32n+31}{,}} \underset{j=4m}{\overset{4m+3}{,}} B[4k + 0, j] \right), \left(\underset{i=32n}{\overset{32n+31}{,}} \underset{j=4m}{\overset{4m+3}{,}} B[4k + 1, j] \right),$$

$$\left(\underset{i=32n}{\overset{32n+31}{,}} \underset{j=4m}{\overset{4m+3}{,}} B[4k + 2, j] \right), \left(\underset{i=32n}{\overset{32n+31}{,}} \underset{j=4m}{\overset{4m+3}{,}} B[4k + 3, j] \right),$$

where the ID variable j is incremented before i as it corresponds to `get_global_id(0)`, and it is therefore written as the innermost $,$ operator.

We see that the reads from A do not depend on j and are therefore repeated for each group of four consecutive work-items, and we introduce the $\times$ operation to reflect repetition of the same memory access as in

$$\underset{j=4m}{\overset{4m+3}{,}} A[i, k] = A[i, k] \times 4$$

This notation allows us to write a single iteration over k as

$$\left(\overset{32n+31}{\underset{i=32n}{,}} A[i,k] \times 4 \right), \left(\overset{4m+3}{\underset{j=4m}{,}} B[4k+0,j] \right) \times 32, \left(\overset{4m+3}{\underset{j=4m}{,}} B[4k+1,j] \right) \times 32,$$

$$\left(\overset{4m+3}{\underset{j=4m}{,}} B[4k+2,j] \right) \times 32, \left(\overset{4m+3}{\underset{j=4m}{,}} B[4k+3,j] \right) \times 32.$$

As a cache line has space for four `float4` elements, we see that the reads from A read the first quarter of 32 consecutive cache lines and the reads from B read four full cache lines. To get full cache lines instead, we consider four consecutive iterations in k together, and we see that those four iterations read 32 full cache lines from A and 16 full cache lines from B. For the moment, we restrict ourselves to considering a single work-group, and we note that these cache lines will never be reused by later operations in the same work-group. We have now arrived at our conclusion for the L1 cache requirements of the loop. If our L1 cache has enough space for 48 cache lines, then we will never read the same value into the L1 cache twice while executing the loop for all work-items in a work-group, as all subsequent uses will be able to reuse the value that is stored in the cache.

After the loop has completed, the work-group additionally has to load and store to C, which needs access to a 32×4 block of 1×4 blocks of C, spanning 32 complete cache lines, meaning that (as long as our L1 cache is at least 32 cache lines large) we will not see any lack of reuse for the elements of C within a work-group.

If we continue to assume that we only have a single work-group at a time, and consider the possibilities for cache reuse between consecutively scheduled work-groups on the same core, we need to consider the state of the L1 cache when work-group (n, m) finishes execution. The L1 cache contains 256 cache lines in total, and the operations on C will have filled 32 of those, so 224 remain for A and B. Each sequence of four iterations needs 48 cache lines, so the number of iterations that have their cache lines still in cache at work-group completion is $4(256 - 32)/48$, or 16, and this lets us see that the work-group size where we may have reuse between work-groups is when we only need 16 sequences of four iterations each in the loop, or 64 iterations, which corresponds to a matrix size of 256×256 (as we chose $\Delta K_{\text{reg.}} = 4$). For larger matrices, no reuse between consecutively scheduled work-groups on the same core is possible.

Arbitrary local work size. For an arbitrary local work size, we have two reasons to redo the above analysis. First, we have the obvious reason that we get a different interleaved read pattern between the work-items within a work-group. Second, we can have more than one work-group simultaneously active on the same core, if we choose a smaller local work size.

With a local work size of (λ_0, λ_1), we need to look at all work-groups that are running simultaneously on the same core. If the total number of work-items on the core is 128 (which seemed optimal in the Sobel study), and if $\lambda_0\lambda_1 = 128$, then we have only a single work-group on the core, but we could have chosen $\lambda_0 = \lambda_1 = 4$, which would give us $128/16 = 8$ work-groups executing simultaneously on a core. As before, it will be beneficial to look at the cache usage over four iterations over k, and we can easily generalize the results we had before to see that a single work-group reads λ_1 full cache lines from A and $4\lambda_0$ full cache lines from B for every four iterations (provided that λ_0 is a multiple of 4).

If $\lambda_0\lambda_1 \leq 64$, we have more than one work-group executing simultaneously on the core. In this case, the work-groups that are simultaneously active on a code will have consecutive values of m and identical values of n. We see that the reads from A read from the same cache lines, so they are reused between the work-groups. We said above that a few work-groups are sent to each core, and we assume that the work-groups we are having active at the same time belong to this set, as we would otherwise not have consecutive group IDs (m, n).[18]

This means that the 128 work-items executing simultaneously on one core use

$$\lambda_1 + 4\lambda_0 \,[\text{number of work-groups}] = \lambda_1 + 4\lambda_0 \frac{128}{\lambda_0\lambda_1} = \lambda_1 + 512/\lambda_1$$

cache lines from the L1 cache for four consecutive iterations in k. As this expression is independent of λ_0, we can select our λ_0 freely (as long as it is a multiple of 4), and the only effect we see (from our analysis so far) is that a larger λ_0 restricts our possible choices for λ_1. With $\lambda_1 = 1, 2, 4, 8, 16, 32, 64, 128$, we see that we require $513, 258, 132, 72, 48, 48, 72, 132$ cache lines, and with room for 256 lines in the L1 cache of each core, the fraction of L1 we need to use is[19] $2.0, 1.0, 0.52, 0.28, 0.19, 0.19, 0.28, 0.52$. Under our assumptions of fully associative cache and perfect execution order between work-items, we would expect all options with a value below 1 to have the same performance (disregarding the effects of L2 and RAM).

As we know that our assumptions are incorrect, though, we need to discuss what happens when executing on a real GPU. First, due to the design of the cache, we will see cache misses before the cache is 100% filled, i.e., earlier than our analysis above would have predicted. The more complicated aspect of execution is that the work-items that are spawned in the order we describe here do not keep the order. When one work-item is stalled on a cache miss, other work-items may overtake it, so we will have active work-items that are executing different iterations (different values of k) at the same time. We refer to this as thread divergence (or work-item divergence), and the fraction of L1 we need is a measure of our robustness to keep having good performance in cases of thread divergence. Thread divergence always happens and is difficult to measure and quantify, but

---

[18]With work-group divergence, i.e., with a few work-items each from many work-groups partially finished on the same core, we might have work-groups with very different `group_ids` simultaneously active on the same core.

[19]The numbers are also shown in Table 12.2.

we can qualitatively say that the longer the program runs, the stronger divergence we see. This implies that the benefits of a low L1 cache utilization fraction have a stronger impact on performance for large matrix sizes.

The innermost index. Now that we have discussed cache usage, we will return to one aspect of the NN variant that we did not discuss before, namely the choice to use j as the innermost index in the sequencing of operations. We have chosen the order by using `global_id(0)` for the index j and `global_id(1)` for the index i in our CL C kernels. The argument we will provide here holds only for the NN versions, and is not applicable for the NT versions.

If we again consider the memory read sequence for the scalar NN variant, and only look at a single iteration and a single work-group, we see

$$\left(\underset{i=0}{\overset{\lambda_1-1}{,}} \underset{j=0}{\overset{\lambda_0-1}{,}} A[i,k] \right), \left(\underset{i=0}{\overset{\lambda_1-1}{,}} \underset{j=0}{\overset{\lambda_0-1}{,}} B[k,j] \right)$$

$$= \left(\underset{i=0}{\overset{\lambda_1-1}{,}} A[i,k] \times \lambda_0 \right), \left(\underset{j=0}{\overset{\lambda_0-1}{,}} B[k,j] \right) \times \lambda_1,$$

but we could instead have swapped the roles of the `global_id`s and gotten

$$\left(\underset{j=0}{\overset{\lambda_1-1}{,}} \underset{i=0}{\overset{\lambda_0-1}{,}} A[i,k] \right), \left(\underset{j=0}{\overset{\lambda_1-1}{,}} \underset{i=0}{\overset{\lambda_0-1}{,}} B[k,j] \right)$$

$$= \left(\underset{i=0}{\overset{\lambda_0-1}{,}} A[i,k] \right) \times \lambda_1, \left(\underset{j=0}{\overset{\lambda_1-1}{,}} B[k,j] \times \lambda_0 \right).$$

We will now look for the number of cache-line switches in the execution of those reads. For the former case, the reads from A are described by $\underset{i=0}{\overset{\lambda_1-1}{,}} A[i,k] \times \lambda_0$, which switches cache line λ_1 times (and between those switches, we read from the same matrix element λ_0 times). For different values of i we read from different rows of the matrix, and separate rows are always on separate cache lines.[20] Staying with the first version, but looking at B, we see that we switch matrix element $\lambda_0\lambda_1$ times, as every read is from a different element than the previous read, and we perform $\lambda_0\lambda_1$ reads. We note, however, that we switch between consecutive elements in memory, which means that we only have $\lambda_0\lambda_1/16$ cache line switches, as we can fit 16 matrix elements into a cache line. For the second version, with the indices in the other order, analogous considerations show that we switch matrix element $\lambda_0\lambda_1$ times for A and λ_1 times for B, but

---

[20]Except for very small matrices, of course, but those cases do not require cache analysis anyway.

we again step between consecutive memory locations in B, which means that the number of cache-line switches is only $\lambda_1/16$ for B. If we add the cache line switches together for A and B, we have $\lambda_0\lambda_1/16 + \lambda_1$ and $\lambda_0\lambda_1 + \lambda_1/16$ for the two versions, respectively. With λ_0 and λ_1 between 4 and 64, the first version will always need fewer cache-line switches than the latter.[21] In cases where we do have cache misses (e.g., due to thread divergence), this should improve the performance by reducing the concurrent cache needs within an iteration.

12.5.7   L1 Cache Analysis of Blocked NT Kernel

For the blocked NT kernel, we can analyze the L1 cache utilization in the same way as for the NN kernel. We start by noting that work-item (j, i), in iteration k, performs the memory accesses

$$A[2i, k], A[2i + 1, k], B[2j, k], B[2j + 1, k],$$

and we see that we should again consider four iterations over k, to get full cache lines:

$$A[2i, k+0], A[2i+1, k+0], B[j, k+0], B[2j+1, k+0];$$
$$A[2i, k+1], A[2i+1, k+1], B[j, k+1], B[2j+1, k+1];$$
$$A[2i, k+2], A[2i+1, k+2], B[j, k+2], B[2j+1, k+2];$$
$$A[2i, k+3], A[2i+1, k+3], B[j, k+3], B[2j+1, k+3].$$

During execution of the first four iterations, the first work-group, with its $\lambda_0\lambda_1$ work-items, accesses

$$\overset{4}{\underset{k=0}{,}} \left[\left(\overset{\lambda_1-1}{\underset{i=0}{,}} \overset{\lambda_0-1}{\underset{j=0}{,}} A[2i, k] \right), \left(\overset{\lambda_1-1}{\underset{i=0}{,}} \overset{\lambda_0-1}{\underset{j=0}{,}} A[2i+1, k] \right), \right.$$
$$\left. \left(\overset{\lambda_1-1}{\underset{i=0}{,}} \overset{\lambda_0-1}{\underset{j=0}{,}} B[2j, k] \right), \left(\overset{\lambda_1-1}{\underset{i=0}{,}} \overset{\lambda_0-1}{\underset{j=0}{,}} B[2j+1, k] \right) \right]$$

and the first set of M simultaneous work-groups accesses

$$\overset{4}{\underset{k=0}{,}} \left[\left(\overset{M-1}{\underset{m=0}{,}} \overset{\lambda_1-1}{\underset{i=0}{,}} \overset{m\lambda_0+\lambda_0-1}{\underset{j=m\lambda_0}{,}} A[2i, k] \right), \left(\overset{M-1}{\underset{m=0}{,}} \overset{\lambda_1-1}{\underset{i=0}{,}} \overset{m\lambda_0+\lambda_0-1}{\underset{j=m\lambda_0}{,}} A[2i+1, k] \right), \right.$$
$$\left. \left(\overset{M-1}{\underset{m=0}{,}} \overset{\lambda_1-1}{\underset{i=0}{,}} \overset{m\lambda_0+\lambda_0-1}{\underset{j=m\lambda_0}{,}} B[2j, k] \right), \left(\overset{M-1}{\underset{m=0}{,}} \overset{\lambda_1-1}{\underset{i=0}{,}} \overset{m\lambda_0+\lambda_0-1}{\underset{j=m\lambda_0}{,}} B[2j+1, k] \right) \right],$$

---

[21] The roles of λ_0 and λ_1 are interchanged between the two versions, but the first one is still always better.

λ_1	1	2	4	8	16	32	64	128
Cache lines (NN)	513	258	132	72	48	48	72	132
L1 fraction (NN)	2.0	1.0	0.52	0.28	0.19	0.19	0.28	0.52
Cache lines (NT)	258	132	72	48	48	72	132	258
L1 fraction (NT)	1.0	0.52	0.28	0.19	0.19	0.28	0.52	1.0

Table 12.2. L1 cache utilization for the $1 \times 4 \times 4$ blocked NN and the $2 \times 4 \times 2$ blocked NT kernels. We note that if we want to choose $\lambda_0 = 4$, we are restricted to $\lambda_1 \leq 32$.

where m was incremented as an outer index to both i and j, as we create all work-items in the first work-group before creating the first work-item in the second work-group. We again share the accesses to A, and these four iterations over k will need $2\lambda_1$ cache lines from A and $2M\lambda_0$ cache lines from B, and as before, we have $M = 128/(\lambda_0\lambda_1)$, giving a total L1 usage of

$$2\lambda_1 + 2\lambda_0 \frac{128}{\lambda_0\lambda_1} = 2\lambda_1 + \frac{256}{\lambda_1}.$$

If we compare with the result of the NN implementation, we get the L1 utilization fractions shown in Table 12.2. By comparing with the results with the previous ones, we see that while we had a preference for $\lambda_1 = 16$ or $\lambda_1 = 32$ for the $1 \times 4 \times 4$ blocked (NN) version, the $2 \times 4 \times 2$ blocked (NT) implementation works better with smaller work-groups.

12.5.8 L1 Cache Blocking

We saw above that the L1 cache utilization determined our robustness against thread divergence, but every program will, if we do not interfere with thread scheduling in any way, experience thread divergence. For large enough matrices, this will always lead to performance degradations in the kernels we have discussed so far. Our strategy to get around this issue is to introduce yet another level of blocking and to rewrite the algorithm with this additional level of block-matrix multiplication.

As a means of relating this level of blocking to the discussion about register blocking, we now introduce a much larger ΔK, so that we have two: the $\Delta K_{\text{reg.}}$ introduced previously, and the new ΔK_{cache}. After each set of ΔK_{cache} iterations in the loop, we reassemble all work-items in the work-group to ensure that no thread divergence appears within the work-group.

Relating the change to the actual code, we insert a barrier operation between every ΔK_{cache} iterations in the loop. As this only limits thread divergence within a work-group, we will still have to take into account the divergence between work-groups that will limit L1 cache sharing between different work-groups. It therefore seems as if we should expect that this method will work best when there is only one simultaneously active work-group on each core. The full kernel is shown in Listing 12.13.

```
#define di ((uint)2)
#define dj ((uint)2)
#define dk ((uint)32)

kernel void
sgemm(global float4 const *A, global float4 const *B,
  global float2 *C, float alpha, float beta, uint n)
{
  uint j = get_global_id(0);
  uint i = get_global_id(1);
  uint nv4 = n >> 2;

  float4 ab = (float4) 0.0f;
  for (uint k = 0; k < nv4; k += dk)
  {
    for (uint kk = 0; kk < dk; ++kk)
    {
      float4 a0 = A[ 2*i    *nv4 + kk+k];
      float4 a1 = A[(2*i+1)*nv4 + kk+k];

      float4 b0 = B[ 2*j    *nv4 + kk+k];
      float4 b1 = B[(2*j+1)*nv4 + kk+k];

      ab += (float4)(dot(a0, b0), dot(a0, b1),
              dot(a1, b0), dot(a1, b1));
    }
    barrier(CLK_GLOBAL_MEM_FENCE);
  }

  uint ix = 2*i*(n>>1) + j;
  C[ix]          = alpha * ab.s01 + beta * C[ix];
  C[ix + (n>>1)] = alpha * ab.s23 + beta * C[ix + (n>>1)];
}
```

Listing 12.13. Cache-blocked implementation: `cacheblockedNT`. The constants `di`, `dj`, and `dk` correspond to our ΔI, ΔJ, and ΔK_{cache}, respectively.

The benefit of the barrier is that we can get the same L1 cache sharing for large matrices as we had for small matrices. The cost of executing the barrier is due to the fact that we have to reassemble all work-items of the work-group at regular intervals. If no thread divergence occurs, this means that all work-items need to enter into the barrier, which takes time proportional to the number of work-items, and then all work-items need to exit from the barrier, which again takes a number of cycles proportional to the number of work-items involved. This means that the effective cost of a barrier is the number of cycles it takes, times the number of work-items that are taking part in the barrier, or at least[22] $2\lambda_0^2 \lambda_1^2$. It is therefore beneficial for the actual execution time of the barrier to

---

[22]Executing the `barrier` instruction takes $2\lambda_0\lambda_1$ cycles, and in this time the $\lambda_0\lambda_1$ work-items involved are prevented from performing other work, which means that the work lost due to the `barrier` instruction is $2\lambda_0^2\lambda_1^2$. Again, the description is simplified but sufficient for our needs (e.g., while the last work-item exits from the barrier, the first work-item is already performing work again).

have small work-groups. As the work-group divergence that is a consequence of small work-groups will hurt cache sharing between work-groups, we have two competing behaviors, and we need to find a good compromise. We may therefore want to select a small work-group size to ensure that barriers are cheap (and an NT algorithm, as we say that it goes better with small work-groups). On the other hand, we will want to choose a large work-group size, as we want to keep work-group divergence small, and therefore want to have only a small number of active work-groups.

We also have to find a good compromise for the value of the parameter ΔK_{cache}. It must be small enough to keep thread divergence low, but we also need to ensure that we do not execute the barrier too often (to keep the cost of executing the barriers low).

The barrier is executed $N/(\Delta K_{\text{reg.}}\Delta K_{\text{cache}})$ times, with a cost of $2\lambda_0^2\lambda_1^2$ cycles each time, and we want to ensure that this cost is small compared to the number of memory operations. The number of memory operations performed by the work-group between two consecutive barriers is $\Delta K_{\text{cache}}(\Delta I\Delta K_{\text{reg.}} + \Delta K_{\text{reg.}}\Delta J)\lambda_0\lambda_1$, and our condition for ΔK_{cache} becomes

$$\Delta K_{\text{cache}}(\Delta I\Delta K_{\text{reg.}} + \Delta K_{\text{reg.}}\Delta J)\lambda_0\lambda_1 > 2\lambda_0^2\lambda_1^2,$$

which we rewrite as

$$\Delta K_{\text{cache}} > \frac{2\lambda_0\lambda_1}{(\Delta I\Delta K_{\text{reg.}} + \Delta K_{\text{reg.}}\Delta J)}.$$

For the $2 \times 4 \times 2$ blocking with a large work-group size, we find that we need

$$\Delta K_{\text{cache}} > \frac{2[\#\text{active threads}]}{8 + 8} = \frac{256}{16} = 16.$$

For our kernel, we have chosen $\Delta K_{\text{cache}} = 32$.

12.5.9 Page Table Lookups

One aspect that we have not yet discussed but that is important for the performance of the NN and NT versions, is the way they affect the memory management unit. The physical memory is partitioned into areas called *pages*, and the abstract pointer space is also partitioned into pages in a similar way. Every page that we use in the pointer space must correspond to a page in physical memory, and information about this mapping is stored in page tables. When we try to access memory using a pointer, we need to find out which page it points to in pointer space, and which page that corresponds to in the physical memory space. The process of looking up a page in the page tables is costly, and we want to perform as few page table lookups as possible when executing our kernel.[23] Going back

---

[23]This description is simplified but sufficient for our current purposes.

to the scalar kernels, to keep the discussion simple, the memory accesses of a work-group of the scalar NN kernel looks like

$$\sum_{k=0}^{N} \left[\left(\sum_{i=0}^{\lambda_1-1} \sum_{j=0}^{\lambda_0-1} A[i,k] \right), \left(\sum_{i=0}^{\lambda_1-1} \sum_{j=0}^{\lambda_0-1} B[k,j] \right) \right],$$

and we see that it needs to access data from all rows of B but only from a single row of A. The scalar NT kernel instead reads from

$$\sum_{k=0}^{N} \left[\left(\sum_{i=0}^{\lambda_1-1} \sum_{j=0}^{\lambda_0-1} A[i,k] \right), \left(\sum_{i=0}^{\lambda_1-1} \sum_{j=0}^{\lambda_0-1} B[j,k] \right) \right],$$

which accesses only one row each of A and B. This means that, if the matrices are much larger than the size of a page, the work-group in the NN variant needs to access memory from many more pages than the NT variant, although they access the same number of bytes. We must expect that the need to access more pages implies a need to perform a larger number of page table lookups, which decreases performance.

We should look at the memory accesses for the work-groups that are active at the same time, and not just a single work-group, but the conclusion will be the same: the NN version needs to perform a larger number of page table lookups than the NT version. The conclusion also remains the same when we look at blocked versions, as we are still in the situation that all work-items access the entire column from B in the NN versions.

If we turn to a cache-blocked NN version, we have a barrier that we introduced to prevent thread divergence, and although we still need a larger number of lookups in the NN version than in the NT version, we do not need as many at the same time as in the scalar and blocked NN versions, as the barrier ensures that the work-items that are simultaneously active only want to access a limited number of pages at once.

To summarize the discussion of page tables, cache-blocking should improve the situation slightly over the scalar and blocked NN versions, but for large matrices, we must expect the NT versions to have a performance advantage over the NN versions.

12.5.10   Performance

Performance metrics. The primary performance metric is the number of floating-points operations (nflops) per second (FLOPS). For each output element $C[i,j]$, $(2N-1)+1 = 2N$ FLOPS are required to compute the dot product of $A[i,*] \cdot B[*,j]$ and scale it by α, one multiplication to scale $C[i,j]$ by β, and one addition to obtain the final result. Thus, nflops $= 2N^2(N+1)$. Dividing nflops by execution time in nanoseconds (10^{-9} seconds) gives GFLOPS (10^9 FLOPS).

Size	sNN	sNT	bNN	bNT	cbNN	cbNT
96	2.0	2.0	8.0	11.2	5.1	7.4
192	2.0	2.1	8.4	13.0	5.1	8.1
384	2.0	2.1	7.6	13.2	6.4	10.1
768	2.0	2.1	7.5	13.1	6.6	10.0
1440	2.0	2.1	7.4	13.1	6.5	9.3
2880	1.6	2.0	6.8	10.8	6.1	9.2

Table 12.3. Performance in GFLOPS for some variants and matrix sizes. For each matrix size and kind of implementation, we have only selected one number, and it may, e.g., use different blocking parameters at different sizes. The columns show the best performance we see in GFLOPS for scalar (s), blocked (b), and cache-blocked (cb) variants of non-transposed (NN) and transposed (NT) SGEMM implementations.

Overall trends. In Table 12.3, we show performance numbers for different kinds of implementations and different matrix sizes. Variation within one kind is not shown, and different rows in the same column can contain results for different variants of the same kind (e.g., different blocking parameters or work-group sizes).

   We see that the NT versions perform better than NN versions and that blocked versions are better than scalar versions, as expected. While already the smallest shown matrix size appears sufficient for the scalar versions, the blocked and (more strongly) the cache-blocked variants need larger amounts of work to reach their best performance.

   Our experiments with larger matrices, where performance is heavily influenced by system effects like thread-divergence, are not shown in the table, due to variations in results.

Cache-blocking. One surprising result in the table is the large difference between the blocked and cache-blocked variants, where the introduction of cache-blocking seems to come at a large cost. This impression is misleading and due to our selection of data. We only display the best performance achieved for each kind of implementation, and we saw in the Sobel results that the number of registers plays a crucial role in determining performance. For the best blocked NT implementation we have, the corresponding cache-blocked versions use more registers, which prevents us from keeping 128 simultaneous threads per core. Due to the limited number of threads, this version is not our best cache-blocked implementation, as we have other variants that use fewer registers. The columns bNT and cbNT therefore display results for different implementations. If we instead consider (nearly) identical implementations of $1 \times 4 \times 4$ blocked and cache-blocked NT variants (shown in Table 12.4), we see much larger similarities in the top results, and we also see the large difference in the median result for large matrices.

Work-group divergence. For large workloads, work-group divergence will start to appear, and this will affect performance. The occasional very good performance

Size	Blocked		Cache-Blocked	
	Median	High	Median	High
96	9.3	9.4	7.0	7.4
192	10.5	10.6	8.0	8.1
384	9.9	10.0	9.9	10.0
768	9.7	9.9	9.7	10.0
1440	9.6	9.9	9.1	9.3
2880	1.1	9.4	9.2	9.2

Table 12.4. Performance in GFLOPS for $1 \times 4 \times 4$ blocked and cache-blocked NT implementations. Each implementation was run three times for each matrix size and each local work-group size. The median and best results from the nine runs are listed in the table.

results with blocking versions probably appear in runs where we see no or very little work-group divergence, whereas the much lower median result shows that the typical case has lower performance.

Cache-blocking, introduced to stifle thread divergence, also has an effect in preventing work-group divergence, thereby decreasing the variability.

The cost of a barrier. In our previous estimate of the cost of executing a barrier instruction, we assumed that we would have one work-item per cycle entering into the barrier, and then one work-item per cycle exiting. In reality, with thread divergence, we do not have the ideal case of one work-item entering the barrier every cycle, as the first work-item will be a few instructions ahead of the last one. Instead, all work-items will have to wait for the last one to arrive at the barrier. The actual cost of the barrier can therefore be significantly higher than our estimate, if a few work-items of the work-group are far behind in executing the program.

12.5.11 Summary

We started from scalar versions of a generic matrix multiplication and then transformed the initial kernels, successively arriving at more elaborate implementations. We discussed the reason behind the transformations, and we discussed how the transformations took advantage of aspects of the hardware. We started by introducing vector operations, and then we focused on the memory system and in particular on the L1 cache. We also discussed execution times, as measured on an Arndale development board, and we found that the qualitative results were as we expected, although a quantitative comparison shows that our simplifying assumptions are not always satisfied.

Acknowledgments

The authors gratefully acknowledge the work of their colleagues at ARM's Media Processing Group.

Bibliography

[ARM 13] ARM. "Mali OpenCL SDK v1.1." http://malideveloper.arm.com/ develop-for-mali/sdks/mali-opencl-sdk, 2013.

[Howes et al. 10] Lee Howes, Anton Lokhmotov, Alastair F. Donaldson, and Paul H. J. Kelly. "Towards Metaprogramming for Parallel Systems on a Chip." In *Workshop on Highly Parallel Processing on a Chip (HPPC)*, LNCS 6043, pp. 36–45. Berlin: Springer-Verlag, 2010.

[Ryoo et al. 08] Shane Ryoo, Christopher I. Rodrigues, Sam S. Stone, John A. Stratton, Sain-Zee Ueng, Sara S. Baghsorkhi, and Wen-mei W. Hwu. "Program optimization carving for GPU computing." *Journal of Parallel and Distributed Computing* 68:10 (2008), 1389–1401.

Hybrid Ray Tracing on a PowerVR GPU

Gareth Morgan

13.1 Introduction

Ray tracing and rasterization are often presented as a dichotomy. Since the early days of computer graphics, ray tracing has been the gold standard for visual realism. By allowing physically accurate simulation of light transport, ray tracing renders extremely high-quality images. Real-time rendering, on the other hand, is dominated by rasterization. In spite of being less physically accurate, rasterization can be accelerated by efficient, commonly available GPUs and has mature standardized programing interfaces.

This chapter describes how an existing raster-based game engine renderer can use ray tracing to implement sophisticated light transport effects like hard and soft shadows, reflection, refraction, and transparency, while continuing to use rasterization as the primary rendering method. It assumes no prior knowledge of ray tracing.

The PowerVR Wizard line of GPUs adds hardware-based ray tracing acceleration alongside a powerful rasterizing GPU. Ray tracing acceleration hardware vastly improves the efficiency and therefore the performance of the techniques described.

13.2 Review

13.2.1 Conceptual Differences between Ray Tracing and Rasterization

In a ray tracer, everything starts with the initial rays (often called primary rays). Typically, these rays emulate the behavior of a camera, where at least one ray is used to model the incoming virtual light that gives color to each pixel in a framebuffer. The rays are tested against the scene's geometry to find the closest intersection, and then the color of the object at the ray's intersection point is evaluated. More precisely, the outgoing light that is reflecting and/or scattering from the surface in the direction of the ray is computed. These calculations often involve creating more secondary rays because the outgoing light from a surface depends on the incoming light to that surface. The process can continue recursively until the rays terminate by hitting a light-emitting object in the scene or when there is no light contributed from a particular ray path.

Contrast this with rasterization, where the driving action is the submission of vertices describing triangles. After the triangles are projected to screen space, they are broken into fragments and the fragments are shaded. Each datum is processed independently and there is no way for the shading of one triangle to directly influence another unrelated triangle in the pipeline.

Ray tracing enables inter-object visibility, but the tradeoff is that every piece of the scene that could possibly be visible to any ray must be built and resident prior to sending the first ray into the scene.

13.2.2 GPU Ray Tracing

Early 3D games, such as *Quake*, all implemented their own rasterizers in software on the CPU. Eventually, the power of the dedicated hardware in the GPU outweighed the efficiency of the special purpose rasterizer built for the game, and today almost all game renderers take advantage of a hardware abstraction API, such as OpenGL. Today, ray tracing is at a similar stage of evolution. For flexibility and portability, you can implement your own bespoke ray tracer and, performance aside, all of the techniques we describe should work. In this chapter, however, we will use OpenRL.

OpenRL is the ray-tracing API that can take advantage of the dedicated ray tracing hardware in the PowerVR Wizard architecture. OpenRL is conceptually based on OpenGL ES and, like OpenGL ES, is highly configurable by allowing shaders to implement the behavior in certain sections of the process. You can download the OpenRL SDK, including the library, code examples, and documentation at http://community.imgtec.com/developers/powervr/openrl-sdk/.

If you don't want to use OpenRL, you are free to write your own ray tracer and all of these techniques from this chapter will still work. Alternatively, there are several open source ray-tracing projects available, such as LuxRays [LuxRender 14] or Cycles [Blender 14], that take advantage of the GPU for parallel execution. Unfortunately, if you choose to go this route, dedicated ray-tracing hardware acceleration will not provide any speed benefit.

13.2.3 The Simplest Ray Tracer Using OpenRL

To start out, we need to make the geometry available to OpenRL so the rays have something to intersect. This is done by assembling the geometry into primitive

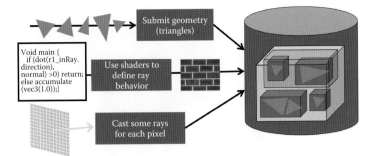

Figure 13.1. Ray tracing overview.

objects. Each primitive object represents a conceptual object within the scene—for example, the glass top of a coffee table could be a primitive object. They are defined in world space, and their state is retained from one frame to the next.

Each primitive object needs to know how to handle rays that intersect it. This is done by attaching a ray shader to the object. The ray shader runs whenever a ray intersects a piece of geometry. It can be used to define the look of the object's material or, more specifically, the behavior of the material when interacting with rays. A ray shader can be thought of as a conceptual analogy to a fragment shader in rasterization. There is, however, one big difference between OpenRL shaders and traditional raster shaders: OpenRL shaders can emit rays, and hence trigger future shader invocations. This feedback loop, where one ray intersection results in secondary rays being emitted, which in turn causes more ray intersections, is a vital part of the ray-tracing process. In OpenRL shaders, this process is implemented via the built-in functions `createRay()` and `emitRay()`. The built-in variable `rl_OutRay` represents the newly created ray. This ray structure is made up of ray attributes, some of which are built-in, such as `direction` and `origin`, and some of which can be user defined.

In the aforementioned glass coffee table example, the ray shader would define the appearance of a glass tabletop by emitting secondary rays based on the material properties stored in the primitive object (such as color and density). Those secondary rays will intersect other objects in the scene, defining how those objects (for example, the base of the table or the floor it is resting on) contribute to the final color of the glass tabletop.

The final step in our simple ray tracer is to create the primary rays. In OpenRL, a frame shader is invoked once for every pixel and is used to programmatically emit the primary rays.

The simplest camera is called a pinhole camera. This name comes from the fact that every light ray passes through the exact same point in space, or pinhole aperture, and therefore the entire scene is in perfect focus.

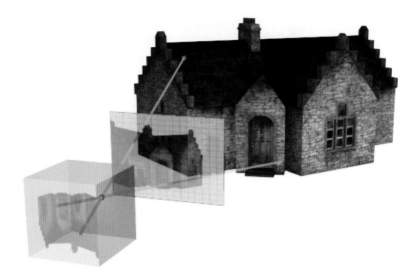

Figure 13.2. Pinhole camera

```
void main() {
  vec3 direction = vec3((rl_FrameCoord/rl_FrameSize-0.5).xy,1.0);
  createRay();
  rl_OutRay.origin           = cameraPosition;
  rl_OutRay.direction        = direction;
  emitRay();
}
```

Listing 13.1. Pinhole camera frame shader.

Simulating a pinhole camera using ray tracing is as easy as emitting a primary ray for every pixel of the image. These rays all share the same origin, which is conceptually the focal point of the light, or the center of the camera's aperture. The direction of the ray is the vector from the ray's origin through the center of the pixel being traced.

13.2.4   Light, Rays, and Rendering

James Kajiya wrote, "All rendering methods are attempting to model the same physical phenomenon, that of light scattering off of various surfaces" [Kajiya 86]. In a pure ray tracer like the example above, rays simulate the light in reverse, starting at the camera and finding a path backward to an illumination source. In this backward propagation model, rays are a means of estimating the incoming light from a specific direction.

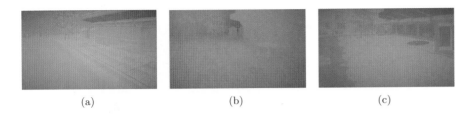

(a)   (b)   (c)

Figure 13.3. G-buffer contents: (a) normals, (b) positions, and (c) material IDs.

Some highly specular materials, like glass, propagate light in a direction that is largely dependent on the direction of the incoming light, while diffuse materials like plaster will scatter incoming light across a whole hemisphere.

A ray is fundamentally a line. It has zero thickness and its intersection with a surface is therefore a point.[1] In order to approximate a diffuse material, renderers often emit many rays to estimate the continuous function of incoming light from all directions.

13.3 Combining Ray Tracing with Rasterization

Raster-based renderers rely on a variety of techniques to calculate the light that is illuminating a surface. Some of these are simplistic, like a universal directional light source that casts no shadows, and some are more complex, like prebaked light maps. Ray tracing adds another tool to your toolbox: the ability to cast rays into the scene to compute light transport and occlusion.

But how do you get a ray tracer, based on a world-space database of the entire scene, to work with a rasterizer that only understands individual screen-space fragments? By taking advantage of the deferred shading architecture used by many modern rasterized renderers [Hargreaves and Harris 04]. In deferred shading, instead of performing the lighting calculations in the fragment shader, the properties of the fragment are simply written into a geometry buffer or *G-buffer*.

After the first pass, this G-buffer contains a 2D screen-space texture for each surface property (such as normal, position, albedo, and material information). Critically, these surface properties are in now in world space. In deferred shading, this G-buffer is then used as an input to a second, screen-space lighting pass. This means lighting calculations are carried out only on the visible fragments.

In our hybrid rendering technique, this screen-space lighting step is replaced by the ray tracer. The G-buffer is used as an input to the frame shader, so rather than emitting rays from a camera, the primary rays are emitted directly

---

[1]OpenRL allows a ray's spread to be tracked as it travels through the scene, and this enables ray shaders to perform mipmapping during texture samples and differential functions within the shader. However, a ray will only intersect one point on one surface.

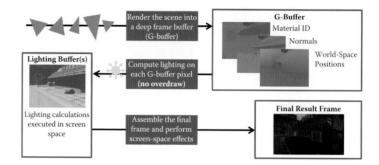

Figure 13.4. Deferred shading pipeline.

```
uniform sampler2D normalTexture;
uniform sampler2D positionTexture;

void main()
{
 vec2 uv = rl_FrameCoord.xy / rl_FrameSize.xy;
 vec4 normal = texture2D(normalTexture, uv);
 vec4 position = texture2D(positionTexture, uv;

 if(normal.w==0.0) return; //No fragment was rendered for this
                           //pixel

 IlluminateSurface(normal, position);
}
```

Listing 13.2. Hybrid frame shader.

from the surface. The results from the ray tracer render are then returned to the rasterizer, where they are composited, along with the albedo color from the original G-buffer, to produce the final frame.

Each G-buffer component is bound to a 2D texture uniform in the frame shader, and those textures are sampled for each pixel. This provides the world-space surface properties required to start tracing rays directly from the surface defined by that pixel, without emitting any camera rays.

On a pixel-by-pixel basis, the frame shader can then decide which effects to implement for that fragment and how many rays each effect uses based on the material properties stored in the G-buffer. This allows the application to use its ray budget on surfaces where raytraced effects will add most to the look or the user experience.

Currently, hybrid ray tracing requires using two different APIs—one for ray tracing (OpenRL) and one for rasterization; a separate OpenRL render context must be created for the ray-tracing operations. Every frame, the contents of the G-buffer must be transferred to the ray tracer, and the results must be returned

```
rlBindTexture(RL_TEXTURE_2D, normalTxt_RL);
rlTexImage2D( RL_TEXTURE_2D,
            0,
        RL_RGBA,
        windowWidth,
        windowHeight,
        0,
        RL_RGBA,
        RL_FLOAT,
        NULL);
normalTxt_EGL = eglCreateImageKHR(
                dpy,
                openRLContext,
                EGL_RL_TEXTURE_2D_IMG,
                (EGLClientBuffer)normalTxt_RL,
                NULL);
```

Listing 13.3. Create an EGL image bound to an OpenRL texture.

to the rasterizer for final frame render. On platforms where it is available, EGL can be used to avoid this extra copy by sharing the contents of these textures between the ray tracer and the rasterizer. Listing 13.3 shows how each OpenRL texture object is bound on an EGL image object to achieve this.

The rest of this chapter will discuss some effects that can be added to your raster-based renderer by taking advantage of the light simulation provided by ray tracing.

13.4 Hard Shadows

Shadows are important optical phenomena, caused by objects blocking the path between a light emitter and a surface. The nature of ray tracing, which has an inherent understanding of the world-space layout of the scene, makes it very well suited to shadow rendering.

Rendering physically correct hard shadows simply requires shooting a single ray from the surface to the light. If the ray intersects any scene geometry, it is discarded; if it reaches the light, then the surface is shaded, typically using the traditional Lambertian lighting calculation (the "N dot L" diffuse lighting equation used in 3D graphics for many years).

Ray tracing on PowerVR takes advantage of an optimization that is possible with these kind of rays, referred to as *shadow rays*. As you are not interested in *what* the shadow ray hits, only *whether* it hits anything before reaching its endpoint, an optimization is possible. The intersection algorithm can terminate at the first triangle collision, rather than continuing until it tests all triangles to find the closest collision. In OpenRL shaders, this property is set on the ray using the `occlusionTest` ray attribute. This feature is used in conjunction with the `defaultPrimitive` ray attribute, which defines the ray shader that will be executed

```
vec3 toLight = lightPosition - rl_IntersectionPoint;

createRay();
rl_OutRay.maxT = length(toLight);
rl_OutRay.direction = normalize(toLight);
rl_OutRay.occlusionTest = true;
rl_OutRay.defaultPrimitive = lightPrimitive;
emitRay();
```

Listing 13.4. Emitting a shadow ray.

if the ray fails to hit any geometry. Finally, the distance to the light is calculated and assigned to the ray's `maxT` attribute.[2] These attributes collectively mean that the shader will run when there is no occluding geometry in the way, so light can be accumulated into the framebuffer. If occluding geometry is encountered, the ray is dropped and no light is accumulated. The shader fragment in Listing 13.4 shows how to implement hard shadows using these ray attributes.

13.5 Soft Shadows

In 3D graphics, lights are often approximated as infinitesimally small points. In real life, however, lights are not infinitesimally small. From the point of view of the shadowed surface, lights have a nonzero area. This causes soft shadows with fuzzy edges. These edges are called the *penumbra region*. This phenomenon occurs on parts of the shadowed surface where some of the light area is visible and some is occluded. Scattering media like clouds or dust can also create soft shadows because the light is no longer originating from a single point source.

Rendering soft shadows using ray tracing is also conceptually simple. At each surface point, instead of shooting a single ray, as in the hard shadow case, we shoot multiple rays.

The ray directions are calculated based on a table precomputed on the host CPU. Each ray is shaded identically to the hard shadow case except it is assigned a weight so the total contribution of all the rays is the same as for a single ray. This weight can be encoded in a user-defined ray attribute.

What this technique is actually doing is performing Monte Carlo integration to estimate what percentage of the light is visible at the surface point. The domain we are integrating over is the solid angle representing the total light area visible at the surface, and each ray is in fact a point sample in that domain. The more samples we generate, the better our approximation will be.

---

[2]It is a historical convention in ray tracing to express the distance a ray *travels* between the origin and the intersection point. In OpenRL, `maxT` is a far clipping distance, past which no objects are evaluated for intersection.

```
float weight = 1.0/float(numSamples);
int ii,jj;
for(ii = 0; ii < numLights; ii = ii + 1)
{
  mat4 lightMatrix = lightToWorld[ii];
  for(jj = 0; jj < numSamples; jj = jj + 1)
  {
    vec4 samplePos = lightMatrix * samples[jj];
    vec3 toLight   = samplePos.xyz - rl_IntersectionPoint;

    createRay();
    rl_OutRay.maxT = length(toLight);
    rl_OutRay.direction = toLight/rl_OutRay.maxT;
    rl_OutRay.color = vec3(weight);
    rl_OutRay.occlusionTest = true;
    rl_OutRay.defaultPrimitive = lightPrimitive;
    emitRay();
  }
}
```

Listing 13.5. Emitting multiple shadow rays.

We could use pseudorandom numbers to generate our ray directions, however numerical analysis theory tells us that for small numbers of rays, this will produce a poor approximation of the integral. This is because random numbers will have uneven coverage over the domain. There are a number of other sequences that will be more likely to produce a better distribution over the domain. The book *Physically Based Rendering* by Matt Pharr and Greg Humphreys contains an excellent overview of sampling theory regarding ray tracing [Pharr and Humphreys 04, Chapter 7].

There are many techniques that can be used to reduce the number of rays emitted for each pixel but still produce a good estimate of the lighting integral. One that works well with hybrid ray tracing is interleaved sampling [Keller and Heidrich 01]. This technique takes advantage of the continuity between adjacent pixels so that the final pixel color for one pixel is calculated using the ray tracing results from its neighbors.

13.6   Reflections

Reflections are another optical phenomenon that are well suited for simulation with ray tracing. They are an important aspect of rendering many material types, not just perfectly reflective materials such as chrome and mirrors.

Reflections are caused by light bouncing off of a surface in a manner defined by the law of the reflection. This is an ancient physical law first codified by Euclid in the third century BC. It says that when light hits a perfectly reflective surface, it is reflected at the same angle as the incident angle.

```
void IlluminateSurface(vec4 normal, vec4 position)
{
  float reflectivity = position.w; //Surface reflectivity
  if(reflectivity>0.0)
  DoReflection(normal, position.xyx, reflectivity);
}
```

Listing 13.6. Using surface properties.

Rendering reflections using ray tracing is very simple, and in fact how to do so is suggested by looking at any textbook diagram of the law of reflection. When shading the reflective surface, we simply emit an extra ray from the surface to generate the reflection color. The direction of this reflection ray is calculated by reflecting the direction of the incoming ray about surface normal. When the reflection ray collides with objects in the scene, it should be shaded as if it were a primary ray; in this way, the surface that is visible in the reflection will contribute its color to the original surface.

When rendering reflections using a hybrid approach, there are several additional implementation details that must be handled. Firstly, we have to decide whether the pixel we are shading is reflective. We can do this by encoding our reflectivity in the G-buffer when we rasterize out fragments into it, then reading it back in our frame shader to decide if we need a reflection ray.

Another issue is that we are emitting our primary rays from a surface defined by a G-buffer pixel, so we don't have an incoming ray to reflect. Therefore, we have to calculate a "virtual" incoming ray based on the view frustum used by the rasterizer. In this example, we pass in the corners of the view frustum as four normalized vec3s, and then we can calculate the virtual ray's direction by interpolating between the corners based on the pixel position. We then reflect this ray around the normal defined by the G-buffer producing our reflection ray direction. The built-in RLSL function `reflect` is used to perform this calculation.

Finally, when our reflection ray hits a surface, we need to make sure the result is the same as when the same surface is viewed directly. So the output from the ray shader for a reflection ray must match the result of the compositing fragment shader that produces the final color for directly visible surfaces.

13.7 Transparency

Transparency is a fundamental physical property that is not handled well by rasterization. Rasterization approximates transparency using alpha blending. Transparent objects are sorted by distance from the camera and rendered after the opaque objects, in an order starting at the most distant. Transparency is approximated in the raster pipeline by having each fragment combine a percentage of its color with the value already in the framebuffer.

```
vec3 CalcVirtualInRay()
{
 vec2 uv = rl_FrameCoord.xy/rl_FrameSize.xy;
 vec3 left = mix(frustumRay[0],   frustumRay[1],   uv.y);
 vec3 right = mix(frustumRay[2],   frustumRay[3],   uv.y);
 vec3 cameraRay = mix(left,   right,   uv.x);

 return cameraRay;
}

void DoReflection(vec4 normal,vec3 position, float reflectivity)
{
 vec3 inRay = CalcVirtualInRay();
 vec3 reflection = reflect(inRay, normal);

 createRay();
 rl_OutRay.direction          = reflection;
 rl_OutRay.origin             = position;
 emitRay();
}
```

Listing 13.7. Reflection in hybrid renderer.

Alpha blending causes many artifacts, as it bares little relation to how transparency works in real life. Transparency is caused by light traveling through a transparent medium, where some wavelengths are absorbed and some are not. Ray tracing can be used to simulate transparency, independent of vertex submission order and without any of the artifacts and problems inherent in alpha blending.

To render a transparent surface, we emit a transparency ray from the back side of the surface, with the same direction as the incoming ray. If the surface is translucent, the ray's color will have its color ray attribute modulated with the color of the surface. This transparency ray is treated exactly the same as a reflection ray. The final color that the transparency ray contributes to the pixel will be modulated by the color of the transparent surface it traveled through. In this example, the surface transparency is stored in the alpha channel of the surface color. If the surface is completely transparent, the ray has 100% intensity, and as the surface becomes opaque, the ray's intensity approaches zero.

Simple ray-traced transparency of this kind does not take into account the behavior of many transparent materials. The physics of what happens when light travels from one transparent medium to another is more complicated than presented above. Some light is reflected off the surface (according the law of reflection discussed earlier) and some light bends, or refracts, changing its direction based on the relative speed of light in the two media.

This too can be represented in a ray tracer using a simple combination of a transparency ray and a reflection ray. The percentage of the light that is reflected versus refracted is defined by Fresnel's equations and can be approximated using a power function.

```
void DoTransparency(vec4 normal,vec3 position, vec4 color)
{
 vec3 inRay = CalcVirtualInRay();

 createRay();
 rl_OutRay.direction   = inRay;
 rl_OutRay.origin      = position;
 rl_OutRay.color       = (1.0-color.a)*rl_InRay.color*color.rgb;
 emitRay();
}
```

Listing 13.8. Emitting a transparency ray.

```
float incidentDot    = dot(inRay, normal);
vec3  atten = vec3(1.0);
float powTerm = pow((1.0-abs(incidentDot)), fresnelExp);
float fres = KrMin+(Kr-KrMin)*powTerm;

if (rl_FrontFacing)
  ior = 1.0 / ior;
else {
  /* Beer's Law to approximate attenuation. */
  atten  = vec3(1.0) - materialColour;
  atten *= materialDensity * -rl_IntersectionT;
  atten  = exp(atten);
}

createRay();
rl_OutRay.direction = refract(rl_InRay.direction, normal, ior);

/* For Total Internal Reflection, reflect() returns 0.0 */
if (rl_OutRay.direction == vec3(0.0)) {
  rl_OutRay.direction = reflect(inRay, normal);
}

rl_OutRay.color *= (1.0 - fres) * atten;
emitRay();
```

Listing 13.9. Refraction shader.

13.8 Performance

Performance in a ray-tracing GPU is a big topic that cannot be covered by one section of this chapter. Hopefully this section contains enough information to provide a framework to begin to optimize your engine.

13.8.1 Rays per Pixel

The most obvious performance metric to measure is how many rays your engine is using. Because each ray can trigger a shader that can potentially emit many more rays, this is not always easy. To address this, OpenRL includes a tool called

Figure 13.5. A sample heat map showing the most expensive pixels. Note the internal ray bouncing on the refractive glass objects can generate many rays.

Profiler. Profiler can provide a heat map that displays a visual representation of the number of rays that were cast for each pixel. This view can be useful to spot a potential shader problem or a problematic interaction between shaders.

Naturally, some effects are just more expensive, so some variation in the heat map is expected. But if some effects require more rays than can be sustained across the entire frame, it is important to design the game so that those pixels never fill the entire frame. Other options are to build in a mechanism to dynamically limit the effect quality up front based on the viewing position, or progressively use more rays until you have consumed the time allotted for the frame. This is sometimes necessary to maintain a stable frame rate.

13.8.2 Bottlenecks within the Ray Tracer

If the number of rays is within the expected ranges, but the performance is not what you had hoped for, then you may have encountered one of several other bottlenecks.

The Wizard architecture has a peak ray flow, measured in rays per second. For the PowerVR GR6500, that is 300 MRays/second. The architecture is not designed to exceed the peak ray flow, so if your measured performance is within 80% of the peak-ray-flow number, the best optimization opportunity is to reduce the number of rays you are casting.

If your performance is substantially below the peak ray flow, the bottleneck is geometry processing, executing shaders, or traversing rays (testing the rays against the scene geometry to find the best hit).

Geometry processing can be ruled out by ensuring that the geometry remains static from one frame to the next. To do this, make sure that no primitive objects

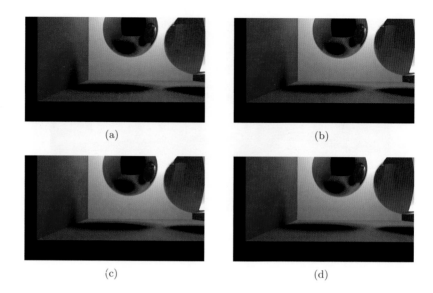

Figure 13.6. An unfiltered soft shadow computation using (a) one, (b) two, (c) four, and (d) eight rays per pixel. The quality gradually improves as more rays are used.

are created, removed, or modified, and that uniforms that affect a vertex shader are not modified.

The cost of ray traversal is a direct function of the geometric complexity of the scene. If reducing the complexity of your meshes yields a large performance gain, then the ray tracer may be bottlenecked on traversal.

The most difficult factor to isolate is the shader. As in a rasterizer, one valuable test may be to reduce the complexity of the shaders in the scene, for example, by replacing the material ray shaders with a simple shader that visualizes the normal at the ray intersection point. In ray tracing, however, this may also mask the problem by avoiding the emission of secondary rays (and hence less ray traversal).

Keep in mind that, in the Wizard architecture, ray and frame shaders execute on exactly the same shading hardware as the vertex and fragment shaders used in rasterization. Furthermore, they share exactly the same interface to memory. This means that a heavy raster shader could bog down the system for ray tracing or vice versa.

13.9   Results

All of the screenshots in Figures 13.7–13.12 were rendered with between one and four rays per pixel, measured as a frame-wide average.

Figure 13.7. Shadows and ray-traced transparency.

Figure 13.8. Multiple shadow casting lights.

Figure 13.9. Reflections and refraction.

Figure 13.10. High-quality ray-traced shadow from a highly detailed occluder.

Figure 13.11. Soft shadows from multiple lights.

Figure 13.12. Reflections and transparency.

13.10   Conclusion

This chapter described one way of adding the sophisticated light transport simulation of ray tracing to a raster-based renderer. By using ray tracing as a tool like this, the physically accurate rendering techniques that have long been used in ray-tracing production renderers can be added to real-time renderers. As ray-tracing acceleration becomes more wide spread in consumer GPUs, many other techniques will likely be developed as computer graphics developers explore innovative ways to add ray tracing to their products.

Bibliography

[Blender 14] Blender. "Cycles Render Engine." *Blender 2.61 Release Notes*, http: //wiki.blender.org/index.php/Dev:Ref/Release_Notes/2.61/Cycles, accessed August 19, 2014.

[Hargreaves and Harris 04] Shawn Hargreaves and Mark Harris. "Deferred Shading." Presented at NVIDIA Developer Conference: 6800 Leagues Under the Sea, San Jose, CA, March 23, 2004. (Available at http://http. download.nvidia.com/developer/presentations/2004/6800_Leagues/6800 _Leagues_Deferred_Shading.pdf.).

[Kajiya 86] James T Kajiya. "The Rendering Equation." *Computer Graphics: Proc. SIGGRAPH '86* 20:4 (1986), 143–150.

[Keller and Heidrich 01] Alexander Keller and Wolfgang Heidrich. "Interleaved Sampling." In *Proceeding of the 12th Eurographics Workshop on Rendering Techniques*, edited by S. J. Gortler and K. Myszkowski, pp. 269–176. London: Springer-Verlag, 2001.

[LuxRender 14] LuxRender. "LuxRays." http://www.luxrender.net/wiki/ LuxRays, accessed July 19, 2014.

[Pharr and Humphreys 04] Matt Pharr and Greg Humphreys. *Physically Based Rendering*. San Francisco: Morgan Kaufmann, 2004.

14

Implementing a GPU-Only Particle-Collision System with ASTC 3D Textures and OpenGL ES 3.0

Daniele Di Donato

14.1 Introduction

Particle simulation has always been a part of games to realize effects that are difficult to achieve in a rasterizer systems. As the name suggests, particles are associated with the concept of small elements that appear in huge numbers. To avoid the complexity of real-world physics, the particles used in graphics tend to be simplified so they can be easily used in real-time applications. One of these simplifications is to consider each particle independent and not interacting with each other, which makes them suitable for parallelization across multiple processors.

The latest mobile GPUs support OpenGL ES 3.0, and the new features added gives us the right tools for implementing this simulation. We also wanted to enable a more realistic behavior, especially concerning collisions with objects in the scene. This can be computationally expensive and memory intensive since the information of the geometry needs to be passed to the GPU and traversed, per simulation step, if we want to parallelize the traditional CPU approach. With the introduction of ASTC [Nystad et al. 12] and its support for 3D textures, we are now able to store voxelized data on mobile devices with huge memory savings. This texture can be used in the OpenGL pipeline to read information about the scene and use it to modify the particle's trajectory at the cost of a single texture access per particle. The following sections describe all the steps of the particle-system simulation in detail (Figure 14.1).

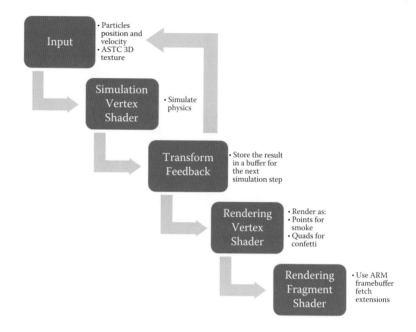

Figure 14.1. Simulation steps.

14.2 GPU-Only Particle System

14.2.1 Gathering Information about the Surroundings

To handle collisions with objects, we need to give the particles knowledge of their surroundings. This is achieved using a 3D texture describing uniform voxels of our 3D scene. For each voxel, we check if it's occupied by parts of the object and we store informations for that location. For voxels that end up on the surface of the mesh, we store a normal direction, while for internal voxels, we store the direction to the nearest surface and the amount of displacement from the current voxel to the nearest voxel on the surface. To achieve this, we used a freely available software called Voxelizer [Morris 13]. Voxelizer uses 32-bit floats for the mentioned values, so we convert them to 16-bit half-floats. This reduces the space needed by the data to be stored in a 3D texture. ASTC allows converting 16-bit per channel values, representing half-floats in our case, for the same memory cost. This gives us a better precision compared to using 8-bit values.

14.2.2 Compression Using ASTC 3D

The ASTC texture compression format is a block-based compression algorithm that is able to compress 2D and 3D textures in LDR or HDR format. Compared to

Block Dimension	Bit Rate (bits per pixel)
$3 \times 3 \times 3$	4.74
$4 \times 3 \times 3$	3.56
$4 \times 4 \times 3$	2.67
$4 \times 4 \times 4$	2.0
$5 \times 4 \times 4$	1.60
$5 \times 5 \times 4$	1.28
$5 \times 5 \times 5$	1.02
$6 \times 5 \times 5$	0.85
$6 \times 6 \times 5$	0.71
$6 \times 6 \times 6$	0.59

Table 14.1. ASTC 3D available block sizes.

other compression algorithms, ASTC offers more parameters to tune the quality of the final image (more details are available in [Smith 14]). The main options are the block size, the quality settings, and an indication of the correlation within the color channels (and the alpha channel if present). For the 3D format, ASTC allows the block sizes described in Table 14.1

Because the block compressed size is always 128 bits for all block dimensions and input formats, the bit rate is simply 128/(number of texels in a block). This specifies the tradeoff between quality and dimension of the generated compressed texture. In Figure 14.2, various ASTC compressed 3D texture have been rendered using slicing planes and various block sizes.

The other parameter to choose is the amount of time spent finding a good match for the current block. From a high-level view, this option is used to increase the quality of the compression at the cost of more compression time. Because this is typically done as an offline process, we can use the fastest option for debug

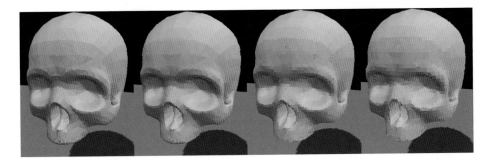

Figure 14.2. From left to right: uncompressed 3D texture, ASTC 3D $3 \times 3 \times 3$ compressed texture, ASTC 3D $4 \times 4 \times 4$ compressed texture, and ASTC 3D $5 \times 5 \times 5$ compressed texture.

purposes and compress using the best one for release. The options supported by
the free ARM ASTC evaluation codec [ARM Mali 15a, ARM Mali 15c] are *very
fast, fast, standard, thorough*, and *exhaustive*. The last parameter to set is the
correlation within the color channels. The freely available tools also allows us to
use various preset configuration options based on the data you want to compress.
For example, the tool has a preset for 2D normal maps compression that treats the
channels as uncorrelated and also uses a different error metric for the conversion.
This preset is not available for 3D textures, so we set the uncorrelation using
the fine-grained options available. Note that the ASTC compression tool used
does not store negative numbers, even in case of half-float format. This is due to
the internal implementation of the ASTC algorithm. Because our data contains
mostly unit vectors, we shifted the origin to be at $[1, 1, 1]$ so that the vectors
resides in the $[0, 0, 0]$ to $[2, 2, 2]$ 3D cube.

14.2.3   Statistics of the Savings

Compressing the 3D texture using ASTC gave us a huge amount of memory
saving, especially thanks to its ability to compress HDR values at the same cost
as LDR values. As can be seen from Table 14.2, the memory saving can reach
nearly 90% with the subsequent reduction of memory read bandwidth, and hence
energy consumption. The memory read bandwidth has been measured using
ARM Streamline profiling tool on a Samsung Galaxy Note 10.1, 2014 edition.
We measured the average read bandwidth from the main memory to the L2
cache of the GPU running the demo for around two minutes for each ASTC
texture format we used. The energy consumption per frame is an approximation
computed using ARM internal reference values for DDR2 and DDR3 memory
modules.

14.3   Physics Simulation

The physics simulation is really simple and tries to approximate the physical
behavior. Each particle will be subject to the force of gravity as well as other
forces we choose to apply. Given an initial state $t = 0$ for the particles, we
simulate the second law of motion and compute the incremental movement after
a Δt. The Δt used in the demo is fixed to 16 ms since we assume the demo will
run at 60 fps. Methods that try to solve ordinary and partial derivative equations
using incremental steps are typically called *explicit methods*.

14.3.1   Explicit Methods

To delegate the physics computation to the GPU, we decided to use an explicit
method of computation for the simulation step, since this methods fits well with

	Sphere	Skull	Chalice	Rock	Hand
Texture Resolution	$128 \times 128 \times 128$	$180 \times 255 \times 255$	$255 \times 181 \times 243$	$78 \times 75 \times 127$	$43 \times 97 \times 127$
Texture Size MB					
Uncompressed	16.78	82.62	89.73	5.94	4.24
ASTC $3 \times 3 \times 3$	1.27	6.12	6.72	0.45	0.34
ASCT $4 \times 4 \times 4$	0.52	2.63	2.87	0.19	0.14
ASTC $5 \times 5 \times 5$	0.28	1.32	1.48	0.10	0.07
Memory Read Bandwidth in MB/s					
Uncompressed	644.47	752.18	721.96	511.48	299.36
ASTC $3 \times 3 \times 3$	342.01	285.78	206.39	374.19	228.05
ASCT $4 \times 4 \times 4$	327.63	179.43	175.21	368.13	224.26
ASTC $5 \times 5 \times 5$	323.10	167.90	162.89	366.18	222.76
Energy consumption per frame DDR2 mJ per frame					
Uncompressed	4.35	5.08	4.87	3.45	2.01
ASTC $3 \times 3 \times 3$	2.31	1.93	1.39	2.53	1.54
ASCT $4 \times 4 \times 4$	2.21	1.21	1.18	2.48	1.51
ASTC $5 \times 5 \times 5$	2.18	1.13	1.10	2.47	1.50
Energy consumption per frame DDR3 mJ per frame					
Uncompressed	3.58	4.17	4.01	2.84	1.66
ASTC $3 \times 3 \times 3$	1.90	1.59	1.15	2.08	1.27
ASCT $4 \times 4 \times 4$	1.82	1.00	0.97	2.04	1.24
ASTC $5 \times 5 \times 5$	1.79	0.93	0.90	2.03	1.24

Table 14.2. ASTC 3D texture compression examples with various block sizes.

the transform feedback feature available through OpenGL ES 3.0. For the purpose of the demo, we implemented a simple Euler integration, and each shader execution computes a step of the integration. This implementation is good enough for the demo, but for advanced purposes, a variable time step can be used and each shader execution can split this time step further and compute a smaller integration inside the shader itself.

So, the physical simulation for step $N + 1$ will be dependent on a function of step N and the delta time (Δt) that occurred between the simulation steps:

$$Y(t + \Delta t) = F(Y(t), \Delta t).$$

Due to the time dependency of position, velocity, and acceleration, this method is suitable for use in our simulation.

```
typedef struct _XFormFeedbackParticle
{
    Vec3   Position;
    Vec3   Velocity;
    Vec4   Attrib;
    float  Life;
} XFormFeedbackParticle;

glGenBuffers( 2, m_XformFeedbackBuffers );

glBindBuffer( GL_ARRAY_BUFFER ,
              m_XformFeedbackBuffers[0] );

glBufferData( GL_ARRAY_BUFFER ,
              sizeof( XFormFeedbackParticle ) *
              totalNumberOfParticles ,
              NULL,
              GL_STREAM_DRAW );

glBindBuffer( GL_ARRAY_BUFFER ,
              m_XformFeedbackBuffers[1] );

glBufferData( GL_ARRAY_BUFFER ,
              sizeof( XFormFeedbackParticle ) *
              totalNumberOfParticles ,
              NULL,
              GL_STREAM_DRAW );

//Initialize the first buffer with the particles'
//data from the emitters
unsigned int offset = 0;
for( unsigned int i = 0; i < m_Emitters.Length(); i++ )
{
    glBindBuffer( GL_ARRAY_BUFFER ,
                  m_XformFeedbackBuffers[0] );

    glBufferSubData( GL_ARRAY_BUFFER ,
                     offset,
                     m_Emitters[i]->MaxParticles() *
                     sizeof( XFormFeedbackParticle ),
                     m_Emitters[i]->Particles() );

    offset += m_Emitters[i]->MaxParticles() *
              sizeof( XFormFeedbackParticle );
}
```

Listing 14.1. Transform feedback buffers initialization.

```
const char* xformFeedbackVaryings[4] = { "oParticlePos",
                                         "oParticleVel",
                                         "oParticleAttrib",
                                         "oParticleLife"  };
glTransformFeedbackVaryings( m_XFormFeedbackShader ,
                             4,
                             xformFeedbackVaryings ,
                             GL_INTERLEAVED_ATTRIBS );
```

Listing 14.2. Transform feedback output varyings definition.

Position1	Velocity1	Attrib1	Life1	Position2	Velocity2	Attrib2	Life2	...

Table 14.3. Order of GL_INTERLEAVED_ATTRIBS attributes.

Position1	Position2	Position3	...
Velocity1	Velocity2	Velocity3	...
Attrib1	Attrib2	Attrib3	...
Life1	Life2	Life3	...

Table 14.4. Order of GL_SEPARATE_ATTRIBS attributes.

14.3.2 OpenGL ES Transform Feedback Overview

Transform feedback allows users to store the result of a vertex shader execution into a predefined vertex buffer. This feature fits well with the explicit methods described above, since we can simulate the various steps using two buffers that are swapped at each simulation step (this is usually called ping-ponging). After we generate IDs for the transform feedback buffers using glGenBuffers, we initialize them with a set of random particles. If multiple emitters are present, we can store all their particles in the same buffer so that one step of the simulation can actually update multiple emitters in the scene (see Listing 14.1).

Vertex shaders output various results to the subsequent fragment shader, so we need a way to specify which results should also be written to the predefined output buffer. This can be done after we attach the vertex program that will run the simulation to the main program.

The command glTransformFeedbackVaryings (see Listing 14.2) will check if the specified strings are defined as output of the vertex shaders, and GL_INTERLEAVED_ATTRIBS will tell OpenGL in which layout to store the data. Possible options are GL_INTERLEAVED_ATTRIBS and GL_SEPARATE_ATTRIBS. The former will store the result of the vertex shader in a single buffer and in order as specified by the strings passed to the function and the particles' data will look like Table 14.3. The latter stores each attribute in a separate buffer (see Table 14.4).

During the rendering, we do the following:

1. Set which buffer to use as the destination buffer for transform feedback using the specific GL_TRANSFORM_FEEDBACK_BUFFER flag.

```
glBindBufferBase( GL_TRANSFORM_FEEDBACK_BUFFER,
                  0,
                  m_XformFeedbackBuffers[1] );
```

2. Set which buffer is the source buffer and how the data is stored in it.

```
glBindBuffer( GL_ARRAY_BUFFER, m_XformFeedbackBuffers[0] );
glEnableVertexAttribArray( m_ParticlePositionLocation );
```

```
glEnableVertexAttribArray( m_ParticleVelocityLocation );
glEnableVertexAttribArray( m_ParticleAttribLocation );
glEnableVertexAttribArray( m_ParticleLifeLocation );

//We store in one buffer the 4 fields that represent a particle
// Position: 3 float values for a total of 12 bytes
// Velocity: 3 float values for a total of 12 bytes
// Attrib: 2 float values for a total of 8 bytes
// life: 1 float value for a total of 4 bytes

glVertexAttribPointer( m_ParticlePositionLocation,
                       3,
                       GL_FLOAT,
                       GL_FALSE,
                       sizeof( XFormFeedbackParticle ),
                       0);

glVertexAttribPointer( m_ParticleVelocityLocation,
                       3,
                       GL_FLOAT,
                       GL_FALSE,
                       sizeof( XFormFeedbackParticle ),
                       12);

glVertexAttribPointer( m_ParticleAttribLocation,
                       4,
                       GL_FLOAT,
                       GL_FALSE,
                       sizeof( XFormFeedbackParticle ),
                       24);

glVertexAttribPointer( m_ParticleLifeLocation,
                       1,
                       GL_FLOAT,
                       GL_FALSE,
                       sizeof( XFormFeedbackParticle ),
                       40);
```

3. Enable transform feedback and disable the rasterizer step. The former is done using the `glBeginTransformFeedback` function to inform the OpenGL pipeline that we are interested in saving the results of the vertex shader execution. The latter is achieved using the `GL_RASTERIZER_DISCARD` flag specifically added for the transform feedback feature. This flag disables the generation of fragment jobs so that only the vertex shader is executed. We disabled the fragment execution since the rendering of the particles required two different approaches based on the scene rendered and splitting the simulation from the rendering gave us a cleaner code base to work with.

```
glEnable( GL_RASTERIZER_DISCARD );
glBeginTransformFeedback( GL_POINTS );
```

4. Render the particles as points.

```
glDrawArrays( GL_POINTS, 0, MaxParticles );
```

5. Disable transform feedback and re-enable the rasterizer.

```
glEndTransformFeedback();
glDisable( GL_RASTERIZER_DISCARD );
```

14.3.3 Manage the Physics in the Vertex Shader Using 3D Textures

The attributes of each particle are read in the vertex shader as vertex attributes and used to compute the next incremental step in the physics simulation. First, we compute the total forces acting on the particles. Since this is a very simple simulation, we ended up simulating just the gravity, a constant force, and the air friction. The air friction is computed using the Stokes' drag formula [Wikipedia 15] because the particles are considered to be small spheres:

$$Fd = -6\pi\eta r v,$$

where η is the dynamic viscosity coefficient of the air and is equal to 18.27 μ Pa, r is the radius of the particle (we used 5 μm in our simulation), and v is the velocity of the particle. Since the first part of the product remains constant, we computed it in advance to avoid computing it per particle.

```
//Air friction is given by 6.0 * 3.14 * 5 * 0.000018 = 0.0016956
vec3 totalForce = uConstantForce +
                ( uParticleMass * gravity ) -
                0.0016956 * iParticleVel;

vec3 totalAcceleration = totalForce/uParticleMass;

oparticlePos_worldSpace = iparticle_Pos +
                ( iparticle_Vel * uDeltaT ) +
                ( totalAcceleration * uDeltaTSquared );
```

The new position is then transformed using the transformation matrix derived by the bounding box of the model. This matrix is computed to have the bounding box minimum to be the origin $(0, 0, 0)$ of the reference. Also, we want the area of world space inside the bounding box to be mapped to the unit cube space $(0, 0, 0)$–$(1, 1, 1)$. Applying this matrix to the particle's position in world space gives us the particle's coordinate in the space with the origin at the minimum corner of the bounding box and also scaled based on the dimension of the model. This means that the particles positioned in bounding box space within $(0, 0, 0)$

and $(1, 1, 1)$ have a chance to collide with the object, and this position is actually the 3D texture coordinate we will use to sample the 3D texture of the model.

- Host code.

```
uBoundingBoxMatrix = ( (1.0/max.x-min.x, 0.0,0.0,-min.x),
                       (0.0, 1.0/max.y-min.y, 0.0, -min.y),
                       (0.0, 0.0, 1.0/max.z-min.z, -min.z),
                       (0.0, 0.0, 0.0, 1.0) ) *
                     inverse( ModelMatrix );
```

- Vertex shader.

```
vec4 oParticlePos_BBSpace = uBoundingBoxMatrix *
                            vec4( oparticlePos_worldSpace, 1.0 );

vec4 surfaceNormal =  texture( uCollisionTexture, tex3dCoord );
```

The surface's normal will be encoded in a 32-bit field and stored to be used later in the rendering pass to orient the particles in case of collisions. Due to the discrete nature of the simulation, it can happen that a particle goes inside the object. We recognize this event when sampling the 3D texture since we store a flag plus other data in the alpha channel of the 3D texture. When this event happens, we use the gradient direction stored in the 3D texture plus the amount of displacement that needs to be applied and we "push" the particle to the nearest surface. The push is applied to the particles in the bounding-box space, and the inverse of the uBoundingBoxMatrix is then used to move the particles back to the world space. Discrete time steps can cause issues when colliding with completely planar surfaces since a sort of swinging can appear, but at interactive speeds ($\geq$ 30 fps), this is almost unnoticeable. For particles colliding with the surface of the object, we compute the new velocity direction and magnitude using the previous velocity magnitude, the surface normal, the surface tangent direction, and a bouncing resistance to simulate different materials and particle behavior. We use the particle's mass as sliding factor so that heavier particles will bounce while lighter particles such as dust and smoke will slide along the surface. A check needs to be performed for the tangent direction since the normal and the velocity can be parallel, and in that case, the cross product will give an incorrect result (see Listing 14.3).

The velocity is then used to move the particle to its new position. Because we want to avoid copying memory within the GPU and CPU, the lifetime of all the particles should be managed in the shader itself. This means we check if the lifetime reached 0 and reinitialize the particle attributes such as initial position, initial velocity, and total particle duration. To make the simulation more

```
float slidingFactor = clamp( uParticleMass, 0.0,1.0 );
vec3 velocityDir =  normalize( iparticle_Vel );
vec3 tangentDir = cross( surfaceNormal.xyz, velocityDir );

if( length(tangentDir) < 0.0001 )
{
    tangentDir = getRandomTangentDir( surfaceNormal.xyz, 0.0 );
}

iparticle_Vel = length( iparticle_Vel ) *
                ( surfaceNormal.xyz * slidingFactor +
                  tangentDir.xyz * ( 1.0-slidingFactor ) ) *
                uBouncingResistance;
```

Listing 14.3. Particle-collision behavior.

interesting, some randomness can be added while the particles are flowing and no collision occurred. The fragment shader of the simulation is actually empty. This is understandable since we do not need to execute any fragment work for the simulation results. Also, we have enabled the GL_RASTERIZER_DISCARD to skip all fragment work from being executed. In a way that differs from the OpenGL standard, OpenGL ES needs a fragment shader to be attached to the program, even if is not going to be used.

14.4   Rendering the Particles

After updating the particles' locations, we can render them as we want. In our demo, we decided to render them as smoke particles and as confetti. The light lamp shape on the floor is procedurally generated using its texture coordinates. The shadows are created using a projected texture that is generated from the light point of view. This texture is used for the shadows of the floor as well the ones on the objects. To achieve this we implement an incremental approach:

1. Render the object without color enabled so that its depth is stored in the depth buffer. We need to do this step to prevent particles behind the object (from the point of view of the light) from casting shadows on the object.

2. Render the particles with depth testing on, but not depth writing.

3. Render the object normally using the texture generated at Step 2 for the shadows.

4. Render the object as shadow in the texture from Step 2.

5. Render the floor with the result of Step 4 for the shadows.

This approach can be optimized. For example, we can use two different frame-buffers for the shadow of the floor and on the object so that we avoid incremental renderings (refer to [Harris 14] for more information). To achieve this, we copy the result of the texture created at the end of Step 2 into the other framebuffer and then render the object as shadow on it.

14.4.1 Smoke Scene

In this scene, the smoke (Figure 14.3) is rendered as point sprites since we always want them to face the viewpoint. The smoke is rendered using a noise texture and some mathematics to compute the final color as if it was a 3D volume. To give the smoke a transparent look, we need to combine different overlapping particles' colors. To do so, we used blending and disabled the Z-test when rendering the particles. This gives a nice result, even without sorting the particles based on the Z-value (otherwise we have to map the buffer in the CPU). Another reason for disabling it is to achieve soft particles. From Mali-T600 GPUs onward, we can use a specific extension in the fragment shader called `GL_ARM_shader_framebuffer_fetch` to read back the values of the framebuffer (color, depth, and stencil) without having to render to a texture [Björge 14]. The extension allows us to access a set of built-in variables (`gl_LastFragColorARM`, `gl_LastFragDepthARM`, `gl_LastFrag StencilARM`) from the fragment shader, and for each pixel, the value is based on previous rendering results.

```
#extension GL_ARM_shader_framebuffer_fetch_depth_stencil : enable
#ifdef GL_ARM_shader_framebuffer_fetch_depth_stencil
float dla= (2.0 * uNear) /
          (uFar + uNear - gl_LastFragDepthARM * (uFar - uNear));
#else
    //Texture read fallback
#endif
```

This feature makes it easier to achieve soft particles, and in the demo, we use a simple approach. First, we render all the solid objects so that the Z-value will be written in the depth buffer. Afterward, we render the smoke and we can read the depth value of the object and compare it with the current fragment of the particle (to see if it is behind the object) and fade the color accordingly. This technique eliminates the sharp profile that is formed by the particle quad intersecting the geometry due to the Z-test. During development, the smoke effect looked nice, but we wanted it to be more dense and blurry. To achieve all this, we decided to render the smoke in an offscreen render buffer with a lower resolution compared to the main screen. This gives us the ability to have a blurred smoke (since the lower resolution removes the higher frequencies) as well as lets us increase the number of particles to get a denser look. The current implementation uses a 640×360 offscreen buffer that is up-scaled to 1080p resolution in the final image.

Figure 14.3. Smoke scene.

A naïve approach causes jaggedness on the outline of the object when the smoke is flowing near it due to the blending of the up-sampled low-resolution buffer. To minimize this effect, we apply a bilateral filter. The bilateral filter is applied to the offscreen buffer and is given by the product of a Gaussian filter in the color texture and a linear weighting factor given by the difference in depth. The depth factor is useful on the edge of the model because it gives a higher weight to neighbor texels with depth similar to the one of the current pixel and lower weight when this difference is higher. (If we consider a pixel on the edge of a model, some of the neighbor pixels will still be on the model while others will be far in the background.)

14.4.2 Confetti Scene

In this case, we used quads instead of points since we needed to rotate the particles when they slide along the surfaces (Figure 14.4). Those quads are initialized to `min` $= (-1, -1, 0)$ and `max` $= (1, 1, 0)$. The various shapes are achieved procedurally checking the texture coordinates of the quad pixels. To rotate the quad accordingly, we retrieve the normal of the last surface touched and compute the tangent and binormal vectors. This gives us a matrix that we use to rotate the initial quad position, and afterward we translate this quad into the position of the particle that we computed in the simulation step.

14.4.3 Performance Optimization with Instancing

Even if the quad data is really small, they waste memory because the quads are all initialized with the same values and they all share the same number of vertices and texture coordinates. The instancing feature introduced in OpenGL ES 3.0

Figure 14.4. Confetti scene.

allows us to avoid replication of vertex attribute by defining just one "template" of the mesh we want to render. This template is then instantiated multiple times and the user will vary the parameters (matrices, colors, textures, etc.) to represent multiple meshes with different characteristic with a single draw call (Figure 14.5).

OpenGL ES instancing overview.

1. Bind the buffers that we will use as the template source data.

```
glBindBuffer( GL_ARRAY_BUFFER, m_QuadPositionBuffer );
glEnableVertexAttribArray( m_QuadPositionLocation );
glVertexAttribPointer( m_QuadPositionLocation,
                       3,
                       GL_FLOAT,
                       GL_FALSE,
                       0,
                       (void*)0 );

//Set up quad texture coordinate buffer
glBindBuffer( GL_ARRAY_BUFFER, m_TexCoordBuffer );
glEnableVertexAttribArray( m_QuadTexCoordLocation );
glVertexAttribPointer( m_QuadTexCoordLocation,
                       2,
                       GL_FLOAT,
                       GL_FALSE,
                       0,
                       (void*)0 );
```

2. Set a *divisor* for each vertex attribute array. The divisor specifies how the vertex attributes advance in the array when rendering instances of primitives in a single draw call. Setting it to 0 will make the attribute advance

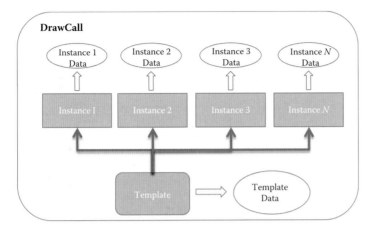

Figure 14.5. OpenGL ES 3.0 instancing.

once per vertex, restarting at the start of each instance rendered. This is what we want to happen for the initial quad position and texture coordinate since they will be the same for each particle (instance) rendered.

```
glVertexAttribDivisor( m_QuadPositionLocation, 0 );
glVertexAttribDivisor( m_QuadTexCoordLocation, 0 );
```

3. For the attributes computed in the simulation step, we would like to shift the vertex buffer index for each of the particles (instances) to be rendered. This is achieved using a divisor other than zero. The divisor then specifies how many instances should be rendered before we advance the index in the arrays. In our case, we wanted to shift the attributes after each instance is rendered, so we used a divisor of 1.

```
glVertexAttribDivisor( m_UpdatedParticlePosLocation, 1 );
glVertexAttribDivisor( m_UpdatedParticleLifeLocation, 1 );
glVertexAttribDivisor( m_UpdatedParticleAttribLocation, 1 );
```

4. Bind the buffer that was output from the simulation step. Set up the vertex attributes to read from this buffer.

```
glBindBuffer( GL_ARRAY_BUFFER, m_XformFeedbackBuffers[1] );

glVertexAttribPointer( m_UpdatedParticlePosLocation,
                       3,
                       GL_FLOAT,
```

```
                            GL_FALSE,
                            sizeof( XFormFeedbackParticle ),
                            0);

glVertexAttribPointer( m_UpdatedParticleAttribLocation,
                            4,
                            GL_FLOAT,
                            GL_FALSE,
                            sizeof( XFormFeedbackParticle ),
                            24);

glVertexAttribPointer( m_UpdatedParticleLifeLocation,
                            1,
                            GL_FLOAT,
                            GL_FALSE,
                            sizeof( XFormFeedbackParticle ),
                            40);
```

5. Render the particles (instances). The function allows to specify how many vertices belong to each instance and how many instances we want to render. Note that when using instancing, we are able to access a built-in variable `gl_InstanceID` inside the vertex shader. This variable specifies the ID of the instance we are currently rendering and can be used to access uniform buffers.

```
glDrawArraysInstanced( GL_TRIANGLE_STRIP, 0, 4, MaxParticles );
```

6. Always set back to 0 the divisor for all the vertex attribute arrays since they can affect subsequent rendering even if we are not using indexing.

```
glDisableVertexAttribArray( m_QuadPositionLocation );
glDisableVertexAttribArray( m_QuadTexCoordLocation );
glVertexAttribDivisor( m_UpdatedParticlePosLocation, 0 );
glVertexAttribDivisor( m_UpdatedParticleAttribLocation, 0 );
glVertexAttribDivisor( m_UpdatedParticleLifeLocation, 0 );
```

14.5   Conclusion

Combining OpenGL ES 3.0 features enabled us to realize a GPU-only particle system that is capable of running at interactive speeds on current mobile devices. The techniques proposed are experimental and have some drawbacks, but the reader can take inspiration from this chapter and explore other options using ASTC LDR/HDR/3D texture as well as OpenGL ES 3.0. In case there is need to sort the particles, the compute shader feature recently announced in the OpenGL ES 3.1 specification will enable sorting directly on the GPU.

An issue derived from the use of a texture is the texture's resolution. This technique can describe a whole 3D static scene in a single 3D texture, but the resolution of it needs to be chosen carefully since too small resolution can cause parts of objects to not collide properly since multiple parts with different normals will be stored in the same voxel. Also, space is wasted if the voxelized 3D scene contains parts with no actual geometry in them but that fall inside the volume that is voxelized. Since we are simulating using a discrete time step, issues can appear if we change the system too fast. For example, we can miss the collision detection in narrow parts of the object if we rotate it too fast.

Bibliography

[ARM Mali 15a] ARM Mali. "ASTC Evaluation Codec." http://malideveloper. arm.com/develop-for-mali/tools/astc-evaluation-codec, 2015.

[ARM Mali 15b] ARM Mali. "Mali Developer Center." http://malideveloper. arm.com, 2015.

[ARM Mali 15c] ARM Mali. "Mali GPU Texture Compression Tool." http://malideveloper.arm.com/develop-for-mali/tools/asset-creation/ mali-gpu-texture-compression-tool/, 2015.

[Björge 14] Marius Björge. "Bandwidth Efficient Graphics with ARM Mali GPUs." In *GPU Pro 5: Advanced Rendering Techniques*, edited by Wolfgang Engel, pp. 275–288. Boca Raton, FL: CRC Press, 2014.

[Harris 14] Peter Harris. "Mali Performance 2: How to Correctly Handle Framebuffers." *ARM Connected Community*, http://community. arm.com/groups/arm-mali-graphics/blog/2014/04/28/mali-graphics -performance-2-how-to-correctly-handle-framebuffers, 2014.

[Morris 13] Dan Morris. "Voxelizer: Floodfilling and Distance Map Generation for 3D Surfaces." http://techhouse.brown.edu/~dmorris/voxelizer/, 2013.

[Nystad et al. 12] J. Nystad, A. Lassen, A. Pomianowski, S. Ellis, and T. Olson. "Adaptive Scalable Texture Compression." In *Proceedings of the Fourth ACM SIGGRAPH/Eurographics Conference on High-Performance Graphics*, pp. 105–114. Aire-la-ville, Switzerland: Eurographics Association, 2012.

[Smith 14] Stacy Smith. "Adaptive Scalable Texture Compression." In *GPU Pro 5: Advanced Rendering Techniques*, edited by Wolfgang Engel, pp. 313–326. Boca Raton, FL: CRC Press, 2014.

[Wikipedia 15] Wikipedia. "Stokes' Law." http://en.wikipedia.org/wiki/Stokes% 27_law, 2015.

15

Animated Characters with Shell Fur for Mobile Devices
Andrew Girdler and James L. Jones

15.1 Introduction

Fur effects have traditionally presented a significant challenge in real-time graphics. On the desktop, the latest techniques employ DirectX 11 tessellation to dynamically create geometric hair or fur strands on the fly that number in the hundreds of thousands [Tariq and Bavoil 08, Lacroix 13]. On mobile platforms, developers must make do with a much smaller performance budget and significantly reduced memory bandwidth. To compound this, mobile devices are increasingly featuring equal or higher resolution screens than the average screens used with desktop systems.

Many artists are today able to create very detailed models of creatures with advanced animations to be used in 3D applications. This chapter will describe a system to animate and render fully detailed meshes of these creatures with a shell fur effect in real time on mobile platforms. This is made possible by utilizing new API features present in OpenGL ES 3.0, including transform feedback and instancing.

We used this technique in the creation of our *SoftKitty* technical demo, which was first shown at Mobile World Conference 2014. It enabled a high-polygon model of a cat to be animated with 12-bone-per-vertex skinning and then rendered with shell fur at native resolution on an Apple iPad Air. Thanks to the optimizations in this chapter, the device was able to render the cat and a high detail environment in excess of 30 fps.

15.2 Overview

This approach is an optimization of the shell fur technique presented by [Kajiya and Kay 89]. Traditionally, combining a shell fur effect with a skinned mesh

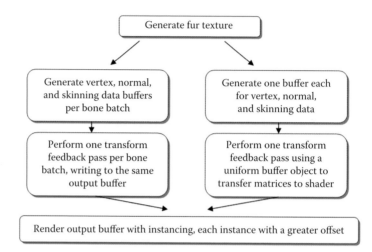

Figure 15.1. Technique overview diagram.

would require the skinned positions to be recomputed for every layer of fur. In addition to this, there would be a separate draw call per layer, resulting in the base mesh being transferred to the GPU multiple times per frame. This is inefficient and, depending on model complexity, possibly not viable on bandwidth-limited platforms.

This approach avoids these issues by first skinning the mesh in a separate transform feedback pass and then using instancing to submit the mesh and create the offset layers of fur with a single draw call. We have also simplified the design of the textures used to create the fur, transitioning from one texture per layer to a single texture for all. There are two approaches to implementing this, the choice of which is decided by model complexity and platform limitations. (See Figure 15.1.)

15.3   Creating a Shell Fur Texture

Traditional shell fur techniques have utilized a separate texture per shell layer to encode the density and length of the strands [Lengyel et al. 01]. An early optimization we used, which was partially necessitated by the use of instancing, was to encode the strand length, and thereby density, onto a single texture. We encoded the length as an integer between 0 (no fur) and the default number of layers and then sampled it in the fur shader to decide whether a strand should be drawn or not. We stored this in the alpha channel of the texture with the intention of storing a color variance (having some strands lighter and some darker than others) in the RGB channels; however, we later removed this as the inherent variance in our diffuse texture was sufficient to give a convincing effect.

```
for (layer < numLayers)
    rand(setSeed)
    length = 1.5f - layer/numLayers
    //hand tuned falloff
    density = inDensity*length
    for i < density
        newxycoords=rand()
        if xycoord.a != layer
            xycoord.a+=1.
```

An alternative approach would be to maintain a single texture per layer and create a 2DTextureArray to pass into the fur instancing shader. This could be explored if more flexibility in the fur was needed, but the single-texture approach was sufficient for our needs and was more bandwidth efficient.

We also created a separate fur length map, using the same UV coordinates as the model's diffuse texture to decide the relative length of the fur for a given location on the model, with white being full length and black being no fur.

15.4 Bone Batches or Single Pass?

We identified two approaches to performing the transform feedback stage for skinning. The first involves performing a separate transform feedback pass for each bone batch, skinning the associated vertices and then appending them into a single output buffer. The second (theoretically more efficient) approach is to export your model with a single batch, pass all the bone matrices into a single pass and skin all the vertices in one go. This avoids the overhead of running multiple transform feedback passes (which may be substantial if the number of batches is high), but depending on the complexity of the model, you may hit an upper limit on the number of uniform matrices that can be passed into a shader. This is an implementation-defined limit that can vary substantially, although we found on several test platforms that using a uniform buffer object (UBO) allowed for a greater number of matrices to be passed in.

Our model had just under 240 bone matrices, as it was designed for offline rendering. If using a model with a near or greater count than this, it would be advisable to use multiple passes, keeping the number of batches to a minimum. If tuning for optimum performance, it would be advisable to test both approaches on your target platform.

15.5 Model Data and Setup

When setting up to performing the transform feedback pass with multiple bone batches, we adopted the approach of having a single output buffer (the size of the entire mesh's vertices and normals) and then two buffers for input—one for

```
glGenTransformFeedbacks(1, &m_TransformFeedbackObject);
glGenBuffers(BONE_BATCHES+1, m_ModelDataBuffer);
// m_ModelDataBuffer[0] is output buffer
glGenBuffers(BONE_BATCHES,m_SkinningDataBuffer);

OutputModelData = new ModelDataStruct[pMesh.nNumVertex];
for(unsigned int i = 0; i < pMesh.nNumVertex; ++i)
{
   //Copy data into OutputModelData
}
glBindBuffer(GL_ARRAY_BUFFER, m_ModelDataBuffer[0]);
glBufferData(GL_ARRAY_BUFFER, sizeof(ModelDataStruct)
   * pMesh.nNumVertex, OutputModelData, GL_STATIC_DRAW);
glBindBuffer(GL_ARRAY_BUFFER, 0);
delete [] OutputModelData;

//loading each batch of vertices into its own buffer
for (unsigned int Batch = 0; Batch < BONE_BATCHES; ++Batch)
{
   //Calculate or retrieve BatchVertexCount
   InputModelData = new ModelDataStruct[BatchVertexCount];
   for(int i = 0; i < BatchVertexCount;++i)
   {
       //Copy data into InputModelData
   }
   glBindBuffer(GL_ARRAY_BUFFER, m_ModelDataBuffer[Batch+1]);
   glBufferData(GL_ARRAY_BUFFER, sizeof(ModelDataStruct)
      * BatchVertexCount, InputModelData, GL_STATIC_DRAW);
   glBindBuffer(GL_ARRAY_BUFFER, 0);
   delete [] InputModelData;

   InputSkinningData = new BoneDataStruct[BatchVertexCount];
   for(int i = 0; i < BatchVertexCount;++i)
   {
       //Copy bone weights and indices into InputSkinningData
   }
   glBindBuffer(GL_ARRAY_BUFFER, m_SkinningDataBuffer[Batch]);
   glBufferData(GL_ARRAY_BUFFER, sizeof(BoneDataStruct)
      * BatchVertexCount, InputSkinningData, GL_STATIC_DRAW);
   glBindBuffer(GL_ARRAY_BUFFER, 0);
   delete [] InputSkinningData;
}
```

Listing 15.1. Creating buffers per bone batch.

vertices and normals and one for skinning data. These input buffers were created per bone batch, containing only the data specific to that bone batch.

If using a single bone batch, the code path in Listing 15.1 can still be used with a batch count of 1. When using the single buffer approach, we created our UBO in the following manner:

```
glGenBuffers(1,&uiUBO);
glBindBuffer(GL_UNIFORM_BUFFER,uiUBO);
uiIndex = glGetUniformBlockIndex(ShaderId, szBlockName);
glUniformBlockBinding(ShaderId,uiIndex,uiSlot);
glBindBufferBase(GL_UNIFORM_BUFFER, uiSlot, uiUBO);
```

```
glUseProgram(m_TransformFeedback.uiId);
glBindTransformFeedback(GL_TRANSFORM_FEEDBACK, m_TFObject);
glEnable(GL_RASTERIZER_DISCARD);
int iTotalVerts = 0;

for (unsigned int Batch = 0; Batch < BONE_BATCHES; ++Batch)
{ //Calculate or retrieve BatchVertexCount
    glBindBufferRange(GL_TRANSFORM_FEEDBACK_BUFFER,0,
        m_ModelDataBuffer[0],iTotalVerts*sizeof(ModelDataStruct),
        BatchVertexCount*sizeof(ModelDataStruct));
    glBeginTransformFeedback(GL_POINTS);
    //Enable Attrib Arrays
    glBindBuffer(GL_ARRAY_BUFFER, m_ModelDataBuffer[Batch+1]);
    //Set Vertex and Normal Attrib pointers
    glBindBuffer(GL_ARRAY_BUFFER, m_SkinningDataBuffer[Batch]);
    //Set Bone Weight and Index Attrib pointers
    glUniform1i(m_TransformFeedback.uiBoneCount,pMesh.sBoneIdx.n);

#if defined(UBO)
    m_matrixPaletteUBO.UpdateData( m_BoneMatrixPalette[0].ptr() );
#else
    glUniformMatrix4fv(m_TransformFeedback.uiBoneMatrices,
        BONE_PALETTE_SIZE,GL_FALSE, m_BoneMatrixPalette[0].ptr());
#endif

    glDrawArrays(GL_POINTS, 0, BatchVertexCount);
    iTotalVerts += BatchVertexCount;
    glEndTransformFeedback();
    //Disable Attrib Arrays
}
glDisable(GL_RASTERIZER_DISCARD);
```

Listing 15.2. Performing the TF pass.

15.6 Animation with TF

In performing the transform feedback (TF) pass, we transform the vertices to their skinned position and write them all into a single output buffer. We bind the specific range of the output buffer to write to before beginning and ending TF for every batch; we also then bind the batch specific buffers for input data. While the input data refers to specific vertices in each batch, the bone indices are relative to the entire bone matrix palette array; as such, we passed in all the bone matrices for every pass either using a standard uniform or a UBO. (See Listing 15.2.)

We then performed the skinning normally in the shader in Listing 15.3.

15.7 Instancing for Fur Shells

We now submit the output of the transform feedback stage as a single buffer to be drawn with instancing. (See Figure 15.2.) We pass in the shell fur texture and the fur length texture, which governs the offset between layers of the fur.

```
#if defined(UBO)
layout(std140) uniform BoneMatrixStruct
{ highp mat4 BoneMatrixArray[NUM_BONE_MATRICES]; };

void main()
{
    gl_Position = vec4(inVertex,1.0); //required
    for (int i = 0; i < BoneCount; ++i)
    {
     //perform skinning normally
    }
    oPosition = position.xyz;
    oNormal = normalize(worldNormal);
}
```

Listing 15.3. TF shader.

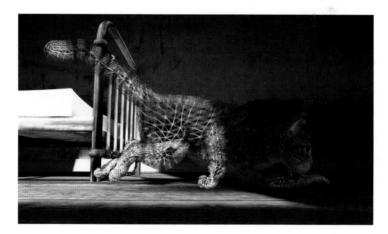

Figure 15.2. Wireframe view of the final model.

We also specify the number of instances to draw, which should be the same as the number of layers used in creating the fur texture. We found with our model, depending on platform and resolution, a count of between 11 and 25 gave good visual results while maintaining workable performance. We bind the `TexCoord` array to a structure that is created when we load our model from disk. (The vertices have not been reordered, so this data is unchanged by the process.) (See Listing 15.4.)

The shell position is then calculated in the shader as shown in Listing 15.5.

Having calculated a base alpha value per layer in the vertex shader, we sample the `StrandLengthTexture` to establish where fur should be drawn and how long it should be. We leave the base layer solid, and we alpha out strands that the random distribution decided should have ended:

```
//Bind Fur Texture, Fur Length Texture, Diffuse Texture
glUniform1i(m_FurShader.uiLayerCount, m_FurLayers);
UpdateShaderMatrices(&m_FurShader,m_WorldFromModel);
glBindBuffer(GL_ARRAY_BUFFER,m_ModelDataBuffer[0]);
//Bind Vertex, Normal Array
glBindBuffer(GL_ARRAY_BUFFER, m_OriginalModelVbo);
//Bind Texcoord Arrays
glEnable (GL_BLEND);
glBlendFunc (GL_SRC_ALPHA, GL_ONE_MINUS_SRC_ALPHA);
glDrawArraysInstanced(GL_TRIANGLES,0,nNumVertex,m_FurLayers);
glDisable(GL_BLEND);
//Disable Attrib arrays
```

Listing 15.4. Submitting the mesh.

```
InstanceID = gl_InstanceID;
oShellDist = (float(InstanceID))/(float(LayerCount)-1.0);
oAlpha = (1.0-pow(oShellDist,0.6)); //tweaked for nicer falloff
shellDist *= texture(ShellHeightTexture,inTexCoord).r;
highp vec3 shellPos = inVertex + inNormal*oShellDist;
gl_Position = ProjectionFromModel *  vec4(shellPos,1.0);
```

Listing 15.5. Instancing shader.

```
highp float alpha = oAlpha;
highp float strandLength = texture(StrandLengthTexture,
                    oTexCoord).a / (float(LayerCount)/255.0);
if(InstanceID > 0 && oShellDist > strandLength) {alpha = 0.0;}
```

15.8 Lighting and Other Effects

In our implementation, we used a minimalist Cook-Torrance BRDF [Schüler 09] to shade the model and fur. (See Figures 15.3 and 15.4 for results.) We experimented with tweaking the alpha values of the fur by hand to achieve a falloff that, when lit, gave a cleaner edge to the fur, avoiding crawling and noise.

For the environment shading, we used a precomputed diffuse reflectance texture and an analytic specular term in the shader. We also stored separate textures for the precomputed shadows so that we could seamlessly merge the shadows cast from the cat into the floor shadow. Having the cat dancing in and out of the shadow was an important part of what we were trying to achieve, and this technique worked well. (See Figure 15.5.) As we were only dealing with a single directional light, we first computed a projected shadow texture for the cat by rendering from outside the window using the preskinned mesh from the transform feedback pass. We then computed the light direction and used this to project the texture to the floor plane situated beneath the cat.

Figure 15.3. Final model lit within the scene.

Figure 15.4. Close-up of fur effect.

Figure 15.5. Model in shadow.

15.9   Conclusion

In moving from skinning every shell individually to using transform feedback, we saw a dramatic performance increase. With a low-polygon early test model on a mobile platform using 18 layers, performance increased from 29 fps to being Vsync limited at 60 fps. We were then able to increase to 30 layers and maintain a framerate above 30 fps. When we later incorporated the changes to the fur texture and incorporated instancing, we saw performance rise to 50 fps. With our final, full-detail model, on a high-performance mobile platform, we were able to run 17 shells on a 1920×1080 display. This gave more than sufficient visual quality and allowed us to render a surrounding scene and other effects, all in excess of 30 fps.

We were able to achieve a pleasing result without the additional use of fins, and our implementation also did not include any force, intersection, or self-shadowing effects. These are all additional avenues that could be explored on higher-performance platforms in the future.

Bibliography

[Kajiya and Kay 89] James T. Kajiya and Timothy L. Kay. "Rendering Fur with Three Dimensional Textures." In *Proceedings of the 16th Annual Conference on Computer Graphics and Interactive Techniques*, pp. 271–180. New York: ACM Press, 1989.

[Lacroix 13] Jason Lacroix. "Adding More Life to Your Characters with TressFX." In *ACM SIGGRAPH 2013 Computer Animation Festival*, p. 1. New York: ACM Press, 2013.

[Lengyel et al. 01] Jerome Lengyel, Emil Praun, Adam Finkelstein, and Hugues Hoppe. "Real-Time Fur over Arbitrary Surfaces." In *Proceedings of the 2001 Symposium on Interactive 3D Graphics*, pp. 227–232. New York: ACM Press, 2001.

[Schüler 09] Christian Schüler. "An Efficient and Physically Plausible Real-Time Shading Model." In *ShaderX 7*, edited by Wolfgang Engel, pp. 175–187. Boston: Cengage, 2009.

[Tariq and Bavoil 08] Sarah Tariq and Louis Bavoil. "Real Time Hair Simulation and Rendering on the GPU." In *ACM SIGGRAPH 2008 Talks*, p. artcle no. 37. New York: ACM Press, 2008.

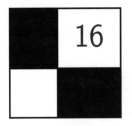

16

High Dynamic Range Computational Photography on Mobile GPUs

Simon McIntosh-Smith, Amir Chohan, Dan Curran, and Anton Lokhmotov

16.1 Introduction

Mobile GPU architectures have been evolving rapidly, and are now fully programmable, high-performance, parallel-processing engines. Parallel programming languages have also been evolving quickly, to the point where open standards such as the Khronos Group's OpenCL now put powerful cross-platform programming tools in the hands of mobile application developers.

In this chapter, we will present our work that exploits GPU computing via OpenCL and OpenGL to implement high dynamic range (HDR) computational photography applications on mobile GPUs. HDR photography is a hot topic in the mobile space, with applications to both stills photography and video.

We explore two techniques. In the first, a single image is processed in order to enhance detail in areas of the image at the extremes of the exposure. In the second technique, multiple images taken at different exposures are combined to create a single image with a greater dynamic range of luminosity. HDR can be applied to an image to achieve a different goal too: as an image filter to create a range of new and exciting visual effects in real time, somewhat akin to the "radioactive" HDR filter from Topaz Labs [Topaz Labs 15].

These HDR computational photography applications are extremely compute-intensive, and we have optimized our example OpenCL HDR code on a range of GPUs. In this chapter, we shall also describe the approach that was taken during code optimization for the ARM Mali mobile GPUs and give the performance results we achieved on these platforms.

We also share the OpenCL/OpenGL interoperability code we have developed, which we believe will be a useful resource for the reader. Surprisingly little is

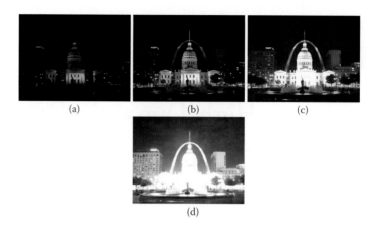

Figure 16.1. Images taken with different exposures: (a) −4 stops, (b) −2 stops, (c) +2 stops, and (d) +4 stops. [Image from [McCoy 08].]

available in the literature on how to efficiently implement HDR pipelines, and even less as real source code. We hope this chapter will address both of these shortcomings.

16.2 Background

Real-world scenes contain a much higher dynamic range of brightness than can be captured by the sensors available in most cameras today. Digital cameras use 8 bits per pixel for each of the red, green, and blue channels, therefore storing only 256 different values per color channel. Real-world scenes, however, can have a dynamic range on the order of about $10^8 : 1$, therefore requiring up to 32 bits per pixel per channel to represent fully.

To compensate for their relatively low dynamic range (LDR), modern digital cameras are equipped with advanced computer graphics algorithms for producing high-resolution images that meet the increasing demand for more dynamic range, color depth, and accuracy. In order to produce an HDR image, these cameras either synthesize inputs taken concurrently from multiple lenses with different exposures, or they take multiple-exposure images in sequential order and combine them into a single scene. Figure 16.1 shows a set of over- and underexposed images of a scene that can be captured in such a way.

The synthesis process produces a 32-bit image encoding the full HDR of the scene. Standard displays, such as computer monitors, TVs, and smartphone or tablet screens, however, only have a dynamic range of around $256 : 1$, which means that they are not capable of accurately displaying the rendered HDR image. Therefore, to display HDR images on a standard display, the images first

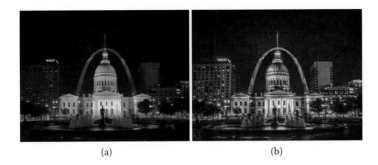

          (a)   (b)

Figure 16.2. HDR images obtained using (a) global and (b) local tone-mapping operators. [Image from [McCoy 08].]

need to be compressed to a lower dynamic range in a way that preserves image detail. This process of compressing an HDR image to a lower dynamic range is called *tone mapping*. Once a 32-bit HDR image is tone mapped, the resulting 8-bit HDR image can then be rendered to standard displays. Figure 16.2 shows examples of the outputs of two different tone-mapping operators (TMOs).

16.2.1 Smartphone Photography

Today, nearly all digital cameras embed EXIF (exchangeable image file format) information about each image [Chaney 15]. This information contains dozens of parameters from the time the picture was taken, including camera aperture, exposure, GPS location, etc. Recently, the photo-sharing network Flickr marked a shift in how people take pictures, noting that the majority of images being uploaded to their site were now being taken using smartphones. Smartphone cameras have greatly improved in the last few years, introducing higher megapixel counts, better lenses, and since 2010 an option to take HDR images [GSM Arena 15]. Increasing use of such cameras has led to the emerging field of *high dynamic range imaging* (HDRI).

To obtain an HDR image, a smartphone takes multiple images in quick succession with different exposures. The motivation behind taking multiple-exposure images is to obtain detail in over- and underexposed parts of the image, which is often otherwise lost due to a camera's auto gain control. These images are then synthesized and a TMO is applied to render the HDR image on the screen.

HDRI blends several LDR images taken at different exposures highlighting light and dark parts of a scene (as in Figure 16.1). These multiple-exposure images take a varying amount of time to acquire. For example, an overexposed image that brings out detail in the dark parts of an image needs to leave the camera shutter open for longer to allow for more light to get through. Therefore, in order to acquire HDR images of a scene in real time, multiple lenses are needed

Figure 16.3. HDR look achieved by Topaz Adjust: (a) original image and (b) HDR image.

looking at the same scene with the use of a beam splitter. Unfortunately, most mobile phones and other handheld cameras do not yet come with the multiple lenses that would be required to acquire multiple-exposure images in real time. For this reason, the HDR TMOs we present in this chapter not only perform well on 32-bit HDR images but also bring out details in a single-exposure LDR image, giving them a HDR look.

Figure 16.3 shows the results of an HDR effect on a single image as obtained by Topaz Adjust, a plug-in for Adobe Photoshop [Topaz Labs 15]. The plugin is able to enhance local gradients that are hard to see in the original image. Furthermore, photographers often manually apply a pseudo-HDR effect on an LDR image to make it more aesthetically pleasing. One way to achieve such a pseudo-HDR effect, as described by Kim Y. Seng [Seng 10], is to create under- and overexposed versions of a well-exposed LDR image. Seng then uses these artificial under- and overexposed images as the basis for creating a 32-bit HDR image before tone-mapping it using a TMO.

16.2.2 Efficient Smartphone Image Processing Pipelines

Currently, most applications running on mobile devices tend to use the CPU, perhaps exploiting SIMD instructions, to run the compute part of the code and use the GPU just for the graphics part, such as compositing and rendering to the screen. However, today's mobile GPUs are now fully programmable compute units in themselves, and through new languages such as OpenCL, or extensions to existing APIs, such as the latest compute shaders in OpenGL, the GPU can also help with the computationally intensive "heavy lifting" required by the application. Using the GPU in this way can result in higher framerates, but there can be more than just a performance advantage from using the GPU for some of the application's computational needs. An experiment carried out by S. Huang et al. to compare the energy consumptions of a single-core CPU, a multicore CPU, and a GPU showed that using the GPU can result in much more energy-efficient computation [Huang et al. 09]. For mobile devices, this energy saving translates into improved battery life, and thus using general-purpose computing on GPUs (GPGPU) has become a hot topic for mobile applications.

One aim of this chapter is to describe an efficient, open source implementation of a pipeline that can be used to capture camera frames and display output of HDR TMOs in real time. The second aim of the example presented in this chapter is to demonstrate an efficient code framework that minimizes the amount of time taken to acquire the camera frames and render the display to output. The pipeline should be such that it can be used for any image-processing application that requires input from a camera and renders the output to a display. This pipeline should also make it possible to create HDR videos.

We present our example pipeline in OpenCL to serve as a real, worked example of how to exploit GPU computing in mobile platforms. We also exploit OpenCL/OpenGL interoperability with the goal of equipping the reader with a working template from which other OpenCL/OpenGL applications can be quickly developed.

16.3 Tone-Mapping Operators

Tone-mapping operators exist for a range of applications. Some TMOs are designed to focus on producing aesthetically pleasing results, while others focus on reproducing as much image detail as possible or maximizing the image contrast. TMOs can be broadly classified into *global* and *local* operators.

Global operators are nonlinear functions that use luminance and other global variables of an input image to obtain a mapping of all the input pixels to the output pixels. Each individual pixel is then mapped in the same way, independent of any neighboring pixels. This spatially uniform characteristic of global TMOs often results in the unfortunate side effect of local contrast reduction. However, because global TMOs are easy to implement and computationally inexpensive (compared to local TMOs), they are prime candidates for use in digital cameras and other handheld devices that might be computationally limited.

Local TMOs have a different mapping for each pixel in the original image. The function used by these operators changes for each pixel depending on the local features of the image. These spatially varying local operators are much slower to compute and harder to implement than global operators and can often result in artifacts in certain areas of the image, making the output look unrealistic. However, if implemented correctly, they generally provide better results than global TMOs, since human vision is mainly sensitive to local contrast.

Figure 16.2 shows the results of applying global and local TMOs to an HDR image obtained by synthesizing the LDR images in Figure 16.1. Even though the global TMO is able to highlight details from each of the exposures, the results of the local TMO are much more aesthetically pleasing, as there is more local contrast in the image.

Reinhard's global TMO. The tonal range of an image describes the number of tones between the lightest and darkest part of the image. Reinhard et al. implemented one of the most widely used global TMOs for HDRI, which computes the tonal range for the output image [Reinhard et al. 02]. This tonal range is computed based on the logarithmic luminance values in the original images.

The algorithm first computes the average logarithmic luminance of the entire image. This average, along with another parameter, is then used to scale the original luminances. Then, to further allow for more global contrast in the image, this approach lets the high luminances often "burn out" by clamping them to pure white. This burning out step is accomplished by computing the smallest luminance value in the original image and then scaling all of the pixels accordingly.

For many HDR images, this operator is sufficient to preserve details in low-contrast areas, while compressing higher luminances to a displayable range. However for very high dynamic range images, especially where there is varying local contrast, important detail can still be lost.

Reinhard's global TMO uses the key value of the scene to set the tonal range for the output image. The key of a scene can be approximated using the logarithmic average luminance $\bar{L}_w$:

$$\bar{L}_w = \exp\left(\frac{1}{N}\sum_{x,y}\log(\delta + L_w(x,y))\right),$$

where $L_w(x,y)$ is the luminance of pixel (x,y), N is the total number of pixels in the image, and δ is a very small value to avoid taking the logarithm of 0 in case there are pure black pixels in the image. Having approximated the key of the scene, we need to map this to middle-gray. For well-lit images, Reinhard proposes a value of 0.18 as middle-gray on a scale of 0 to 1, giving rise to the following equation:

$$L(x,y) = \frac{a}{\bar{L}_w}L_w(x,y), \tag{16.1}$$

where $L(x,y)$ is the scaled luminance and $a = 0.18$. Just as in film-based photography, if the image has a low key value, we would like to map the middle-gray value, i.e, $\underline{\bar{L}}_w$, to a high value of a to bring out details in the darker parts of the image. Similarly, if the image has a high key value, we would like to map $\underline{\bar{L}}_w$ to a lower value of a to get contrast in the lighter parts of the scene. In most natural scenes, occurrences of high luminance values are quite low, whereas the majority of the pixel values have a normal dynamic range. Equation (16.1) doesn't take this into account and scales all the values linearly.

Reinhard's global TMO can now be defined as

$$L_d(x,y) = \frac{L(x,y)\left(1 + \frac{L(x,y)}{L_{\text{white}}^2}\right)}{1 + L(x,y)}, \tag{16.2}$$

where L_{white} is the smallest luminance that we would like to be burnt out. Although L_{white} can be another user-controlled parameter, in this implementation we will set it to the maximum luminance in the image, L_{max}. This will prevent any burn out; however, in cases where $L_{\text{max}} < 1$, this will result in contrast enhancement, as previously discussed.

The operator has a user-controlled parameter, a. This is the key value and refers to the subjective brightness of a scene: the middle-gray value that the scene is mapped to. Essentially, setting a to a high value has an effect of compressing the dynamic range for darker areas, thus allowing more dynamic range for lighter areas and resulting in more contrast over that region. Similarly, decreasing a reduces the dynamic range for lighter areas and shows more contrast in darker parts of a scene. Since the brightness of a scene is very much subjective to the photographer, in this implementation a will be a controllable parameter that can be changed by the user.

The global TMO is one of the most widely implemented TMOs because of its simplicity and effectiveness. It brings out details in low-contrast regions while compressing high luminance values. Furthermore, Equation (16.1) and Equation (16.2) are performed on each pixel independently, and therefore it is fairly straightforward to implement a data parallel version using OpenCL in order to exploit the compute capability of the GPU.

Reinhard's local TMO. Although the global TMO works well in bringing out details in most images, detail is still lost for very high dynamic range images. Reinhard's local TMO proposes a tone reproduction algorithm that aims to emphasize these details by applying *dodging* and *burning*.

Dodging and burning is a technique used in traditional photography that involves restraining light (dodging) or adding more light (burning) to parts of the print during development. Reinhard et al. extended this idea for digital images by automating the process for each pixel depending on its neighborhood. This equates to finding a local key, i.e., a in Equation (16.1), for each pixel, which can then be used to determine the amount of dodging and burning needed for the region. Along with the key value a, the size of each region can also vary depending on the contrast in that area of the image. This size depends on the local contrast of the pixel. To find the optimal size region over which to compute a, Reinhard's approach uses a *center-surround* function at multiple scales. Center-surround functions are often implemented by subtracting two Gaussian blurred images. For this TMO, Reinhard chose to implement the center-surround function proposed for Blommaert's model for brightness perception [Blommaert and Martens 90]. This function is constructed using Gaussian profiles of the form

$$R_i(x, y, s) = \frac{1}{\pi(\alpha_i s)^2} \exp\left(-\frac{x^2 + y^2}{(\alpha_i s)^2}\right).$$

This circularly symmetric profile is constructed for different scales s around each pixel (x, y) in the image. In Bloommaert's center-surround function, the Gaussian profile is then convolved with the image, resulting in response V_i as a function of scale s and luminance $L(x, y)$ for each pixel (x, y):

$$V_i(x, y, s) = L(x, y) \otimes R_i(x, y, s). \tag{16.3}$$

Because the response requires convolving two functions, it can either be performed in the spatial domain or they can be multiplied in the Fourier domain for improved efficiency. The example HDR GPU pipeline described in this chapter makes use of mipmaps as an alternative to the Gaussian profile. Equation (16.4) is the final building block required for Bloommaert's center-surround function:

$$V(x, y, s) = \frac{V_1(x, y, s) - V_2(x, y, s)}{2^\phi a/s^2 + V_1(x, y, s)}, \tag{16.4}$$

where V_1 is the center response function and V_2 is the surround response function obtained using Equation (16.3). The $2^\phi a/s^2$ term in the denominator prevents V from getting too large when V_1 approaches zero. The motive behind having V_1 in the denominator is discussed later. Similarly to the global TMO, a is the key value of the scene, φ is a sharpening parameter, and s is the scale used to compute the response function.

The center-surround function expressed in Equation (16.4) is computed over several scales s to find the optimal scale s_m. This equates to finding the suitably sized neighborhood for each pixel, and therefore plays an important role in the dodging-and-burning technique. An ideal-sized neighborhood would have very little contrast changes in the neighborhood itself; however, the area surrounding the neighborhood would have more contrast. The center-surround function computes the difference between the center response V_1 and surround response V_2. For areas with similar luminance values, these will be much the same, however they will differ in higher-contrast regions. Starting at the lowest scale, the local TMO selects the first scale s_m such that

$$|V(x, y, s_m)| < \epsilon, \tag{16.5}$$

where ε is a user controlled parameter, which we set to 0.05 in our implementation. Equation (16.5) amounts to finding the largest neighborhood around a pixel such that the luminance in the center area is fairly even. Note that $V_1(x, y, s)$ can serve as a local neighborhood average for that pixel. Therefore, this local logarithmic average luminance can be used in place of the global one in Equation (16.2):

$$L_d(x, y) = \frac{L(x, y)}{1 + V_1(x, y, s_m)}. \tag{16.6}$$

A dark pixel in a relatively bright area will satisfy $L < V_1$. In such cases, Equation (16.6) will decrease the L_d of that pixel, which will have the effect of contrast enhancement in that area. Similarly, if a pixel is light in a relatively dark area ($L > V_1$), the local TMO will increase L_d.

$V_1(x, y, s_m)$ plays an important part in controlling the right amount of local contrast in the image. This boils down to choosing the right s_m for each pixel. If s_m is too small, then V_1 will be close to L and Equation (16.6) will reduce to the global operator. However, if s_m is too large, then the resulting tone-mapped image will have halo artifacts around the bright regions.

The set of scale sizes to check can be predetermined. Reinhard's method does not suggest any particular set of scales; however, the implementation proposed by Akyuz [Akyüz 12] suggests using the scale set $\{1, 2, 4, 8, 16, 32, 64\}$. To find the optimal scale s_m, we start from the smallest scale and compute center and surround responses individually for each. To make the algorithm computationally efficient, Reinhard's method suggests setting the center size of the next higher scale to be the size of the current surround. It further suggests maintaining the ratio of 1.6 between the center and surround size; however, since mipmaps are used in this implementation, the next level mipmap can simply be set as the surround.

Just as for the global operator, a is still a user-controlled variable allowing the photographer to obtain more contrast for either dark or light parts of the scene while decreasing the contrast in the other. The local TMO comes with a few more parameters, namely φ and ε. In Equation (16.5), ε serves as a threshold to find the suitable scale s_m for the pixel neighborhood. A small ε causes s_m to be larger and hence results in an increased contrast in the overall image, since there is more contrast at larger scales than smaller ones. On the other hand, φ serves as an edge-enhancing parameter. Increasing φ has more or less the same effects as that of decreasing ε. However, the effects are only noticeable at smaller scales since φ is divided by s^2.

Reinhard's local TMO makes use of traditional photographic techniques to enhance contrast in digital images. The concept behind the local and global operators is more or less the same; however, the local TMO uses information in the pixel's neighborhood to find the suitable "local key" and use that to scale the pixel's luminance. The local TMO is inherently much more compute-intensive due to multiple convolutions required for each pixel to find the suitable neighborhood. This makes the local TMO much more challenging to implement in real time. In this implementation, to minimize the computation required, mipmaps are generated at multiple levels using the OpenGL API instead of using the more compute-intensive Gaussian kernel approach.

Histogram equalization. Contrast enhancement using histogram equalization is one simple way of increasing the global contrast of many images, especially when there isn't much variance between the luminance values in those images. Histogram equalization essentially spreads these densely populated values over the entire luminance range (usually 8-bit), increasing the contrast in low-contrast areas.

The algorithm computes a histogram of the luminance values for an image, calculates its cumulative distribution function (CDF), and then replaces the original histogram with the flattened version of the CDF. The histogram will then have luminance values uniformly distributed over the entire range [UCI iCAMP 10].

Histogram equalization is not an HDR TMO; however, it can be computationally expensive. Our framework is not just limited to HDRI TMOs.

16.4   Related Work

The LDR of cameras has inspired many solutions to produce TMOs for HDR images in recent years. J. Kuang et al. performed a study to compare several existing HDR rendering algorithms [Kuang et al. 07]. In their study, they implemented nine different algorithms and carried out psychophysical experiments whereby they required human observers to evaluate the rendered image. Their results could be useful when selecting an HDR algorithm to implement based solely on the output image. However, the paper does not provide a comparative performance analysis between techniques. In this chapter, we will show results from implementations of several TMOs and compare their performance on various GPUs.

Sing Bing Kang et al. proposed a method to generate an HDR video by taking multiple-exposure images in quick succession [Kang et al. 03]. They did this by automatically determining the temporal exposure bracketing during capture, motion-compensating information between neighboring images, and tone mapping for viewing the results. We take a different approach in this chapter, as we will focus on processing single-exposure images as opposed to multiple images of different exposures. The technique presented by Kang et al. is quite effective, however the frame rate is limited by the rate at which the camera can vary exposures. Motion between exposures can become a problem, and so Kang's method required an algorithm to account for motion between the images. Their implementation was too slow for real-time image processing.

TMOs, in particular local operators, are computationally expensive and therefore currently require a GPU implementation to be able to operate in real time. There have been several proposed real-time implementations of Reinhard's global and local TMOs [Akyüz 12, Krawczyk et al. 05, Chiu et al. 11, Kiser et al. 12]. However, the real-time OpenGL implementation proposed by Akyuz in [Akyüz 12] is most relevant to this research topic. Akyuz presented an HDRI pipeline on the GPU for Reinhard's global and local TMOs. Although the implementation is in OpenGL (as opposed to OpenCL), it provides an insight on how the algorithm can be modified for a GPGPU implementation. We can also use the results from Akyuz's work as an efficiency benchmark for the OpenCL implementation we present in this chapter.

Perhaps the most closely related work to ours is that by Chris McClanahan [McClanahan 11]. McClanahan created a Linux and Android application that uses a single video camera to create tone-mapped HDR images in real time. The implementation uses OpenCV and OpenMP but does not appear to include a GPGPU implementation. Furthermore, the frame rate of the Linux implementation is very low, even on low-resolution images. Nevertheless, McClanahan's work provides a benchmark against which we can compare.

16.5 GPGPU Using OpenCL

Traditionally, a GPU was designed for one task: speeding up the processing of an image that ends up being rendered to a screen. Today's GPUs are now highly data parallel computational engines, making them really good at performing the same calculation over and over on different data.

Upon evaluating the HDR TMO discussed in this chapter, it should be obvious that often similar operations are applied on each individual pixel in the image. Therefore, these algorithms should benefit from being executed on a GPU. However, in order to take advantage of the highly concurrent nature of a GPU, the algorithms have to be programmed to take advantage of it. Implementing algorithms in such a way is called general purpose computing on GPUs (GPGPU).

This brings us nicely to OpenCL (Open Computing Language). OpenCL is a cross-platform open standard for parallel programming across different kinds of hardware, and can target both CPUs and GPUs, and from embedded SoCs to high-end desktop, workstation, and server GPUs. The framework is standardized by the Khronos Group, which includes ARM, Imagination, Qualcomm, AMD, Intel, NVIDIA, IBM, Samsung, Apple, and most of the other vendors in the CPU/GPU space.

OpenCL 1.0 was released in late 2008, and support by multiple CPU and GPU vendors appeared by mid-2009. Since its initial release, OpenCL has evolved rapidly through two minor releases (OpenCL 1.1 in 2010 and 1.2 in 2011) and a major OpenCL 2.0 release in late 2013. The rapid pace of evolution in the OpenCL standard is challenging for programmers to track and absorb. These modifications to the standard have been necessary, due to the rapid pace of evolution in computer hardware.

This section will now focus on the core features of OpenCL—those that have not changed much since the introduction of the first standard. We explain OpenCL in terms of its key models:

- platform model,

- execution model,

- memory model.

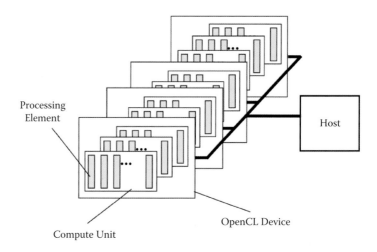

Figure 16.4. The OpenCL platform model with a single host and multiple devices. Each device has one or more compute units, each of which has one or more processing elements.

The *platform* model is presented in Figure 16.4 and consists of a host and one or more devices. The *host* is a familiar CPU-based system supporting file I/O, user interaction, and other functions expected of a system. The *devices* are where the bulk of the computing takes place in an OpenCL program. Example devices include GPUs, many-core coprocessors, and other devices specialized to carry out the OpenCL computations. A device consists of one or more compute units (CUs) each of which presents the programmer with one or more processing elements (PEs). These processing elements are the finest-grained units of computation within an OpenCL program.

The platform model gives programmers a view of the hardware they can use when optimizing their OpenCL programs. Then, by understanding how the platform model maps onto different target platforms, programmers can optimize their software without sacrificing portability.

OpenCL programs execute as a fine-grained SPMD (single program, multiple data) model. The central ideal behind OpenCL is to define an index space of one, two, or three dimensions. Programmers map their problem onto the indices of this space and define a block of code, called a *kernel*, an instance of which runs at each point in the index space.

Consider the matrix multiplication OpenCL kernel in Listing 16.1. Here we have mapped the outermost two loops of the traditional sequential code onto a 2D index space and run the innermost loop (over k) within a kernel function. We then ran an instance of this kernel function, called a *work item* in OpenCL terminology, for each point in the index space.

```
__kernel void mat_mul(const unsigned int Order,
                      __global const float *A,
                      __global const float *B,
                      __global       float *C)
{
  int i, j, k;
  i = get_global_id(0);
  j = get_global_id(1);
  for (k = 0; k < Order; k++)
    C[i*Order+j] += A[i*Order+k] * B[k*Order+j];
}
```

Listing 16.1. A parallel matrix multiply as an OpenCL kernel.

A more detailed view of how an OpenCL program executes is provided in Figure 16.5, which summarizes the OpenCL *execution* model. The global index space, in this case two dimensions each of size 16, implies a set of work items that execute a kernel instance at each point. These work items are grouped together into blocks with the same shape as the global index space. Blocks of work items, called *work groups*, cover the full index space.

Logically, the work items in a single work group run together. Hence, they can synchronize their execution and share memory in the course of their computation. This is not the case, however, for the work groups. There are no ordering constraints among the work groups of a single kernel instance; hence, there are no synchronization constructs among work groups. This limitation has important implications for sharing data, which we will cover as part of the memory hierarchy discussion.

To a programmer used to the flexibility of programming with threads (e.g., Pthreads, Java threads, etc.), these restrictions on synchronization may seem onerous. They were included in the OpenCL execution model, however, for a good reason. OpenCL is designed for high-throughput parallel computing typically associated with highly data parallel algorithms. High performance is achieved by creating a large internal work pool of work groups that are ready to execute. A scheduler can then stream these runnable work groups through the compute units of a device to keep them fully occupied.

Because compute devices such as GPUs may have their own discrete memories, a heterogeneous platform often cannot provide a single coherent address space. The *memory* model in OpenCL, therefore, takes this into account by defining how the memory in OpenCL is decomposed into different address spaces aligned with the platform model. We present this concept in Figure 16.6.

Starting at the bottom of Figure 16.6, consider the host memory. As the name implies, *host memory* is defined by the host and only directly visible to the host (although this is relaxed in OpenCL 2.0). The next layer in the memory hierarchy is the *global memory*, which includes a read-only memory segment called the

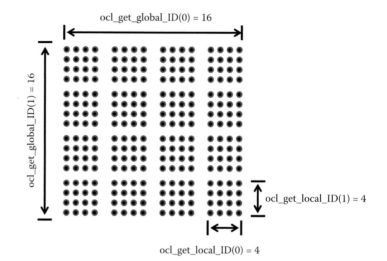

Figure 16.5. A problem is decomposed onto the points of an N-dimensional index space ($N = 1$, 2, or 3), known in OpenCL as an `NDRange`. A kernel instance runs at each point in the `NDRange` to define a work item. Work items are grouped together into work groups, which evenly tile the full index space.

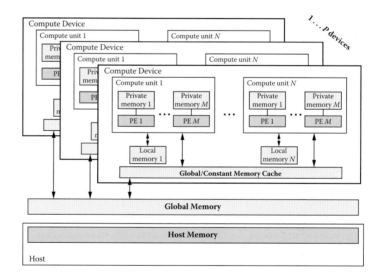

Figure 16.6. The memory model in OpenCL 1.X and its relationship to the platform model. Here, P devices exist in a single context and therefore have visibility into the global/constant memory.

constant memory. Global and constant memories hold OpenCL memory objects and are visible to all the OpenCL devices involved in a computation (i.e., within the context defined by the programmer). The onboard DRAM of a discrete GPU or FPGA will typically be mapped as global memory. It is worth noting that, for discrete devices, moving data between host memory and global memory usually requires transferring data across a bus, such as PCI Express, which can be relatively slow.

Within an OpenCL device, each compute unit has a region of memory local to the compute unit called *local memory.* This local memory is visible only to the processing elements within the compute unit, which maps nicely onto the OpenCL execution model, with one or more work groups running on a compute unit and one or more work items running on a processing element. The local memory within a compute unit corresponds to data that can be shared inside a work group. The final part of the OpenCL memory hierarchy is *private memory,* which defines a small amount of per work-item memory visible only within a work item.

Another important OpenCL buffer type for any application that wants to mix OpenCL and OpenGL functionality, is the *textured images* buffer. These are available in 2D and 3D and are a global memory object optimized for image processing, supporting multiple image formats and channels. There is a one-to-one correspondence between an OpenCL textured image and certain OpenGL textures. In fact, as discussed later, this correspondence can be taken advantage of to optimize the framework we will present in this chapter.

Data movement among the layers in the memory hierarchy in OpenCL is explicit—that is, the user is responsible for the transfer of data from host memory to global memory and so on. Commands in the OpenCL API and kernel programming language must be used to move data from host memory to global memory, and from global memory to either local or private memory.

16.6   OpenGL ES and Android

OpenGL is a "cross-platform graphics API that specifies a standard software interface for 3D graphics processing hardware" [Android 15]. OpenGL ES is a subset of the OpenGL specification intended for embedded devices. Although a powerful API in itself, the main use of OpenGL ES in the implemented Android version of our HDR framework is to provide image acquisition and to render the output of our OpenCL TMO kernels to the display. All of the manipulation of the images in our example framework is performed by OpenCL kernels.

16.6.1   OpenCL and OpenGL Interoperability

One of the main hurdles in achieving a real-time implementation of an Android pipeline to process and render camera images is the transfer of image data to and from the GPU's memory. Although the camera input is stored on the GPU, existing image-processing applications tend to transfer the data to the host device (the CPU), where they serially process the data and render it to the display using OpenGL. Clearly this process can cause several inefficient transfers of data back and forth between the CPU and GPU.

What is required is an approach that avoids any unnecessary memory transfers between the GPU's memory and the host's memory. OpenCL/OpenGL interoperability supports this approach. Input from the camera can be acquired in the form of an OpenGL ES texture using Android's `SurfaceTexture` object. OpenCL then allows a programmer to create a textured image from an OpenGL texture, which means that the camera data doesn't need to be transferred to the host, instead staying resident in the GPU from image acquisition all the way to rendering the output of the OpenCL kernels to the screen. Furthermore, even on the GPU, the data doesn't actually move as we switch between OpenCL and OpenGL; instead it just changes ownership from OpenGL to OpenCL and back again. To achieve this pipeline, interoperability between OpenCL and OpenGL ES needs to be established.

16.6.2   EGL

To enable OpenCL and OpenGL ES interoperability, the OpenCL context must be initialized using the current display and context being used by OpenGL ES. OpenGL ES contexts are created and managed by platform-specific windowing APIs. EGL is an interface between OpenGL ES and the underlying windowing system, somewhat akin to GLX, the X11 interface to OpenGL with which many readers might already be familiar.

To avoid unnecessary use of memory bandwidth, the implementation makes use of OpenGL ES to bind the input from the camera to a texture. An OpenGL ES display and context is then created by acquiring a handle to the Android Surface. The context and display are then used to create a shared OpenCL context. This shared context allows OpenCL to have access to the camera texture and therefore to perform computations upon it. Because the Android OS has only recently included support for such APIs, to date not many examples have appeared in this area.

16.7   Implementing an HDR Pipeline Using OpenCL and OpenGL ES

TMOs work best on a 32-bit HDR image obtained by synthesizing multiple LDR images of various exposures. The 32-bit HDR image is then processed to obtain an 8-bit HDR image that combines details from each of the original LDR images.

To achieve a real-time implementation of the HDRI pipeline, multiple cameras are required, with each capturing a different-exposure image and therefore capturing the full dynamic range of the scene among them. However, as discussed earlier, since we are aiming for an implementation on a smartphone with a single camera, we will only have single-exposure images available to us as input for our real-time pipeline. This section discusses the design and implementation details of a GPU pipeline using OpenCL to achieve an HDR look on single-exposure images.

For the example HDR pipeline presented in the rest of this chapter, we used OpenCL v1.1, since this version is supported by all mobile GPU vendors at the time of writing. We also used OpenGL ES 4.2 since this is the version of GL currently supported by the Android OS. We have also written the code in C/C++ in order to achieve the best performance possible (OpenCL/GL bindings for Java, Python, etc. exist, but would not have given the necessary performance).

16.7.1 Pseudo-HDR Pipeline with Image Synthesis

Multiple-exposure images are a set of under- and overexposed LDR images highlighting details in bright and dark regions of a scene, respectively. It's common practice to adjust an image's brightness and contrast to highlight its dark or bright regions. Since here we are limited to using a single-exposure image as the input for our process, we can use a set of such adjusted images as inputs to the pseudo-HDR pipeline.

This is a commonly used approach. For example, Seng manually created a set of over- and underexposed images from a single RAW image using Photomatix [Seng 10]. He then used Photomatix's HDR feature to synthesize and tone-map the pseudo-underexposed and pseudo-overexposed images to create a pseudo-HDR image. This section discusses how this method can be automated. Figure 16.7 shows the modified pipeline to obtain a pseudo-HDR image using single-exposure images.

Step 1: Contrast adjustment. To employ Seng's method for our psuedo-HDR pipeline, we first need to create multiple-exposure images by adjusting the contrast of a well-exposed original image. Here we create multiple images such that each output image brings out details in a certain dynamic range. For our purposes, we used Photomatix to create the under- and overexposed versions of our original input image.

Step 2: Image synthesis. To obtain an HDR image, the multiple-exposure LDR images of a scene are first synthesized. An HDR pixel I_j can be obtained as follows:

$$I_j = \frac{\sum_{i=1}^{N} \frac{p_{ij} w(p_{ij})}{t_i}}{\sum_{i=1}^{N} w(p_{ij})}, \tag{16.7}$$

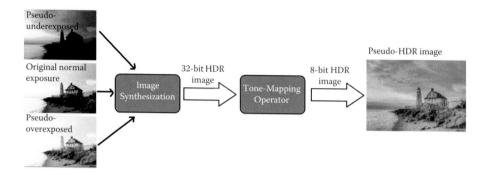

Figure 16.7. Pseudo-HDR pipeline that takes multiple input images with a range of contrasts.

where N is the number of LDR images, $w(p_{ij})$ is the weight of pixel ij, and t_i is the exposure time of the LDR image i.

The serial implementation of Equation (16.7) is straightforward and is therefore not presented here. The algorithm simply iterates over each pixel, computes its luminance and weight, and uses those with the image exposure to calculate the 32-bit HDR pixel color.

Clearly the calculation of each pixel is independent of all the others, and so this natural data parallelism is ideal for a GPU implementation.

Listing 16.2 shows the OpenCL kernel implemented for the image synthesis process. Since the number of LDR images can vary, the kernel is passed a 1D array, `LDRimages`, containing all the images. The 1D array is of type `unsigned char`, which is sufficient to store each 8-bit color value per pixel.

The `if` statement on line 10 ensures that the work items don't access out-of-bound memory. The `for` loop on line 14 uses Equation (16.7) to synthesize the LDR pixels from different images into an HDR pixel. Once an HDR pixel is calculated, it is stored in the 1D array `HDRimage`. The array `HDRimage` is of type `float`, which is sufficient to store the higher dynamic range of the pixel.

Step 3: Automating contrast adjustment. We now have a 32-bit HDR image. The three tone-mapping algorithms we have previously described can now be used to tone map the 32-bit HDR image, producing an 8-bit HDR image that can be rendered on most displays. Their implementation is discussed in more detail later on in this chapter.

16.7.2   HDR Tone-Mapping Operators

This section will describe the OpenCL implementations of the three tone-mapping algorithms.

```
1  //LDRimages contains num_images LDR images
2  //exposures contains num_images exposures, one for each LDR image
3  //HDRimage is the output synthesised 32-bit image.
4  kernel void stitch( __global uchar* LDRimages,
5                      __global float* exposures,
6                      __global float* HDRimage) {
7
8    int gid = get_global_id(0); //ID in the entire global memory
9
10   if (gid < IMAGE_SIZE) {
11     float weightedSum = 0;
12     float3 hdr, ldr;
13     hdr.x = hdr.y = hdr.z = 0;
14     for (int i=0; i < NUM_IMAGES; i++) {
15       ldr.x = LDRimages[i*IMAGE_SIZE*4 + (gid*4 + 0)];
16       ldr.y = LDRimages[i*IMAGE_SIZE*4 + (gid*4 + 1)];
17       ldr.z = LDRimages[i*IMAGE_SIZE*4 + (gid*4 + 2)];
18
19       float luminance = getPixelLuminance(ldr);
20       float w = weight(luminance);
21       float exposure = exposures[i];
22
23       hdr.x += (ldr.x/exposure) * w;
24       hdr.y += (ldr.y/exposure) * w;
25       hdr.z += (ldr.z/exposure) * w;
26
27       weightedSum += w;
28     }
29
30     HDRimage[gid*4 + 0] = hdr.x/(weightedSum + 0.000001);
31     HDRimage[gid*4 + 1] = hdr.y/(weightedSum + 0.000001);
32     HDRimage[gid*4 + 2] = hdr.z/(weightedSum + 0.000001);
33     HDRimage[gid*4 + 3] = getPixelLuminance(hdr);
34   }
35 }
```

Listing 16.2. OpenCL kernel for image synthesis.

Histogram equalization. The histogram equalization algorithm first computes the brightness histogram of the image. A cumulative distribution function (CDF) of the histogram is then created, which in turn is used to create a new set of brightness values for the image. This process requires several steps, described below.

Brightness histogram. In OpenCL, writes to global memory cannot be synchronized between work items in different work groups. Therefore, a global histogram array can't be used to accumulate the results, as it would result in race conditions between work items. Instead, local histogram arrays are used—one for each work group. The results of these per-work-group histograms are written to global memory, which are then safely merged together into a single histogram by a separate kernel.

The code to perform this partial histogram is included in Listing 16.3 (see kernels `partial_hist` and `merge_hist`). These take an LDR image as an

```
1 const sampler_t sampler = CLK_NORMALIZED_COORDS_FALSE | ↩
      CLK_ADDRESS_NONE | CLK_FILTER_NEAREST;
2
3 //Kernel to perform histogram equalization using the modified
4 //brightness CDF
5 kernel void histogram_equalisation( read_only image2d_t input_image,
6                    write_only image2d_t output_image,
7                    __global uint* brightness_cdf) {
8   int2 pos;
9   uint4 pixel;
10  float3 hsv;
11  for (pos.y = get_global_id(1); pos.y < HEIGHT; pos.y += ↩
        get_global_size(1)) {
12    for (pos.x = get_global_id(0); pos.x < WIDTH; pos.x += ↩
          get_global_size(0)) {
13      pixel = read_imageui(image, sampler, pos);
14
15      hsv = RGBtoHSV(pixel);  //Convert to HSV to get hue and
16                             //saturation
17
18      hsv.z = ((HIST_SIZE-1)*(brightness_cdf[(int)hsv.z] - ↩
          brightness_cdf[0]))
19          /(HEIGHT*WIDTH - brightness_cdf[0]);
20
21      pixel = HSVtoRGB(hsv);  //Convert back to RGB with the
22                             //modified brightness for V
23
24      write_imageui(output_image, pos, pixel);
25    }
26  }
27 }
```

Listing 16.3. OpenCL kernel to equalize the image histogram.

input and, allocating one pixel to each work item, compute the brightness value for each pixel. Once the brightness value is computed, the index corresponding to that value is incremented in the local histogram array `l_hist`. To ensure correct synchronization among different work items, a `barrier` call is made just before writing to the shared `l_hist` array. Once the `l_hist` array has been modified, the results are written to the global partial histogram array. The `merge_hist` kernel then merges the partial histograms together. This kernel is executed with global size of 256, so as to have a one-to-one correspondence between the work items and the indices of the image histogram. For this last kernel, each work item computes the sum over all the partial histograms for the index value corresponding to the work item's ID. Once the sum is computed, the final histogram value for this work item is then set to this sum.

Cumulative distribution function. Computing the cumulative distribution function is an operation that is not so well suited for GPGPU, due to the sequential nature of the algorithm required to compute it. Several OpenCL SDKs provide implementations of a parallel scan, which can be used to compute the cumulative distribution function of a histogram. However, since the histogram is only of size 256, it is not very computationally expensive to compute this sequentially.

Histogram equalization. Once the CDF of the original histogram has been computed, it can be used to compute new brightness values for each pixel; see Listing 16.3. Once the RGB pixel is obtained from the image using an OpenCL image sampler, it is converted to HSV format on line 14. Using the formulation discussed earlier, we then compute the equalized brightness value for this pixel. The HSV value with the modified V is then converted to RGB on line 19, before the results are written to the image.

Unlike previous kernels, this kernel is executed in 2D. This is because the output image is a textured 2D image as opposed to a 1D buffer.

16.7.3   Reinhard Global Tone-Mapping Operator

Reinhard's global TMO iterates over the entire image twice, once to compute $L_{\max}$ and $\bar{L}_w$ and a second time to adjust each pixel according to these values and the key value (a) of the scene.

Computing $L_{\max}$ and $\bar{L}_w$. As discussed previously, the $L_{\max}$ of a scene is the largest luminance value, whereas $\bar{L}_w$ is the average logarithmic luminance of a scene. Calculating these values serially is straightforward; however, to obtain them using an OpenCL kernel, we will need to perform a reduction over the entire image. As described in [Catanzaro 10], the fastest way to perform a reduction is in a two-stage process. Here, each work item i performs reduction operations over the following array indices:

$$\{i + n \times \texttt{global\_size} | i + n \times \texttt{global\_size} < \texttt{array\_size}\}, \forall n \in N.$$

The result from this equation is then stored in the local array, and reduction is then performed over this local array. The output of this stage of the reduction is one partial reduction value for each work group. The second stage of the two-stage reduction requires execution of a separate kernel, which simply performs reduction over these partial results.

The input image to the kernel is a 2D texture image, therefore it's natural to want to run this kernel in 2D. However, this requires implementing a novel 2D version of the above two-stage reduction. The main difference is that now each work item (x, y) performs reduction operations over the image pixels at positions:

$$\{(x + m \times gx, y + n \times gy) \mid (x + m \times gx, y + n \times gy) < (\texttt{imagewidth}, \texttt{imageheight})\},$$
$$\forall m, n \in N,$$

where gx and gy are the global sizes in the x and y dimensions, respectively.

```
1 const sampler_t sampler = CLK_NORMALIZED_COORDS_FALSE | ←
      CLK_ADDRESS_NONE | CLK_FILTER_NEAREST;
2
3 //This kernel computes logAvgLum by performing reduction
4 //The results are stored in an array of size num_work_groups
5 kernel void computeLogAvgLum(   __read_only image2d_t image,
6                   __global float* lum,
7                   __global float* logAvgLum,
8                   __local float* logAvgLum_loc) {
9
10   float lum0;
11   float logAvgLum_acc = 0.f;
12
13   int2 pos;
14   uint4 pixel;
15   for (pos.y = get_global_id(1); pos.y < HEIGHT; pos.y += ←
        get_global_size(1)) {
16     for (pos.x = get_global_id(0); pos.x < WIDTH; pos.x += ←
          get_global_size(0)) {
17       pixel = read_imageui(image, sampler, pos);
18       //lum0 = pixel.x * 0.2126f + pixel.y * 0.7152f + pixel.z * ←
          0.0722f;
19       lum0 = dot(GLtoCL(pixel.xyz), (float3)(0.2126f, 0.7152f, 0.0722f←
          ));
20
21       logAvgLum_acc += log(lum0 + 0.000001f);
22       lum[pos.x + pos.y*WIDTH] = lum0;
23     }
24   }
25
26   pos.x = get_local_id(0);
27   pos.y = get_local_id(1);
28   const int lid = pos.x + pos.y*get_local_size(0); //Local ID in
29                                     //one dimension
30   logAvgLum_loc[lid] = logAvgLum_acc;
31
32   //Perform parallel reduction
33   barrier(CLK_LOCAL_MEM_FENCE);
34
35   for(int offset = (get_local_size(0)*get_local_size(1))/2; offset > ←
        0; offset = offset/2) {
36     if (lid < offset) {
37       logAvgLum_loc[lid] += logAvgLum_loc[lid + offset];
38     }
39     barrier(CLK_LOCAL_MEM_FENCE);
40   }
41
42   //Number of workgroups in x dim
43   const int num_work_groups = get_global_size(0)/get_local_size(0);
44   const int group_id = get_group_id(0) + get_group_id(1)*←
        num_work_groups;
45   if (lid == 0) {
46     logAvgLum[group_id] = logAvgLum_loc[0];
47   }
48 }
```

Listing 16.4. OpenCL kernel to compute L_{max} and $\bar{L}_w$.

The 2D kernel used to compute such a reduction is shown in Listing 16.4. As described above, first each work item (x, y) computes the sum and maximum of luminances over a range of image pixels (line 17–25). This sum and maximum is then stored in local arrays at an index corresponding to the pixel's position. A wave-front reduction is then performed over these local arrays (lines 36–42), and the result is then stored in the global array for each work group. The `finalReduc` kernel is then used to perform reduction over the partial results, where `num_reduc_bins` is the number of work groups in the execution of the `computeLogAvgLum` kernel. Once the sum over all the luminance values is computed, we take its average and calculate its exponential.

Once we have calculated $L_{\max}$ and $\bar{L}_w$, these values are plugged into Equation (16.7), with $L(x,y) = L_w(x,y)\frac{a}{\bar{L}_w}$, $L_{\text{white}} = L_{\max}$, and $L_w(x,y)$, the luminance of pixel (x,y). Once the values of $L_{\max}$ and $\bar{L}_w$ have been computed, the rest of the computation is fully data parallel, thus benefitting from a GPGPU implementation. Due to limited space, the OpenCL kernel is not presented here as it only requires a simple modification of the serial implementation.

16.7.4 Reinhard Local Tone-Mapping Operator

Reinhard's local TMO is similar to the global TMO in that it also computes the average logarithmic luminance of the entire image. To do this, the `computeLog AvgLum` and `finalReduc` kernels used for Reinhard's global TMO are modified so that they do not compute $L_{\max}$. Instead, the local TMO computes the average logarithmic luminance over various-sized neighborhoods for each pixel. For greater performance, these kernels are all fused together into one master kernel called `reinhardLocal`, as shown in Listing 16.5.

```
1  const sampler_t sampler = CLK_NORMALIZED_COORDS_FALSE | ↵
        CLK_ADDRESS_NONE | CLK_FILTER_NEAREST;

2
3  //Computes the mapping for each pixel as per Reinhard's Local TMO
4  kernel void reinhardLocal(  __read_only image2d_t input_image,
5                __write_only image2d_t output_image,
6                __global float* lumMips,
7                __global int* m_width,
8                __global int* m_offset,
9                __global float* logAvgLum_acc) {
10
11     float factor = logAvgLum_acc[0];
12
13     //Assumes Phi is 8.0
14     constant float k[7] = {
15        256.f * KEY / ( 1.f*1.f ),
16        256.f * KEY / ( 2.f*2.f ),
17        256.f * KEY / ( 4.f*4.f ),
18        256.f * KEY / ( 8.f*8.f ),
19        256.f * KEY / (16.f*16.f),
20        256.f * KEY / (32.f*32.f),
21        256.f * KEY / (64.f*64.f)
22     };
23
```

```
24    int2 pos, centre_pos, surround_pos;
25    for (pos.y = get_global_id(1); pos.y < HEIGHT; pos.y += ←
          get_global_size(1)) {
26      for (pos.x = get_global_id(0); pos.x < WIDTH; pos.x += ←
            get_global_size(0)) {
27        surround_pos = pos;
28        float local_logAvgLum = 0.f;
29        for (uint i = 0; i < NUM_MIPMAPS-1; i++) {
30          centre_pos = surround_pos;
31          surround_pos = centre_pos/2;
32
33          int2 m_width_01, m_offset_01;
34          m_width_01  = vload2(0, &m_width[i]);
35          m_offset_01 = vload2(0, &m_offset[i]);
36
37          int2 index_01 = m_offset_01 + (int2)(centre_pos.x, ←
              surround_pos.x);
38          index_01 += m_width_01 * (int2)(centre_pos.y, surround_pos←
              .y);
39
40          float2 lumMips_01 = factor;
41          lumMips_01 *= (float2)(lumMips[index_01.s0], lumMips[←
              index_01.s1]);
42
43          float centre_logAvgLum, surround_logAvgLum;
44          centre_logAvgLum   = lumMips_01.s0;
45          surround_logAvgLum = lumMips_01.s1;
46
47          float cs_diff = fabs(centre_logAvgLum - surround_logAvgLum←
              );
48          if (cs_diff > (k[i] + centre_logAvgLum) * EPSILON) {
49            local_logAvgLum = centre_logAvgLum;
50            break;
51          } else {
52            local_logAvgLum = surround_logAvgLum;
53          }
54        }
55
56        uint4 pixel = read_imageui(input_image, sampler, pos);
57
58        float3 rgb = GLtoCL(pixel.xyz);
59        float3 xyz = RGBtoXYZ(rgb);
60
61        float Ld  = factor / (1.f + local_logAvgLum) * xyz.y;
62        pixel.xyz = convert_uint3((float3)255.f * \
63          clamp((pow(rgb.xyz/xyz.y, (float3)SAT)*(float3)Ld), 0.f, ←
              1.f));
64
65        write_imageui(output_image, pos, pixel);
66      }
67    }
68  }
```

Listing 16.5. OpenCL kernels for Reinhard's local tone-mapping operator.

Computing HDR luminance. To recap, for each pixel the local TMO creates a Gaussian kernel to compute the average logarithmic luminance in a neighborhood. However, Gaussian kernels are expensive to compute, therefore this implementation makes use of OpenGL mipmaps.

Mipmaps of the luminance values are created at different scales and then used as an approximation to the average luminance value at that scale. Using OpenGL's API, mipmaps up to Level 7 are computed. The `reinhardLocal` kernel in Listing 16.5 gets passed these seven mipmaps in the array `lumMips`. The `for` loop on line 29 is the core of this TMO. Each mipmap is iterated over to obtain the average logarithmic luminance at that scale. Lines 37 to 45 compute the center and surround functions V_1 and V_2 used in Equation (16.4). Lines 47 to 53 compute V as in Equation (16.4) and checks whether it is less than ε (Equation (16.5)) to determine the appropriate average logarithmic luminance, $V_1(x, y, s_m)$, for that pixel. Once the optimal center function V_1 is computed, the remaining code implements Equation (16.6) to obtain the HDR luminance for that pixel.

Writing to output. Having computed the HDR luminance array L_d, the local tone-map kernel simply modifies the luminance values to reflect the new dynamic range. We first obtain the original RGB pixel, convert it to (x, y, z), modify its luminance, and convert it back to RGB.

16.8 Android Implementation

One of the contributions of this chapter is the fully working Android Open-CL/OpenGL pipeline, which we will describe in this section. The overall aim of the pipeline is to acquire camera frames, process them in OpenCL, and render the output to the screen using OpenGL. Ideally, the pipeline should be fast enough to allow for real-time image processing. This means that the time between acquiring a camera frame and passing it to OpenCL should be negligible. Our example pipeline achieves this by avoiding the image transfer between the GPU and the host by using OpenCL/OpenGL interoperability. Using this approach, the camera texture is kept on the GPU, and just before the OpenCL kernels are executed, the ownership of the texture is transferred to OpenCL.

To achieve OpenCL–OpenGL interoperability, an OpenCL context must first be initialized using the current OpenGL context as per the OpenCL specification. Then, OpenCL memory objects are created using the OpenGL data objects. Just before enqueing the OpenCL kernels, the ownership of the data objects is passed from OpenGL to OpenCL. Once the OpenCL kernels are executed, the OpenGL objects can be released so that they can be used as the basis for rendering. This section discusses the implementation details of this pipeline.

Java Native Interactive. Our example Android application is written in Java; however, the OpenCL kernel execution code is in C++ for performance reasons. Therefore, to call various C++ functions from the Android application we make use of the Java Native Interface (JNI).

OpenCL. To enable OpenCL and OpenGL ES interoperability, the OpenCL context must be initialized using the current display and context being used by

OpenGL ES. OpenGL ES contexts on Android are created and managed by EGL, the previously described interface between OpenGL ES and the underlying windowing system. Therefore, to create an OpenCL context for interoperability, the properties array must be initialized such that it holds the EGL context and display.

There are two classes in the Android framework API that allow a developer to create and manipulate graphics with the OpenGL ES API: `GLSurfaceView` and `GLSurfaceView.Renderer`.

GLSurfaceView. This class provides a canvas where we can draw and manipulate objects using OpenGL ES API calls. More importantly, `GLSurfaceView` manages an EGL display that enables OpenGL ES to render onto a surface. Therefore, by using `GLSurfaceView`, we don't have to worry about managing the EGL windowing life cycle.

GLSurfaceView.Renderer. This defines the methods required for drawing graphics in `GLSurfaceView`. When `GLSurfaceView` is instantiated, it must be provided with a renderer class that extends `GLSurfaceView.Renderer`. This is further discussed later on in the chapter.

OpenCL texture image. After the OpenCL context has been successfully initialized, OpenCL image textures can be created for the kernels from the camera input.

Convert GL_TEXTURE_EXTERNAL_OES to GL_TEXTURE_2D. A `SurfaceTexture` object can be used to capture frames from the camera as an OpenGL ES texture. The `SurfaceTexture` object is initialized using an OpenGL ES texture ID. However, the texture ID must be bound to the `GL_TEXTURE_EXTERNAL_OES` texture target. Unfortunately, as per the OpenCL specification, when creating an OpenCL texture image from an OpenGL texture, `GL_TEXTURE_EXTERNAL_OES` isn't a valid texture target. Therefore, the `GL_TEXTURE_EXTERNAL_OES` is used instead to create a `GL_TEXTURE_2D` texture.

Then the fragment shader in Listing 16.6 is executed. Note that since we are sampling from `GL_TEXTURE_EXTERNAL_OES`, the directive

```
extensionGL_OES_ EGL_image_external : require
```

must be declared in the fragment shader. This results in the contents of the `GL_TEXTURE_EXTERNAL_OES` target texture being copied to the `GL_TEXTURE_2D` texture rather than being rendered to the display. At this point we now have an OpenGL ES `GL_TEXTURE_2D` texture on the GPU which contains the camera data.

```
1 extension GL_OES_EGL_image_external : require
2
3 precision mediump float;
4 uniform samplerExternalOES sTexture;
5 varying vec2 texCoord
6
7 void main() {
8   gl_FragColor = texture2D(sTexture, texCoord);
9 }
```

Listing 16.6. Fragment shader that samples from a `GL_TEXTURE_ EXTERNAL_OES` texture.

```
1 mem_images[0] = clCreateFromGLTexture2D(m_clContext,
2         CL_MEM_READ_ONLY, GL_TEXTURE_2D, 0, in_tex, &err);
3 err = clEnqueueAcquireGLObjects(m_queue, 1, &mem_images[0], 0, 0, 0);
4   runCLKernels();   //Function to run OpenCL kernels
5 err = clEnqueueReleaseGLObjects(m_queue, 1, &mem_images[0], 0, 0, 0);
```

Listing 16.7. Creating an OpenCL image from an OpenGL texture.

Create an OpenCL image from OpenGL 2D texture. Using JNI, the C++ global state is then instructed to use the previously created OpenCL context to create an OpenCL texture image from the provided input texture ID. Combining OpenCL and OpenGL allows OpenCL kernels to modify the texture image on the GPU, but before the kernels can access the texture data, the host needs to create an OpenCL memory object specifically configured for this purpose (line 1 in Listing 16.7).

16.8.1   Render Output to Display

Having applied TMO to an LDR image, the results now need to be displayed on the Android device. To do so, we create another OpenGL texture and instruct the OpenCL kernels to render the output to that instead. Then, once the OpenCL kernels have been executed, an OpenGL fragment shader can be used to render the contents of the output texture.

One important design point to note is that OpenGL and OpenCL cannot simultaneously access the same data. The OpenCL kernels need to acquire exclusive access to the data, which can be achieved by making a call to `clEnqueue` `AcquireGLObjects`. Once the data has been acquired, OpenCL kernels to process this data can then be enqueued. Finally, for OpenGL ES to be able to reuse the texture, the OpenCL context must give up the exclusive access to the texture (for example, see line 5 in Listing 16.7).

Once the OpenCL kernels have been executed and access to the textures is given up, the contents of the resulting texture can be rendered to the display in Java (Listing 16.8).

```
precision mediump float;
uniform sampler2D sTexture;
varying vec2 texCoord;
void main() {
  gl_FragColor = texture2D(sTexture, texCoord);
};
```

Listing 16.8. Java code to render the result texture to the display.

16.8.2 GLSurfaceView.Renderer

Extending GLSurfaceView.Renderer requires implementation of the following methods.

onSurfaceCreated. This method is called by the Android framework every time the EGL context is created or recreated. Aside from when the application first starts, this typically happens when the Android device wakes up after going to sleep.

Because the OpenCL context relies on the OpenGL ES context created from EGL, it is important to ensure that the OpenCL context is recreated every time this method gets called. Therefore, in onSurfaceCreated, we make calls to C++ through JNI to initialize the OpenCL properties. These OpenCL properties are then used to create a new OpenCL context, which in turn is used to execute the OpenCL kernels.

Building OpenCL kernels and initializing OpenCL memory objects every time a new frame is available can be quite expensive. However, these OpenCL objects can't simply be created only when the app starts, as they rely on an active OpenCL context. Therefore, the following tasks are also carried out when onSurfaceCreated is called:

- creating OpenCL command queue,

- creating and building the TMO OpenCL program,

- creating all the required kernels,

- creating buffers and textured images,

- setting kernel arguments.

onDrawFrame. This method repeatedly gets called by the GLSurfaceView.Renderer API and is responsible for rendering objects to the display. Therefore, this method is the ideal place to execute the tone-mapping process.

First, `updateTexImage` is called to update the camera texture with the latest available frame. An OpenGL ES 2D texture is then created from the camera texture as described earlier. The texture ID of this texture is then passed to the C++ global state, where the OpenCL tone-mapping kernels are executed to create a pseudo-HDR effect on the image. Once the tone-mapping process has finished, the output texture is then rendered to the display.

`onSurfaceChanged`. This method is called when the surface size changes. However, the method is redundant here as the orientation is locked in our example application.

16.8.3 Mipmap Generation

Mipmaps are used for our implementation of Reinhard's local TMO. OpenGL ES provides built-in functionality to generate the complete chain of mipmaps by making a call to `glGenerateMipmap`. Once generated, the corresponding OpenCL textures can be created by making a call to `clCreateFromGLTexture2D()`. However, executing the said function returns an error, which as per the OpenCL specification is raised when the "OpenGL implementation does not support creating from nonzero mipmap levels" [Khronos 15].

To get around this, an OpenCL kernel (called `channel_mipmap`) was implemented, which, when executed, generates the next level mipmap. As discussed previously, for Reinhard's local TMO, we set the number of mipmaps to 8.

16.8.4 Reading from an OpenGL Texture

When called from an OpenCL kernel, `read_imageui` returns the RGBA value of a pixel at a specified coordinate. The returned pixel values represent an 8-bit color each and therefore should be in the range of $\{0, \ldots, 255\}$.

However, while testing our example application, we ran into problems with Qualcomm's OpenCL implementation on their Snapdragon chipset. Their OpenCL implementation (incorrectly) returns values ranging between 0 and 15,359. Moreover, there is no linear mapping between the original 8-bit values and the ones returned by `read_imageui`, making it nontrivial to obtain the original 8-bit color values.

Using linear interpolation on a subset of the reversed mapping, we have managed to generate a suitable polynomial function. However, this polynomial is of a very high degree and therefore is quite computationally expensive to execute. Instead, we have produced a function called `GL_to_CL()`, which is a combination of four linear functions and a quartic function. (Of course, this bug may be fixed in their OpenCL implementation at some stage.)

Device (32-bit GFLOPS)	Peak performance Bandwidth (GB/s)	Global Memory per CU (KB)	Local Memory
ARM Mali T604	68	12.8	–
NVIDIA GTX 760	2258	192	48
Intel i3-3217U	29	25.6	32
Qualcomm Adreno 330	129	12.8	8

Table 16.1. Specifications for the devices under test.

16.9 Performance of Our HDR Effects

Each of the TMOs we have implemented has been run on images of different sizes to measure their performances. These tests were carried out on a range of devices, as detailed below.

First, we have an ARM Mali-T604–based device: an Arndale development board sporting a Samsung Exynos 5 5250 processor. This processor includes two ARM Cortex A-15 CPU cores and a four-core Mali T604 GPU. A second device in our test is an Android-based Sony Xperia Z Ultra smartphone. This device comes with an embedded Qualcomm Snapdragon 800 quad-core processor and Adreno 330 GPU. Other OpenCL-compatible devices used to analyze the results are an NVIDIA GTX 760 and an Intel i3-3217U CPU. Table 16.1 lists the relevant specifications for each of these devices.

The GFLOPS figure is a measure of peak performance—in this case, billions of single precision floating point operations per second. Global and local memory are the amount of memory resources available to an OpenCL kernel at the time of execution. If an OpenCL kernel exhausts its local memory, then any overspill is typically stored in global memory instead, with correspondingly slower access speeds.

Reinhard global TMO performance. Reinhard's global TMO iterates over the entire image twice; once to compute $L_{\max}$ and $\bar{L}_w$, and a second time to adjust each pixel according to these values and the key value (a) of the scene. To achieve a real-time implementation, the kernels need to be executed in less than 33 milliseconds (30 fps). Figure 16.8 compares the execution times of different-sized images, all running the same OpenCL code on the ARM Mali T604 and NVIDIA GTX 760 platforms.

The NVIDIA GTX 760, being a fast, discrete, desktop GPU, executes the OpenCL kernels on all image sizes in less than 2.5 ms, achieving more than 400 fps at 1080p. This is much faster than the equivalent OpenGL implementation by Akyuz, which achieved 103 fps on a 1024×768 image, albeit on much slower hardware. The ARM Mali T604 GPU can process the two smaller images fast enough to render the output in real time. However, processing a 1080p image is slightly borderline, coming in at about 28 fps. With a little more optimization, 30 fps is probably achievable on this platform.

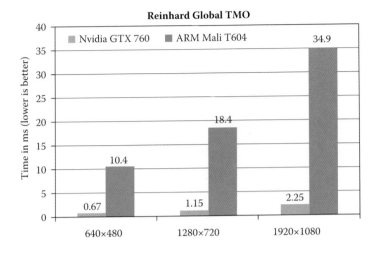

Figure 16.8. Reinhard's global TMO timings (lower is better).

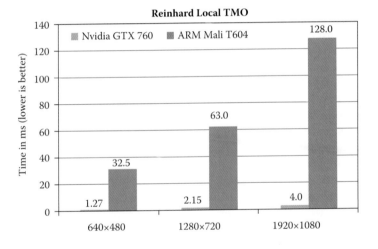

Figure 16.9. Reinhard's local TMO timings (lower is better).

Reinhard local TMO performance. Because Reinhard's Local TMO requires iterating over multiple sizes of neighborhood for each pixel, the algorithm is much more computationally expensive than its global TMO counterpart. Analyzing the results in Figure 16.9, we see that the desktop GPU again processes all the images in less than 33 ms to achieve a real-time implementation. Our OpenCL implementation achieves 250 fps (4.0 ms) on a 1920×1080 image compared to Akyuz's OpenGL implementation, which has a frame rate of 103 fps on a slightly smaller (1027×768) image.

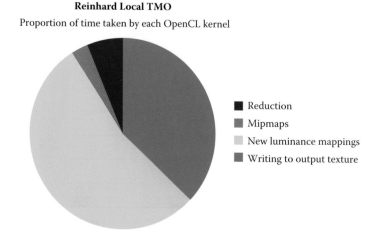

Reinhard Local TMO

Proportion of time taken by each OpenCL kernel

- Reduction
- Mipmaps
- New luminance mappings
- Writing to output texture

Figure 16.10. The fraction of total time spent in each kernel within Reinhard's local TMO.

For the more data-expensive and computationally expensive local TMO, the ARM Mali T604 GPU achieves real-time performance for the 640×480 image size (30.8 fps), but doesn't exceed our 30 fps goal for the two larger image sizes, instead achieving 15.9 fps on a 1280×720 image and 7.8 fps for the 1920×1080 HD image.

A closer look at the execution time of each kernel shows that most of the time is spent in computing the luminance mappings used to scale each luminance value from the original image (Figure 16.10). These mappings are computed based on the luminance of the scene.

When recording a video or taking a picture, the luminance of the scene doesn't vary much between frames. We could therefore take advantage of this to achieve a higher frame rate by only computing a new set of mappings once every few frames, as opposed to computing them for every frame.

Histogram equalization. Although not an HDR TMO, histogram equalization is a demonstration that our example Android pipeline is not limited to just HDR TMOs and can be used for other classes of image-processing applications that require input from a camera and render the output to a display.

Figure 16.11 shows the execution times of our histogram equalization example OpenCL code, this time on a different set of our target devices. Once again, the desktop GPU is the fastest device. However it is interesting to note that the Intel CPU performs this benchmark much faster than the Adreno 330 GPU, demonstrating that this code is memory bandwidth limited rather than compute limited.

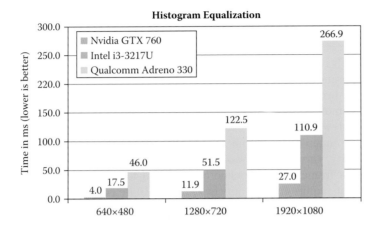

Figure 16.11. Histogram equalization performance results.

16.9.1 Performance Summary

Overall, the example OpenCL kernel implementations presented in this chapter perform better than any previously reported results. Upon closer inspection of the various TMO algorithms we have implemented, Reinhard's global TMO is the least compute intensive. It can achieve real time on 720p images across all the devices we have tested. As expected, the desktop GPU performed best, achieving a frame rate far greater than 30 fps across all the algorithms and all the different-sized images. However, many embedded GPUs are now capable to achieving 30 fps or better for certain image sizes, a very interesting result that shows that real-time HDR pipelines are now within reach for some mobile platforms. We encourage the reader to try the code for themselves and benchmark the hardware platforms of their choice.

16.10 Conclusions

The main contributions of this chapter are

- a description of HDR TMO that can be used to create a pseudo-HDR effect on an image;

- an efficient GPGPU OpenCL/OpenGL implementation of the above algorithms;

- a pipeline that captures camera images, tone-maps them using the above OpenCL implementations, and renders the output to display;

- a demonstration of a working OpenCL–OpenGL interoperability that avoids any unnecessary data transfer in the example pipeline.

For a scene where the overall luminance is very low, Reinhard's TMOs work very well by adjusting the luminance of the image to highlight details in both the dark and the bright regions. The OpenCL implementations of these algorithms have been demonstrated to be efficient and portable. An Android pipeline was also described, which acquired camera frames, tone-mapped them using OpenCL kernels, and rendered the output to a display. Using OpenGL ES and OpenCL interoperability, this pipeline was further optimized to avoid any data transfer of the camera frames. The pipeline can be used for other image-processing applications that require input from the camera. To demonstrate this, an OpenCL histogram equalization program has also been provided.

Bibliography

[Akyüz 12] Ahmet Oğuz Akyüz. "High Dynamic Range Imaging Pipeline on the GPU." *Journal of Real-Time Image Processing: Special Issue* (2012), 1–15.

[Android 15] Android. "OpenGL ES." http://developer.android.com/guide/topics/graphics/opengl.html, accessed May 6, 2015.

[Blommaert and Martens 90] Frans J. J. Blommaert and Jean-Bernard Martens. "An Object-Oriented Model for Brightness Perception." *Spatial Vision* 5:1 (1990), 15–41.

[Catanzaro 10] Bryan Catanzaro. "OpenCL Optimization Case Study: Simple Reductions." *AMD Developer Central*, http://developer.amd.com/resources/documentation-articles/articles-whitepapers/opencl-optimization-case-study-simple-reductions/, August 24, 2010.

[Chaney 15] Mike Chaney. "Understanding Embedded Image Information." *Steve's Digicams*, http://www.steves-digicams.com/knowledge-center/understanding-embedded-image-info.html, 2015.

[Chiu et al. 11] Ching-Te Chiu, Tsun-Hsien Wang, Wei-Ming Ke, Chen-Yu Chuang, Jhih-Siao Huang, Wei-Su Wong, Ren-Song Tsay, and Cyuan-Jhe Wu. "Real-Time Tone-Mapping Processor with Integrated Photographic and Gradient Compression Using 0.13 μm Technology on an ARM SoC Platform." *Journal of Signal Processing Systems* 64:1 (2011), 93–107.

[GSM Arena 15] GSM Arena. "Apple iPhone 4 Specifications." http://www.gsmarena.com/apple_iphone_4-3275.php, 2015.

[Huang et al. 09] Song Huang, Shucai Xiao, and Wu-chun Feng. "On the Energy Efficiency of Graphics Processing Units for Scientific Computing." In *Proceedings of the 2009 IEEE International Symposium on Parallel & Distributed Processing*, pp. 1–8. Washington, CD: IEEE Computer Society, 2009.

[Kang et al. 03] Sing Bing Kang, Matthew Uyttendaele, Simon Winder, and Richard Szeliski. "High Dynamic Range Video. *ACM Transactions on Graphics* 22:3 (2003), 319–325.

[Kiser et al. 12] Chris Kiser, Erik Reinhard, Mike Tocci, and Nora Tocci. "Real-Time Automated Tone Mapping System for HDR Video." In *Proceedings of the IEEE International Conference on Image Processing*, pp. 2749–2752. Piscataway, NJ: IEEE, 2012.

[Krawczyk et al. 05] Grzegorz Krawczyk, Karol Myszkowski, and Hans-Peter Seidel. "Perceptual Effects in Real-Time Tone Mapping." In *Proceedings of the 21st Spring Conference on Computer Graphics*, pp. 195–202. New York: ACM, 2005.

[Khronos 15] Khronos Group. "Khronos OpenCL Standard." http://www.khronos.org/opencl/, accessed May 6, 2015.

[Kuang et al. 07] Jiangtao Kuang, Hiroshi Yamaguchi, Changmeng Liu, Garrett M, and Mark D. Fairchild. "Evaluating HDR Rendering Algorithms." *ACM Trans. Appl. Perception* 4:2 (2007), Article no. 9.

[McClanahan 11] Chris McClanahan. "Single Camera Real Time HDR Tonemapping." *mcclanahoochie's blog*, http://mcclanahoochie.com/blog/portfolio/real-time-hdr-tonemapping/, April 2011.

[McCoy 08] Kevin McCoy. "St. Louis Arch Multiple Exposures." *Wikipedia*, https://en.wikipedia.org/wiki/File:StLouisArchMultExpEV-4.72.JPG, May 31, 2008.

[Reinhard et al. 02] Erik Reinhard, Michael Stark, Peter Shirley, and James Ferwerda. "Photographic Tone Reproduction for Digital Images." *ACM Transactions on Graphics* 21:3 (2002), 267–276.

[Seng 10] Kim Seng. "Single Exposure HDR." *HDR Photography by Captain Kimo*, http://captainkimo.com/single-exposure-hdr/, February 25, 2010.

[Topaz Labs 15] Topaz Labs. "Topaz Adjust." http://www.topazlabs.com/adjust, 2015.

[UCI iCAMP 10] UCI iCAMP. "Histogram Equalization." *Math 77C*, http://www.math.uci.edu/icamp/courses/math77c/demos/hist_eq.pdf, August 5, 2010.

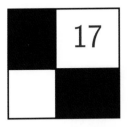

17

Efficient Soft Shadows
Based on Static Local Cubemap
Sylwester Bala and Roberto Lopez Mendez

17.1 Overview

Contemporary mobile GPUs are very powerful and rich in features that make game and application content shine while preserving high performance. As developers want to make use of the latest features, we cannot forget about two very important factors. First, for a game to be successful, it must target as many people as possible around the world. This can be achieved only when using a lower set of features of the GPU because not everyone has a high-specification mobile device. Second, how can you make the player engage with your game for as long as possible? On mobile devices in particular it becomes a challenge because energy source is coming from a battery. Even though ARM's technology is designed for low energy consumption, developers cannot forget that a battery has finite energy capacity. In this chapter we address this problem and help developers to deliver even better quality, higher performance, and longer battery life when playing games. As the subject is very wide and could be addressed to many areas of real-time graphics software development, we want to narrow the scope to one visual effect: soft shadows. We introduce a novel technique of rendering semi-dynamic soft shadows. Although the technique is robust, it cannot be applied for all use cases, and we also explain in which cases you may make the most of this technique.

17.2 Introduction

In this chapter you will learn about a novel soft shadows technique based on local cubemaps. (See the example in Figure 17.1.) We believe that with this you will be able to develop high-quality semi-dynamic shadows of your local environment and at the same time preserve high performance and allow for longer battery life.

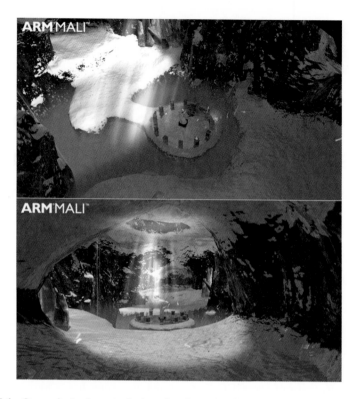

Figure 17.1. Our soft shadows technique has been implemented in the Ice Cave project.

What makes this really interesting is that it can save a lot of bandwidth because it uses a static cubemap texture. The cubemap texture size can be lower than the screen resolution and the quality still will be really good. On top of that, the texture can be compressed, for instance by using ASTC, and can use even less bandwidth. In the next section you will find out more about the technique.

17.3   Algorithm Overview

The overall algorithm is very simple and consists of two steps. The first step is to create a static local cubemap texture, and it is recommended to do this offline as then you can compress the texture and achieve even better performance. The second step is to apply shadows in a scene. In this step most of the work is done in the fragment shader. Having information about light(s) and the bounding volume, you can calculate a vector to the light; then, having this vector, you can calculate the intersection with the bounding volume. Once the intersection point is known, you need to build a vector from the cubemap's position to the

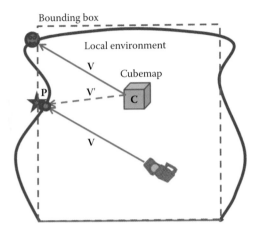

Figure 17.2. Using a proxy geometry to apply the local correction.

intersection point and use this vector to fetch the texel from the cubemap texture. The alpha channel of the texel determines how much shadow needs to be applied to the current fragment.

The two steps are explained in detail later in the chapter.

17.4   What Is a Local Cubemap?

Before we dive further into the explanation of this technique, it would be good to understand what we mean by "local cubemap." A local cubemap is more than the cubemap texture type, which is supported by most GPUs today. You can hardly find a device with a GPU that does not support the cubemap texture type. The cubemap texture has been supported since early versions of OpenGL, even before shaders were introduced. The local cubemap technique has been known in the industry for while [Bjork 04, Czuba 10, Lagarde and Zanuttini 12, Lopez 14].

If we render a cubemap in a local environment and intend to use it in the conventional way, it will not produce the desired results. In Figure 17.2 the camera is looking in the direction of $\mathbf{V}$ to the star. If we use this vector to retrieve the texture from the cubemap, what we really get will be a texel with the smiley face instead of the star.

In order to obtain the star instead of the smiley face, we need to use a new vector $\mathbf{V'} = \mathbf{CP}$ from the cubemap to the intersection point $\mathbf{P}$ of the view vector $\mathbf{V}$ with the boundary. As the boundary can be arbitrary, we simplify the problem of finding the intersection point by using a proxy geometry. The simplest proxy geometry is the bounding box.

The bounding volume describes the boundaries of the local environment where the cubemap is valid and in which the shadows from the cubemap should be applied. In other words, the bounding volume is a geometric approximation of your local environment that must be created in such a way that the cube faces of the volume are as close to the geometry as possible. For instance, in a four-walled room with floor and ceiling, it is fairly easy to create a bounding volume (local environment) because the bounding box describes perfectly the geometry. If you take another example with uneven walls, unlike the room, such as a cave, then an artist needs to compromise the undulated walls and create an approximated cube bounding volume for this geometry.

We come this way to the concept of the local cubemap. The *local cubemap* consists of

- a cubemap texture;

- two extra data, which are position and bounding volume (bounding box);

- the local correction procedure.

Fetching texels from the local cubemap is done with the same shader function that is used for fetching texels from the cubemap textures. The only difference is that the vector used to point out which texel should be fetched needs to be local corrected according to the cubemap's generation position and the bounding volume.

17.5   Creating a Shadow Cubemap

It has already been mentioned that a local cubemap contains a cubemap texture, a world position, and a bounding volume in the world space of the local environment. Now, you need to decide from which point of your scene the cubemap texture should be rendered. Most of the time, the most suitable position is the center of the room, but it does not have to be exactly in the center.

Now you are ready to render your local environment to the cubemap texture. You need to render your scene six times, once for each face. The main idea of this technique is to store the transparency (or, in other words, occlusion) in the alpha channel of your local environment into the cubemap texture. (See Figure 17.3.) An individual texel of the cubemap determines how much light can reach the local environment from outside of the bounding volume.

Along with the alpha value you can also store color values, as you may want to make color-tinted shadows. The color-tinted shadow may give you really interesting results, for example, a stained glass window in the room casting different colors of shadows. You can also reuse the color for reflections, refractions, and other effects, but the main component will be transparency.

It is important to mention that at this stage you are not storing any information related to the lights.

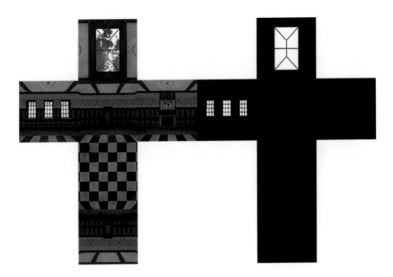

Figure 17.3. An example of a generated cubemap with alpha channel.

17.6 Applying Shadows

Once you have created the local shadow cubemap, it is time to apply shadows to your local environment. Applying shadows is fairly easy and straightforward. It requires fetching a texel from the cubemap texture using the fragment-to-light vector and applying the amount of shadow based on the texel alpha value.

The procedure to render the shadows is practically the same for point and directional light sources.

In the case of a point light source, the fragment-to-light vector can be built directly in the fragment shader or can be obtained by the interpolation of the vertex-to-light vector.

In the case of a directional light source, we just need to replace the vertex-to-light vector (or the fragment-to-light vector) with the light direction vector.

Having the to-light vector—for either type of light, directional or point—you need to apply local correction on this vector before fetching the texel from the cubemap. The vector correction can be done in the following way (see also Figure 17.4):

Input parameters:

> `EnviCubeMapPos`—the cubemap origin position
>
> `BBoxMax`—the bounding volume (bounding box) of the environment
>
> `BBoxMin`—the bounding volume (bounding box) of the environment
>
> `v`—the vertex/fragment position in world space
>
> `L`—the normalized vertex-to-light vector in world space

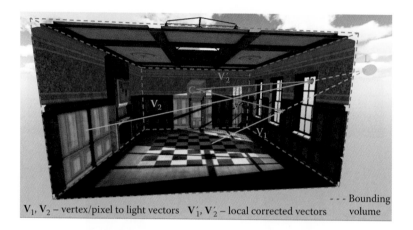

$\mathbf{V_1, V_2}$ – vertex/pixel to light vectors $\mathbf{V'_1, V'_2}$ – local corrected vectors   - - - Bounding volume

Figure 17.4. Representation of local correction of a vector according to the cubemap position and the bounding volume.

Output value:

Lp—the corrected vertex-to-light vector which needs to be used to fetch a texel from the shadow cubemap.

There may be many other methods of correcting the vector. The one that we used is listed in Listing 17.1.

```
// Working in the world coordinate system
vec3 intersectMaxPointPlanes = (BBoxMax - V) / L;
vec3 intersectMinPointPlanes = (BBoxMin - V) / L;

// Find only intersections in the forward direction of the ray.
vec3 largestRayParams = max(intersectMaxPointPlanes,
                            intersectMinPointPlanes);

// The smallest value of the ray parameters is the distance
// to the intersection point.
float dist = min(min(largestRayParams.x, largestRayParams.y),
                 largestRayParams.z);

// Find the position of the intersection point.
vec3 intersectPositionWS = V + L * dist;

// Get the local corrected vector.
Lp = intersectPositionWS - EnviCubeMapPos;
```

Listing 17.1. A vector local correction.

```
float shadow = texture(cubemap, Lp).a;
```

Listing 17.2. Fetching a texel from the shadow cubemap.

All the code in Listing 17.1 is executed in the fragment shader. Now, having the Lp corrected vector from the fragment to the light position, you can fetch the texel from the cubemap texture as shown in Listing 17.2.

The alpha channel from the texel represents how much shadow (intensity of the shadow) to apply on the currently processing fragment. At this moment, once you have completed this stage and run your application, you can set the light position in an arbitrary place and see the semi-dynamic shadows change according to the light position. (See Figure 17.5.)

You can have more than one light in the scene, but you need to implement the vector correction individually per light. However, the texel fetching should be from the same cubemap texture. For other improvements of this technique, see the next sections.

Figure 17.5. The hard shadows from the static cubemap.

```
float texLod = length(IntersectPositionWS - V);
```

Listing 17.3. The distance calculation from the fragment to the intersection point.

17.7 Smoothness

This section is the most interesting section of this chapter because once you do what is described here, you will make your shadows look amazing! In the real world you can observe nonuniform shadow penumbra. The farther away the object that is casting shadows, the more blurred the edge of the shadow becomes and the less intense it gets. There are many factors causing this phenomenon, but the main factor is the area size of the light source. This also indirectly implies light bouncing (radiosity) in the real world. This technique allows you to achieve similar, if not the same, shadows effects in your scene. On top of that, you will achieve even better performance as the softness effect requires lower mipmap levels, which requires less bandwidth.

All you need to do is make sure you enabled trilinear filtering to your cubemap texture. Then, in the rendering process you need to calculate a distance from the fragment position to the intersection point of the light vector against the bounding volume. This distance has already been calculated in the local correction process (Listing 17.1), and you can reuse it here. Use the distance to fetch a texel from the cubemap texture accordingly. The distance should be normalized to the maximum distance within your local environment and the number of mipmaps in the cubemap texture. But there is an even simpler approach. You can expose a single float parameter that is a multiplier of the distance and help to fine tune the shadows effect to the desired quality level that fits to the local environment. Listings 17.3–17.5 show step by step what you need to code in order to achieve desired results:

1. Calculate the distance from the fragment position to the intersection point (Listing 17.3).

2. Normalize the distance to the number of mipmap levels of your cubemap texture. The easiest approach we found ourselves is to expose a single float parameter that then is multiplied by the distance (Listing 17.4).

```
texLod *= distanceNormalizer;
```

Listing 17.4. Normalize the distance to the cubemap level of detail.

```
shadow = textureLod(cubemap, Lp, texLod).a;
```

Listing 17.5. Fetching a texel from the shadow cubemap with level of detail.

3. At this stage, fetch the right texel with the right mipmap level by reusing the above calculation results (Listing 17.5).

After implementing the above, you should be able to see pretty dynamic smooth shadows in your project, as in Figure 17.6.

17.8 Combining the Shadow Technique with Others

As mentioned earlier, the bounding volume needs to be approximated to the local environment. The closer the bounding volume is defined to the real geometry, the less error-prone is the technique. This technique will work for geometry that is near the boundaries of the local environment (bounding volume). For instance,

Figure 17.6. The soft shadows from the static cubemap.

Figure 17.7. The cubemap technique combined with shadowmap: with no shadowmap (left) and with the shadowmap producing shadows for the chesspieces (right).

the room in Figure 17.6 is the most suitable environment for this technique as each wall is defined on the boundaries of the volume.

Dynamic objects may also be problematic. Producing shadows of dynamic objects using this technique is not suitable because it would require updating all six faces of the cubemap texture every frame. However, dynamic objects can still receive shadows from the cubemap though they cannot cast shadows. If you require dynamic objects that cast shadows, we recommend using other techniques. The main idea behind this technique is to make the cubemap texture static, containing pre-baked intensity of all static geometries and the surroundings. Other objects within the scene such as dynamic objects need to be rendered with another technique for the instance shadowmap. Whichever technique is chosen for rendering shadows from dynamic objects, there is an easy mathematical calculation involved in merging the results into one final result, as in Figure 17.7.

17.9 Performance and Quality

Our soft shadows technique, unlike other shadow techniques, does not require writing to memory whether rendering to a depth texture, stencil, or color of the framebuffer object.

In comparison, when shadowmaps are used, very often, if not at every frame, the depth texture needs to be updated. When updating the depth texture, data must be flushed from the GPU to the memory. Then, when applying shadows, data needs to be transferred back from the main memory to the GPU as a texture. Also, updating the depth texture often requires extra CPU-side work such as culling and resubmitting occluder geometry for rendering the shadow map. Another disadvantage of using shadowmaps is that you cannot use ASTC texture compression, which is designed to reduce bandwidth traffic.

The technique requires reading memory as many times as the number of lights per frame. On top of that, when using lower mipmap levels for the softness effect, there is even less data to be transferred. Therefore, the technique won't cause

Figure 17.8. Quality comparison of shadows produced with 512×512 texture resolution: the local cubemap shadows technique (left) and a shadowmap (right).

"unstable texel" artifacts. This is due to the cubemap texture being static and the content not changing from frame to frame, which is not the case when using shadowmap. (See Figure 17.8.)

17.10 Future Work

As you may have noticed, in this chapter we focus mainly on one environment with one local cubemap texture. We have not covered how to deal with more-complex environments that would require more than one cubemap. However, while we have not done any work in this area, we are rather confident that it is very possible to blend multiple cubemap shadows in order to achieve an even more complex shadowing system in a scene.

Another important thing to note here is that we assume the light is always outside of the bounding volume in order to do the calculations in the fragment shader in the most efficient way. We have not covered in this chapter what to do when a light moves from the outside of a bounding volume to the inside. This is a subject for more research.

17.11 Conclusion

What makes the technique described here really interesting is that while it produces high-quality shadows and saves a lot of bandwidth, it does not require any extra GPU features. All it requires is at least OpenGL ES 2.0, and it can be implemented on almost any platform available on the market.

You may find some restrictions with this technique, which were mentioned above, such as that the technique might not be applicable to your current work, but certainly there are many other applications where the technique is suitable. When we first came up with this idea, we thought that it would be applicable only for specific use cases and that we might have not been able to use it for the Ice Cave project. In the end we found that the technique really worked well for the project even though the uneven walls of the cave were far from the approximated bounding volume in some places.

Bibliography

[Bjork 04] Kevin Bjork. "Image-Based Lighting." In *GPU Gems*, edited by Randima Fernando, Chapter 19. Reading, MA: Addison-Wesley, 2004.

[Czuba 10] Bartosz Czuba. "Box Projected Cubemap Environment Mapping." *Gamedev.net*, http://www.gamedev.net/topic/568829-box-projected -cubemap-environment-mapping/?&p=4637262, 2010.

[Lagarde and Zanuttini 12] Sebastien Lagarde and Antoine Zanuttini. "Local Image-Based Lighting with Parallax-Corrected Cubemap." In *ACM SIG-GRAPH 2012 Talks,* article no. 36. New York: ACM, 2012.

[Lopez 14] Roberto Mendez Lopez. "Implementing Reflections in Unity Using Local Cubemaps." http://malideveloper.arm.com/downloads/ ImplementingReflectionsinUnityUsingLocalCubemaps.pdf, 2014.

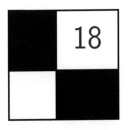

Physically Based Deferred Shading on Mobile

Ashley Vaughan Smith and Mathieu Einig

18.1 Introduction

In order for graphical applications to achieve maximum performance and therefore maximum graphical quality, they need to utilize memory bandwidth as best as possible. This is especially true on mobile devices without large, fast DDR RAM, like discrete GPUs have, and where power is limited through battery life.

This bandwidth bottleneck is even more tangible in the context of deferred shading renderers, where large G-buffers need to be stored and retrieved multiple times during the rendering process. It is possible to take advantage of the fast on-chip memory that exists on tile-based GPUs to prevent unnecessary data transfers, which improves power consumption and increases performance.

This chapter discusses how to achieve minimum main memory bandwidth utilization along with the tradeoffs and benefits to doing so, including power usage. Also discussed is how to take advantage of the savings in time spent reading and writing to main memory by implementing a physically based deferred rendering pipeline. (See the example in Figure 18.1.)

18.2 Physically Based Shading

One key aspect of rendering is trying to reproduce real-world materials in a convincing way. This is a problem that has to be solved both on the engineering side (how do I render shiny metals?) but also on the art side (what colors do I need for a gold material in this specific renderer?), usually leading to either the creation of an impractical number of material shaders that have their own sets of constraints or to simpler shaders that cannot approximate most common materials.

Figure 18.1. An efficient deferred shading renderer.

Physically based shading (PBS) is an attempt at solving the rendering equation [Kajiya 86], but with a more unified shading model than its ad-hoc predecessors [Pharr and Humphreys 04]. While there has been an increasing amount of attention on PBS in the past few years, it should be noted that it does not involve any fundamentally new concept. It should instead be seen as a set of criteria and constraints (for both the developers and artists) that, if respected, should produce an image with plausible materials in most scenarios. Some of the key concepts are as follows:

- Energy conservation: you cannot reflect more light than you receive. This means that the specular intensity is inversely proportional to its size.

- Everything has Fresnel reflections.

- Lighting calculations need to be done in linear space to achieve correct output.

It also formalizes the material parameters:

- Albedo: Formerly known as the diffuse map, with a few notable differences: lighting information should not be present, and this texture is mostly uniform. Metals do not have an albedo color.

- Reflectance: Formerly known as the specular map, expect that in PBS, this is mostly a material constant. Only metals have color information in their reflectance.

Figure 18.2. Specular workflow: albedo (left) and reflectance (right).

Figure 18.3. Metallicness workflow: albedo/reflectance texture (left) and metallicness texture (right).

- Roughness: This is the micro surface data (i.e., the bumps that are too high frequency to be stored in a normal map). It defines the "blurriness" of the specular highlights. This is where artists should focus most of the details. It should also be noted that the roughness textures' mipmap levels should be generated from the original texture and the normal map.

Figure 18.2 shows an example of albedo and reflectance textures for a material with stone and gold.

The albedo and reflectance textures are nearly mutually exclusive: Metals do not have a diffuse component, and insulators can be assumed to have the same constant specular color. This means that they can both be merged into a single texture. An extra mask, representing which areas are to be treated as specular, has to be created. But this saves memory and could be stored as the alpha channel for convenience. See Figure 18.3 for the same material represented using the metallicness workflow.

Using a metallicness workflow requires less memory; however, it also introduces visual artifacts due to texture compression and filtering. The metallicness map should normally be a nearly binary texture, but because of bilinear filtering or mipmapping, sharp transitions between metal and dielectric will become

Figure 18.4. Bright halos caused by the transition between the gold and stone materials.

smooth gradients. This causes the renderer to interpret the color texture as both an albedo and specular map, which may then lead to unnaturally shiny or matte halos, as shown in Figure 18.4.

These issues can generally be fixed by eroding or dilating the metallicness mask around the problematic areas.

18.3   An Efficient Physically Based Deferred Renderer

With the ever-increasing computing power available on mobile chips, state-of-the-art rendering techniques and paradigms such as physically based shading are becoming increasingly feasible on mobile. A deferred renderer is a common way to achieve detailed dynamic lighting [Smith 14]. In the next section we detail how to create an efficient deferred physically based renderer.

18.3.1   A Bandwidth Friendly G-Buffer Setup

Standard deferred shading renderers use multiple passes, each rendering to their own framebuffer, as shown in Figure 18.5. At the end of each render, the content of the on-chip memory is transferred to the main memory, which consumes a prohibitive amount of bandwidth for a mobile GPU.

However, given that each pass relies solely on the previous output and only requires data from the same pixel, it is possible to merge them all into a single large pass and to use the Framebuffer Fetch mechanism [Khronos 13] to bypass the intermediary data transfer. The OpenGL ES Framebuffer Fetch extension

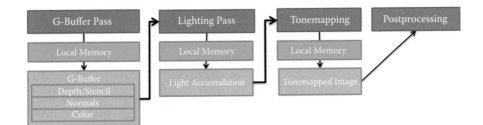

Figure 18.5. Standard deferred shading pipeline.

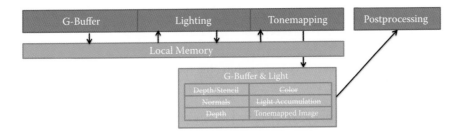

Figure 18.6. Bandwidth-friendly pipeline using Framebuffer Fetch.

allows the shader to treat what is traditionally the output as an input/output register.

Figure 18.6 shows how the pipeline can be modified to limit the amount of data transfer for the G-buffer, lighting, and tonemapping passes. These three passes are merged into one, which has several implications on the G-buffer layout: The HDR light accumulation buffer and tonemapped output are both added to the G-buffer. Furthermore, in order to access the geometry depth in the lighting stage, we pass the current depth through in local memory. Because only the tonemapped output is needed in the subsequent passes, all other attachments should be explicitly discarded to avoid unnecessary data transfer using `glInvalidateFramebuffer()`. It is also possible to reduce the G-buffer size by recycling the normal or color attachments into the tonemapped output.

This pipeline can be improved further: A whole G-buffer is allocated, even though it is never actually written to since its attachments are discarded. Its main use is only to define the data layout to be used for the render pass. The Pixel Local Storage (PLS) extension [Khronos 14] fixes this issue by letting the developer define the data layout in the shaders and write arbitrary data to the on-chip pixel memory. Figure 18.7 shows the same pipeline, improved with PLS: The G-buffer storage is no longer needed, and only one simple RGB color attachment is created for the whole deferred shading renderer.

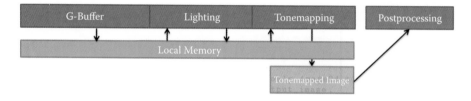

Figure 18.7. Optimal pipeline with Pixel Local Storage.

```
layout(rgb10a2) highp vec4 lightAccumulation_padding;
layout(r32f) highp float depth;
layout(rgba8) highp vec4 normals_roughness;
layout(rgba8) highp vec4 baseColour_padding;
layout(rgba8) highp vec4 specularColour_padding;
```

Listing 18.1. Specular G-buffer setup (160 bits, 142 bits actually used).

PowerVR Rogue series 6 GPUs have 128 bits of per-pixel on-chip memory. It is possible to access up to 256 bits per pixel, at the cost of performance: The spilled data will be transferred back to the main memory, unless it is small enough to fit in a cache. This means that ideally the whole G-buffer and light accumulation buffer would need to fit in 128 bits for a bandwidth-efficient renderer.

Using the specular workflow leads to the data layout in Listing 18.1. Although it is the most flexible and straightforward in terms of assets, and best in terms of quality, it requires 160 bits of storage per pixel, which makes it suboptimal for the hardware because 32 bits may be spilled to main memory per pixel.

Using the metallicness workflow allows us to pack the whole pixel data into 128 bits (see Listing 18.2), which fits nicely in the per-pixel on-chip memory without spilling.

18.3.2 Fast Gamma Approximation

The albedo and reflectance channels of the G-buffer should be stored in gamma space to prevent banding issues. This conversion to and from gamma space is

```
layout(rgb10a2) highp vec4 lightAccumulation_padding;
layout(r32f) highp float depth;
layout(rgba8) highp vec4 normals_roughness;
layout(rgba8) highp vec4 albedoOrReflectance_metallicness;
```

Listing 18.2. Metallicness G-buffer setup (128 bits, 126 bits used).

```
vec3 toGamma(vec3 linearValue) {
  return pow(linearValue, vec3(2.2));
}
vec3 toLinear(vec3 gammaValue) {
  return pow(gammaValue, vec3(1.0/2.2));
}
```

Listing 18.3. Manual gamma correction.

```
vec3 toGamma(vec3 linearValue) {
  return linearValue*linearValue;
}
vec3 toLinear(vec3 gammaValue) {
  return sqrt(gammaValue);
}
```

Listing 18.4. Pseudo-gamma correction.

usually done for free by the hardware as long as the G-buffer relevant attachments are set up as sRGB. However, because the optimized pipeline does not write to a physical G-buffer, this has to be done manually by simply raising to the power of 2.2 (see Listing 18.3).

This can be optimized by assuming a gamma of 2.0, which simplifies the gamma conversion and can be a good compromise between visual quality and speed (see Listing 18.4).

18.3.3 Lighting

We have defined how to input the material parameters to the rendering system. We now define how to input the lighting information. We use and extend physically based rendering techniques from different sources [Lagarde 12]. The types of information we need to include are static diffuse lighting, static specular lighting, and dynamic specular lighting.

An offline renderer is used to generate HDR lightmaps that are used to represent static diffuse lighting information such as shadows and radiosity. As these textures can take up a large memory footprint, they should be compressed to reduce memory usage and improve texture throughput. One such compression format is ASTC, which supports HDR data; however, not all devices currently support HDR ASTC. Non-HDR compression formats such as PVRTC can be used along with an encoding method, RGBM [Karis 09], in which a second texture is used as a scale factor to enable HDR output. The RGB channels should be compressed, but the scale factor channel should be left uncompressed to prevent serious block artifacts. See Listing 18.5 on how to decode this value. Diffuse

```
const float RGBM_SCALE = 6.0;
vec3 RGBMSqrtDecode(vec4 rgbm) {
  vec3 c = (rgbm.a * RGBM_SCALE) * rgbm.rgb;
  return c*c;
}

dualRGBM.rgb = texture(LightmapTexture, uv).rgb;
dualRGBM.a = texture(LightmapTextureScale, uv).r;
vec3 diffuseLight = RGBMDecode(dualRGBM);
diffuseLight *= surfaceColour * (1.0 - surfaceMetallicness);
```

Listing 18.5. Code for calculating the static diffuse lighting information.

lighting can be output into the light accumulation buffer in the geometry pass of the technique. Note that metallic materials do not reflect diffuse lighting.

We use image-based lighting as the input to the static specular lighting. An offline renderer is used to produce a cubemap that represents the lighting from a certain point in space. These cubemaps are converted to Prefiltered mipmaped radiance environment maps (PMREM) using the modified AMD cubemap gen tool [Lagarde 12]. A PMREM is a cubemap filtered by integrating the radiance over a range of solid angles of the hemisphere depending on the mipmap level. During the lighting stage, the surface roughness is used to select which mipmap levels of the cubemap should be sampled (see Listing 18.6). As with the lightmaps, the environment maps are stored in RGBM HDR. Listing 18.6 shows how the static specular lighting is computed, including the implementation of Shlick's approximation of Fresnel [Lagarde 12].

These static specular lights can be rendered in the same way as other dynamic lights in a deferred renderer, with a transparent mesh encompassing the light bounds.

```
// From seblagarde.wordpress.com/2011/08/17/hello-world
vec3 fresRough(vec3 specCol, vec3 E, vec3 N, float smoothness) {
  float factor = 1.0 - clamp(dot(E, N), 0.0, 1.0);
  return specCol + (max(vec3(smoothness), specCol) - specCol) *
    pow(factor, 5.0);
}
vec3 iblSpec(float roughness, vec3 specCol, vec3 N, vec3 V) {
  vec3 iblFresnel = fresRough(specCol, V, N, 1.0 - roughness);
  vec3 refDir = reflect(-V, N);
  float mipLevel = 8.0 * roughness; // 8 mips total
  vec3 envMapResult = RGBMDecode(
    textureLod(SpecularProbe, refDir, mipLevel));
  return envMapResult * iblFresnel;
}
```

Listing 18.6. Code for computing the image-based specular contribution.

For dynamic specular lighting we use the GGX equation [Walter et al. 07]. This takes into account roughness and is designed for a physically based pipeline.

18.3.4 Decals Made Easy

Decals are a popular method for adding extra details to the scene by adding layers of textured transparent geometry. However, this is often limited by the use of fixed function blending, meaning that the decal will be composited to the scene with either an addition or an interpolation.

The Framebuffer Fetch and Pixel local Storage mechanisms allow developers to do programmable blending, meaning complete freedom in how the decals will affect the G-buffer. More importantly, some G-buffer attachments are packed in ways that would prevent naive blending to work properly [Pranckevičius 10], but would be trivial with programmable blending.

It also makes environmental awareness (i.e., knowing what is behind the decal) completely free in terms of bandwidth because the G-buffer no longer needs to be flushed to VRAM before being sampled as a texture.

Finally, programmable blending makes it easy for developers to write selectively to specific outputs (e.g., a decal that only modifies the normals). Writing selectively to framebuffer attachments has always been possible, but with programmable blending, it is no longer defined in the renderer itself but in the shader. This makes it completely transparent to the application, which is convenient and slightly more efficient. With the Pixel Local Storage extension, this goes even further as there is no concept of framebuffer attachment, giving a very fine-grained control over what gets written to what.

18.4 Experiments

Tests were performed on a consumer-available device with a PowerVR series 6 GPU. An analysis of the application using the PowerVR SDK shows that the optimized renderers (Framebuffer Fetch and PLS) execute fewer rendering tasks—meaning that the G-buffer generation, lighting, and tonemapping stages are properly merged into one task. It also shows a clear reduction in memory bandwidth usage between the on-chip and the main memory: a 53% decrease in reads and a 54% decrease in writes (see Figure 18.8). All these optimizations result in a slightly lower frame time but in much lower power consumption, as shown in Figure 18.9. This means longer battery life on mobile devices.

18.5 Conclusion and Future Work

In this chapter, we presented an efficient physically based deferred shading renderer targeted at mobile devices. We have shown how the traditional deferred

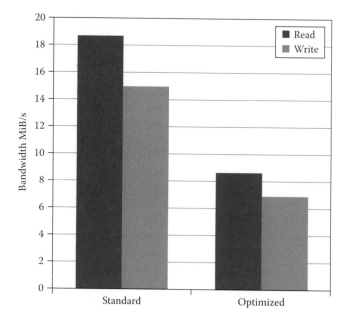

Figure 18.8. Bandwidth comparison.

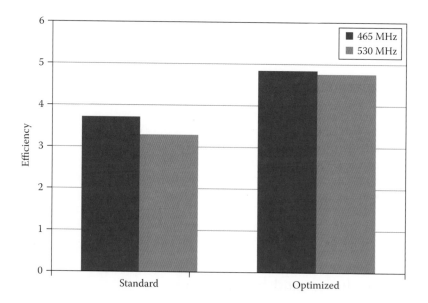

Figure 18.9. Efficiency in FPS (frames per second) per Watt of total system power.

```
layout(r32f) highp float posx;
layout(r32f) highp float posy;
layout(r32f) highp float posz;
layout(rg16f) highp vec2 lightAccumRG;
layout(rg16f) highp vec2 lightAccumB_normalsX;
layout(rg16f) highp vec2 normalsYZ;
layout(rg16f) highp vec2 roughness_metallicness;
layout(r11f_g11f_b10f) highp vec3 albedoOrReflectance;
```

Listing 18.7. Future metallicness workflow PLS G-buffer setup (256 bits).

```
layout(r32f) highp float posx;
layout(r32f) highp float posy;
layout(r32f) highp float posz;
layout(rg16f) highp vec2 lightAccumRG;
layout(rg16f) highp vec2 lightAccumB_roughness;
layout(r11f_g11f_b10f) highp vec3 normals;
layout(r11f_g11f_b10f) highp vec3 albedo;
layout(r11f_g11f_b10f) highp vec3 reflectance;
```

Listing 18.8. Future specular workflow PLS G-buffer setup (256 bits).

shading pipeline could be improved using OpenGL ES extensions such as Framebuffer Fetch and Pixel Local Storage to significantly reduce the amount of necessary bandwidth and therefore power and battery usage. We have proposed an efficient 128-bit G-buffer for PLS that allows state-of-the-art physically based shading, shown how to integrate high-quality static and dynamic lighting, and explained how decals could be made more complex at a lower performance cost.

In the next series of PowerVR GPUs, the available fast storage will increase from 128 to 256 bits per pixel. This gives application developers a wider variety of techniques and optimizations they can take advantage of.

Two examples of possible future G-buffer layouts using 256 bits per pixel are shown in Listings 18.7 and 18.8. Instead of storing depth, the world position is stored, which saves an expensive operation in the lighting stage. All the surface parameters are stored with higher precision, meaning they can all be stored in linear space. This saves an expensive conversion during both the geometry and lighting passes. Normals are also stored in higher precision for better quality. Finally, these G-buffer layouts are also very efficient in terms of ALU usage due to the fact that they are composed mostly of FP16 and FP32 registers, which do not require any packing and unpacking on PowerVR GPUs.

Such a large local storage could also be used for advanced effects such as Order Independent Transparency [Bjørge et al. 14], which could easily be integrated into our proposed deferred pipeline. Transparent objects would be rendered between the lighting and tonemapping stages, reusing the same PLS storage and overwriting it, keeping only the light accumulation data from the previous stage.

Bibliography

[Bjørge et al. 14] Marius Bjørge, Sam Martin, Sandeep Kakarlapudi, and Jan-Harald Fredriksen. "Efficient Rendering with Tile Local Storage." In *ACM SIGGRAPH 2014 Talks, SIGGRAPH '14*, pp. 51:1–51:1. New York: ACM, 2014.

[Kajiya 86] James T. Kajiya. "The Rendering Equation." *SIGGRAPH Comput. Graph.* 20:4 (1986), 143–150.

[Karis 09] Brian Karis. "RGBM Color Encoding." http://graphicrants.blogspot.co.uk/2009/04/rgbm-color-encoding.html, 2009.

[Khronos 13] Khronos. "Framebfufer Fetch." https://www.khronos.org/registry/gles/extensions/EXT/EXT_shader_framebuffer_fetch.txt, 2013.

[Khronos 14] Khronos. "Pixel Local Storage." https://www.khronos.org/registry/gles/extensions/EXT/EXT_shader_pixel_local_storage.txt, 2014.

[Lagarde 12] Sébastien Lagarde. "AMD Cubemapgen for Physically Based Rendering." https://seblagarde.wordpress.com/2012/06/10/amd-cubemapgen-for-physically-based-rendering, 2012.

[Pharr and Humphreys 04] Matt Pharr and Greg Humphreys. *Physically Based Rendering: From Theory to Implementation.* San Francisco: Morgan Kaufmann Publishers, Inc., 2004.

[Pranckevičius 10] Aras Pranckevičius. "Compact Normal Storage for Small G-Buffers." http://aras-p.info/texts/CompactNormalStorage.html, 2010.

[Smith 14] Ashley Vaughan Smith. "Deferred Rendering Techniques on Mobile Devices." In *GPU Pro 5*, edited by Wolfgang Engel, pp. 263–272. Boca Raton, FL: A K Peters/CRC Press, 2014.

[Walter et al. 07] Bruce Walter, Stephen R. Marschner, Hongsong Li, and Kenneth E. Torrance. "Microfacet Models for Refraction Through Rough Surfaces." In *Proceedings of the 18th Eurographics Conference on Rendering Techniques, EGSR'07*, pp. 195–206. Aire-la-Ville, Switzerland: Eurographics Association, 2007.

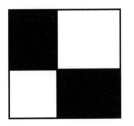

Contributors

Sylwester Bala is an ARM software graphics engineer. In his childhood, he enjoyed building his own bikes when it was sunny and getting familiar with BASIC programming language on C64 when it was raining. As luck would have it, he lived in a rainy land. He worked in the TV broadcast industry for eight years programming real-time graphics engines. Since 2012 he has been part of ARM, and he is responsible for leading development of GPU demonstration software that incorporates the latest mobile technology with highly optimized graphics techniques on the market.

Andrea Bizzotto received his BS and MS degrees in computer engineering from the University of Padua, Italy. After completing college he joined Imagination Technologies, where he developed a range of 3D demos for Imagination's POWERVR Insider ecosystem and published an article in *GPU Pro*. His research interests include 3D graphics, computer vision, image processing, algorithm theory, and software design. More info at www.bizzotto.biz.

Marius Bjørge is a Graphics Research Engineer at ARM's office in Trondheim, Norway. Prior to ARM he worked in the games industry as part of Funcom's core engine team. He has presented research at SIGGRAPH, HPG, and GDC and is keenly interested in anything graphics-related. He's currently looking at new ways of enabling advanced real-time graphics on current and future mobile GPU technology.

Ken Catterall graduated from the University of Toronto in 2005 as a specialist in software engineering. He is currently a leading engineer for Imagination Technologies' business development team, where he has been working since 2006 developing and supporting Imagination's key graphics demos. He has previously contributed to *ShaderX*[6], *ShaderX*[7], and *GPU Pro*.

Amir Chohan is a software developer in the financial industry. He graduated from the University of Bristol with an MEng in mathematics and computer science in 2014, and he developed the prototype of the HDR computational photography pipeline as part of his final-year project.

Ole Ciliox is an experienced freelance graphics programmer. Previously he worked on various technology at Unity and before that at IO Interactive.

Dan Curran is a researcher in the HPC group at the University of Bristol, where his work focuses on the development of efficient algorithms for many-core computer architectures. He has worked on a range of different applications, including computational fluid dynamics, de-dispersion for the SKA, lattice Boltzmann, and computational photography. He is an expert in GPU computing, with a particular focus on OpenCL. Dan graduated with an MEng in computer science in 2012.

Joe Davis graduated from the University of Hull in 2009 with a MEng degree in computer science, where his studies focused on real-time graphics and physics for games. Joe currently works as a developer technology engineer for the Imagination Technologies POWERVR Graphics SDK, where his time is spent developing utilities, demos, and tutorials as well as helping developers optimize their graphics applications for POWERVR-based platforms.

Daniele Di Donato is a senior software engineer in the ARM Demo Team. In his daily job he develops demos for ARM Mali GPU-based devices to showcase the latest OpenGL ES features available on mobile. He obtained an MEng in computer science from the University of Bologna in 2012.

Mathieu Einig has a BSc in computer graphics science and is the technical lead of the PowerVR demo team at Imagination Technologies. He has a passion for generating pretty pixels in real time and has strong interests in real-time raytracing, computer vision, and augmented reality.

Andrew Girdler is a real-time rendering specialist in the graphics demo team at Imagination Technologies, where he works on developing new real-time techniques for embedded graphics platforms. He was an integral part of developing the team's new in-house engine and rendering technologies, including the shell-based fur rendering technique outlined in this book. Andrew is graduating with a degree in computer science from the University of Bath in 2015.

Johan Gronqvist has worked on OpenCL for ARM Mali GPUs over the last three years—writing benchmarks, analysing performance, teaching compute optimization, and optimizing applications for customers as well as for internal use. He is now working on the ARM Mali compiler, focusing on optimizations for GPU compute. From his pre-ARM history he has a PhD in physics, and his GPU interest revolves around understanding how to get more compute performance out of the devices.

James L. Jones graduated with a degree in computer science from Cardiff University and works on real-time graphics demos in the demo team at Imagination Technologies. He is currently focused on physically based rendering techniques for modern embedded graphics platforms and research for demos with Imagination's real-time ray-tracing technology.

Hyunwoo Ki is a graphics engineer at INNOACE Co., Ltd. He is named in the Marquis *Who's Who in the World* (2010 edition). He received an MS in media engineering at Soongsil University and contributed to *ShaderX7* and *Game Programming Gems 8*. He is interested in real-time lighting and shadowing for next-generation graphics engines.

Ramses Ladlani is lead engine programmer at Fishing Cactus, the video game company he co-founded in 2008 with three former colleagues from 10tacle Studios Belgium (a.k.a. Elsewhere Entertainment). When he is not working on the next feature of Mojito, Fishing Cactus's in-house cross-platform engine, he can be found playing rugby or learning his new role as a father. He received his master's degree in computer engineering from Université Libre de Bruxelles.

Anton Lokhmotov has been working in the area of programming languages and tools for 15 years, both as a researcher and engineer, primarily focussing on productivity, efficiency, and portability of programming techniques for heterogeneous systems. In 2015, Anton founded dividiti to pursue his vision of efficient and reliable computing everywhere. In 2010–2015, Antonled development of GPU Compute programming technologies for the ARM Mali GPU series, including production (OpenCL, RenderScript) and research (EU-funded project CARP) compilers. He was actively involved in educating academic and professional developers, engaging with partners and customers, and contributing to open source projects and standardization efforts. In 2008–2009, Anton investigated heterogeneous programming as a research associate at Imperial College London. He received a PhD in computer science from the University of Cambridge in 2008 and an MSc in applied mathematics and physics (summa cum laude) from the Moscow Institute for Physics and Technology in 2004.

Roberto Lopez Mendez is an ARM software graphics engineer. He studied nuclear physics at university, but after a decade working in physics research, he discovered his real passion and since 1995 has been working in 3D graphics for a variety of companies. In 2012 Roberto joined the ARM Demo Team. Since then he has been developing optimized rendering techniques for mobile devices, creating demos that show the capabilities of the latest ARM Mali GPUs. He also regularly delivers workshops at different universities and presents at game-related events.

Simon McIntosh-Smith leads the HPC research group at the University of Bristol in the UK. His background is in microprocessor architecture, with a 15-year career in industry at companies including Inmos, STMicroelectronics, Pixelfusion, and ClearSpeed. Simon co-founded ClearSpeed in 2002 where, as director of architecture and applications, he co-developed the first modern many-core HPC accelerators. In 2003 he led the development of the first accelerated BLAS/LAPACK and FFT libraries, leading to the creation of the first modern accelerated Top500 system, TSUBAME-1.0, at Tokyo Tech in 2006. He joined the University of Bristol in 2009, where his research focuses on efficient algorithms for heterogeneous many-core architectures and performance portability. He is a joint recipient of an R&D 100 award for his contribution to Sandia's Mantevo benchmark suite, and in 2014 he was awarded the first Intel Parallel Computing Center in the UK. Simon actively contributes to the Khronos OpenCL heterogeneous many-core programming standard.

Gareth Morgan has been involved in games and 3D graphics since 1999, starting at Silicon Graphics followed by several games companies including Activision and BAM Studios. Since 2008 he has been a leading software engineer at Imagination Technologies specializing in researching sophisticated rendering techniques using Imagination's ray-tracing technology.

Peter Quayle graduated from the University of Brighton with a degree in computer science. His interest in real-time computer graphics originates from a fascination with the demoscene. Peter currently works at Imagination Technologies as a business development engineer.

Ashley Vaughan Smith is a leading applications engineer at Imagination Technologies and works on creating graphical and compute demos showcasing PowerVR. With a BSc in computer games programming and having worked in the games industry, he enjoys investigating up-coming technologies and graphical techniques, currently including Vulkan and ray tracing.

Stacy Smith is technical lead of the Developer Education team and an engineer within the Demo Team at ARM. This dual role allows her to teach the effects and techniques implemented in the internal graphical demos seen on Mali platforms.

Marco Weber received an MS degree in computer science from Friedrich-Alexander University of Erlangen-Nuremberg with a focus on computer graphics and pattern recognition. Currently, he is a developer technology engineer at Imagination Technologies doing research, implementing demos for new and upcoming technologies, and helping fellow graphics programmers optimize their algorithms and engines for POWERVR-based mobile platforms.

Renaldas Zioma is an experienced graphics programmer working at Unity. Prior to joining Unity, he worked on various technology at DICE.